ETHICS =IN= THOUGHT AND ACTION

Social and Professional Perspectives

WARREN COHEN
University of Hawaii at Manoa

 Ardsley House, Publishers, Inc. • New York

Address orders and editorial
correspondence to:
Ardsley House, Publishers, Inc.
320 Central Park West
New York, NY 10025

ISBN: 1-880157-14-4

Printed in the United States of America

10 9 8 7 6 5 4 3 2 1

To all my students

❖ CONTENTS

Chapter-Opening Pictures

Chapter 1. From "Jurors Listening to Counsel, Supreme Court, New City Hall, New York," *Harper's Weekly*, February 20, 1869. Winslow Homer.

Chapter 2. Businessman. Epson Computers.

Chapter 3. CAT Scanner. NIH.

Chapter 4. From "Shinran Shonan," Buddhist Church of New York. Josh Siegel.

Chapter 5. Malcolm McDowell in *A Clockwork Orange*. Picture Collection, The Branch Libraries, The New York Public Library.

Chapter 6. G & L Recycling, Baltimore. Josh Siegel.

Chapter 7. Outside the "Today" Show. Josh Siegel.

Chapter 8. Pro-Choice Rally. The Picture Collection, The Branch Libraries, The New York Public Library.

Chapter 9. Robert F. Wagner Junior High School, New York City. Josh Siegel.

Chapter 10. Chemist. TRW.

❖ PREFACE

This text is a radical departure from earlier approaches to the questions of ethics. Previously, most ethical discourse has been either sociological or philosophical. Sociological ethicists try to describe ethical behavior; philosophers tell us what we ought to do (or if they worked in the English-speaking world in the middle years of this century, they would have tried to classify ethical language). In devising a text that would be relevant to young people today, I have thrown aside the old barriers between social and philosophical ethics and, instead, have tried to link, or at least describe, both what "is" and "what ought to be."

It will be clear that this book is no didactic treatise, exhorting students to the practice of specific virtues. I believe that telling people what they should do is rarely effective. People have to feel that there is a reason for doing something; furthermore, what you practice is more likely to be imitated than what you preach. Haranguing youths about the sins of drugs does little good if the rhetoric comes from the mouth of a heavy drinker. Youths learn about hypocrisy, not drugs, in such a case. I also do not believe that I have the answers to moral questions; I do not feel that I can tell people, in twenty-five words or less, to do this or that. Nevertheless, I feel that we can profitably talk about what preconditions must exist before anyone can make an ethical choice that is intellectually sound and reasonable. It is to establish these preconditions that this book is dedicated.

On the other hand, we can clearly distinguish this text from the approach of certain members of the "value inquiry" school that was prevalent in the 1970s. In that approach, the teacher did not promote any ethical positions but merely led the class in discussions about ethical issues and allowed the students to come to their own conclusions. I believe that keeping your own ethics out of the situation is impossible. Even to the extent that you succeed in divorcing your own feelings from the moment, you are merely encouraging the students to abide by their own ignorant prejudices. Students cannot discover for themselves what their ethical beliefs are, for they usually lack the tools, the information, and the reasoning skills necessary to make intelligent ethical choices. To sit and let them rattle on in their ignorance is not achieving much, except to set their uninformed opinions in stone.

There is much that responsible teachers can do without telling the students what to think. If we are not telling people what to do, not letting them develop their own opinions, and not teaching either philosophy or sociology, what are we doing? We are, as I said, setting up the preconditions for ethical decision making, letting the students see how to make responsible ethical decisions. This is not an easy task and many students will slip back into the lazy ease of prejudice and rhetoric when out of the classroom. But at least they will have been given a chance to learn how to make intellectually responsible and ethical decisions; most people never have that option.

How do you hold an intellectually responsible ethical position? First of all, you learn as much as you can about the situation; second, you find out as much as possible about the people involved in the situation—their histories, prejudices, and vested interests; third, you look at yourself, your interest in the situation, your own history and prejudices. Consider if your position makes sense logically; consider if you can apply your reasoning to justify your position in this case to other cases; consider the consequences that are likely to occur if your position is adopted. Also, look at your favorite ethical rules to check if your position is consistent with them.

In this text, I try to give the students a sense of the context in which practitioners of various professions make their decisions; what their place is in society, what their vested interests are, what roles they see themselves serving. To this end, readings from the literatures of different professions are presented. Students are given the chance to read the American Bar Association's *Code of*

Professional Conduct as well as the account of an ethical dilemma faced by one young lawyer; the views of a practicing physician on problems in medical ethics; an insider's account of the Congressional debate over acid-rain legislation; and the story of the questionable business practices of a chemical-weapons dealer. Students are also made aware of the often unstated social and/or biological factors that color the ethical decisions of even the most scrupulous professional. An in-depth analysis of a research experiment shows how psychologists have looked at our ethical behavior and the powerful nonrational forces that work on all of us. I thus give the students a sense of the reasons that professionals have for their beliefs so that if students criticize the professionals' ethical behavior, they can do so aware of the factors that have molded their perspectives

The chapter on Zen and Existentialism reveals two philosophical positions that challenge our traditional ways of looking at ethical problems and the rationalizations offered by the ethical codes of lawyers or business people. Both existentialists and Zen practitioners focus on the events of our everyday life, and it seems important in a book on social and professional ethics to remind the reader of these routine activities. The chapter on abortion is edifying because it covers an issue which concerns many different professions. The debate over abortion has been noted for hotheaded rhetoric and lack of reason. Consequently, it can illustrate how the blatant manipulation of language and history can influence one's perception of a problem.

Finally, I also provide the students with the opportunity to read philosophical texts so that they see the elaborate, subtle, and careful reasoning that a philosopher uses to develop a position. This will give them a sense of how careful one should be when developing one's own views. Although we cannot expect the students to show the care of a Kant or a Mill in expressing their own ideas, at least they can hold up the careful writing of the philosophers as models to be emulated.

In this work, I occasionally demonstrate my own opinions and sympathies. I do so not to sell a point of view, but rather to make overt what is so often hidden in textbooks. There is no such

thing as an objective text; the simplest recitation of facts reveals prejudices because the facts chosen show what the commentator considers important. The arrangements of facts in a slightly different order can draw attention to very different things. Even "objective" measures reveal prejudices. Economic indicators like GNPs, per capita income, or trade figures represent the values of a society that considers wealth, measured in capital, to be important and, in some sense, good. Indicators like IQ tests or SATs are taken as objective measures of intelligence or achievement, whereas they really show the individual's ability to perform on these tests. To attribute any kind of significance to these tests is to reveal prejudice. But this type of prejudice, cloaked in "objectivity," has the insidious ability to sound like "the truth." It is not. The opinions of the author in this text are not "the truth," either; but by a clear insistence on these opinions, I hope that no one will mistake them for an objective presentation of material. I do not want to hide behind the veil of an objectivity that does not exist.

❖ TO THE STUDENT

It would be a mistake to look upon this text as a book on philosophy, as its approach to ethics is nontechnical. However, it is necessary for the reader to have some grounding in the philosophical terminology and categories that are used to deal with ethical theories. Ethics as a branch of philosophy goes back to Plato, and no doubt ethical issues were debated for millennia before the ancient Greeks. Categorizing ethical arguments does make it easier to understand how these issues are traditionally approached by philosophers.

Approaches to the Nature of the Good

Philosophers classify ethical arguments in three categories. They can consider the consequences of an action performed; they can consider the rule followed in performing an action; or they can look at the reasons a person uses to justify his or her action. The first approach is called *consequence theory*; the second is called *deontological ethics*; and the third approach is known as *motivist ethics*. We will look at each of these approaches in turn.

Consequence Theory

A consequence theorist is primarily concerned with outcomes. "The end justifies the means" is a classic statement of consequence theory. Among philosophical schools, the utilitarians are the clearest exponents of a consequence-theory approach. They hold that one should always consider the greatest good for the greatest number of people. An action that produces the greatest good is a good action. We shall look at utilitarian thinking when we discuss the writing of John Stuart Mill. It is perhaps worth noting that there are consequence theorists who argue that the goodness of an action can be equated with the degree of pleasure or pain it produces. Other consequence theorists deny this relationship between good and pleasure, arguing that goodness is a unique property and that you cannot reduce "goodness" to the degree of pleasure that is created.

Deontological Ethics

In deontological ethics, the goodness of an action is determined by the degree to which it follows some rule. If we have a rule that says "do not steal," then an action is good to the extent that it conforms to that rule. The obvious difficulty in any deontological ethics is that it may be difficult or impossible to prove that the *rule* itself is good. The advantage to a deontological ethic is that it is always possible to judge any action as good or bad.

Motivist Ethics

In motivist ethics, the goodness or badness of an action is tied to the intentions that a person possesses. An act is good if the person tried to do good. The argument for this position usually begins by noting that the only thing that can be purely good is good intentions. Any act will always lead to consequences that are not purely good. That is why utilitarians are left to justify their position by talking of the *greatest* good for the greatest number, for they are aware that any action is not purely good. For the motivists, the greatest good is not enough; instead, they are searching for something that is unequivocally good.

These positions are not mutually exclusive. Immanuel Kant consistently held both to a deontological and to a motivist ethical position, and it is very easy to see that consequence theorists and motivists are simply looking at ethical questions in different ways. It is precisely the differences among these approaches that are valuable. Ethics is concerned with what is good, and these three approaches offer three very different ways of figuring that out, using different criteria in each case.

In looking at ethical arguments, it is important for the student to be aware of the philosophical starting point of the proponent. This becomes an essential element in understanding what is being said. Frequently, people will try to dispute a position that considers motives by talking about the consequences of the action. Although the point taken may be valid, it does not address the issue in the same way and so is irrelevant as a refutation of the original position. In reading this book, the student should always be aware of the thinking implied in each ethical argument presented.

CHAPTER 1

ETHICS AND THE LAW:
The Individual, Society, and Justice

In this chapter, we consider the ethical implications and limitations of the adversarial justice system, and also the implications for our legal system of the ideas presented in John Stuart Mill's On Liberty. *Selections from Monroe Friedman's discussion of the ethical duties of a lawyer under the adversarial system, brief segments of the American Bar Association's Code of Professional Responsibility, and a case study that illustrates the difficulties of maintaining the proper ethical balance under the present legal system are also included.*

Professional and Personal Ethics

In his book *The Godfather*, Mario Puzo tells the story of a man who was both a ruthless killer and a devoted family man. Within the confines of his own home, he was kind and considerate. But he would kill an outsider for a trivial breach of contract. Obviously, he had two sets of ethical standards—one for home and one for what he called "business." In a very brutal way, this illustrates the distinction between professional and personal ethics.

This distinction is made by lawyers, doctors, scientists, teachers, and businessmen all the time. Teachers frequently insist on classroom behavior that is a far cry from what they tolerate among their own children. Scientists sanction extraordinarily cruel procedures in the name of science. Businessmen often use the word "honest" to describe someone who carefully tiptoes just within the borders of the law. And lawyers are admonished by their own code of legal ethics to defend zealously anyone they retain as a client, even if the client is a psychopathic killer.

In each of these cases, the specific needs and demands of the profession take precedence over personal feelings. These professionals believe that the work situation *demands* a different code of ethics. Often, those outside of the profession are appalled, but the insiders have compelling rationalizations for their behavior.

Lawyers perhaps present the most blatant case of a conflict between personal and professional ethics. The primary duty of a lawyer is to defend a client to the best of his or her ability. The attorney may well be less concerned with justice in the individual case than with doing the best possible for the client. What is more, it is ethically justifiable for the lawyer to behave in this way.

Although it may seem strange that it is ethically justifiable to have someone defend the rights of thieves, rapists, and murderers, it is perfectly consistent with the philosophical orientation of the justice system prevalent in the United States, England, and other English-speaking democracies. All of these countries uphold an adversarial justice system. It is called "adversarial" because the defense attorney and the prosecutor are said to represent contrary interests. The job of the prosecutor in a criminal case is to present the case against the defendant. The job of the defense attorney is to defend his or her client. Since the prosecutor has the entire weight of the elaborate state apparatus behind him or her, it is thought that the defense attorney needs to be forceful to redress the inequality in power between the individual and the state. The defense lawyer need only cast doubt on the guilt of the defendant; there is no need to prove innocence.

The Obligation of Confidentiality

T he following selection describes a rather spectacular case that strained the limits of people's faith in the adversarial justice system. Read the article critically, keeping in mind that many people in the legal profession have strong objections to Professor Freedman's views.

"Where the Bodies Are Buried"[1]

In a recent case in Lake Pleasant, New York, a defendant in a murder case told his lawyers about two other people he had killed and where their bodies had been hidden. The lawyers went there, observed the bodies, and took photographs of them. They did not, however, inform the authorities about the bodies until several months later, when their client had confessed to those crimes. In addition to withholding the information from police and prosecutors, one of the attorneys denied information to one of the victims' parents, who came to him in the course of seeking his missing daughter.

There were interesting reactions to that dramatic event. Members of the public were generally shocked at the apparent callousness on the part of the lawyers, whose conduct was considered typical of an unhealthy lack of concern by lawyers with the public interest and with simple decency. That attitude was encouraged by public statements by the local prosecutor, who sought to indict the lawyers for failing to reveal knowledge of a crime and for failing to see that dead bodies were properly buried. In addition, the reactions of lawyers and law professors who were questioned by the press were ambivalent and confused, indicating that few members of the legal profession had given serious thought to the fundamental questions of administration of justice and of professional responsibility that were raised by the case.

One can certainly understand the sense of moral compulsion to assist the parents and to give the dignity of proper burial to the victims. What seems to be less readily understood—but which, to my mind, throws the moral balance in the other direction—is the obligation of the lawyers to their client and, in a larger sense, to a system of administering justice which is itself essential to maintaining human dignity. In short, not only did the two lawyers behave properly, but they would have committed a serious breach of professional responsibility if they had divulged the information contrary to their client's interest. The explanation to that answer takes us to the very nature of our system of criminal justice and, indeed, to the fundamentals of our system of government.

Let us begin, by way of contrast, with an understanding of the role of a criminal defense attorney in a totalitarian state. As expressed by law professors at the University of Havana, "the first job of a revolutionary lawyer is not to argue that his client is innocent, but rather to determine if his client is guilty and, if so, to seek the sanction which will best rehabilitate him."

Similarly, a Bulgarian attorney began his defense in a treason trial by noting that: "In a Socialist state there is no division of duty between the judge, prosecutor, and defense counsel. . . . The defense must assist the prosecution to find the objective truth in a case." In that case, the defense attorney ridiculed his client's defense, and the client was convicted and executed. Sometime later the verdict was found to have been erroneous, and the defendant was "rehabilitated."

The emphasis in a free society is, of course, sharply different. Under our adversary system, the interests of the state are not absolute, or even paramount. The dignity of the individual is respected to the point that even when the citizen is known by the state to have committed a heinous offense, the individual is nevertheless accorded such rights as counsel, trial by jury, due process, and the privilege against self-incrimination.

A trial is, in part, a search for truth. Accordingly, those basic rights are most often characterized as procedural safeguards against error in the search for truth. Actually, however, a trial is far more than a search for truth, and the constitutional rights that are provided by our system of justice may well outweigh the truth-seeking value—a fact which is manifest when we consider that those rights and others guaranteed by the Constitution may well impede the search for truth rather than further it. What more effective way is there, for example, to expose a defendant's guilt than to require self-incrimination, at least to the extent of compelling the defendant to take the stand and respond to interrogation before the jury? The defendant, however, is presumed innocent; the burden is on the prosecution to prove guilt beyond a reasonable doubt, and even the guilty accused has an "absolute constitutional right" to remain silent and to put the government to its proof.

Thus, the defense lawyer's professional obligation may well be to advise the client to withhold the truth. As Justice Jackson said: "Any lawyer worth his salt will tell the suspect in no uncertain terms to make no statement to police under any circumstances." Similarly, the defense lawyer is obligated to prevent the introduction of evidence that may be wholly reliable, such as a murder weapon seized in violation of the Fourth Amendment, or a truthful but involuntary confession. Justice White has observed that although law enforcement officials must be dedicated to using only truthful evidence, "defense counsel has no comparable obligation to ascertain or present the truth. Our system assigns him a different mission. . . . [W]e . . . insist that he defend his client whether he is innocent or guilty."

Such conduct by defense counsel does not constitute obstruction of justice. On the contrary, it is "part of the duty imposed on the most honorable defense counsel," from whom "we countenance or require conduct which in many instances has little, if any, relation to the search for truth." The same observation has been made by Justice Harlan, who noted that "in fulfilling his professional responsibilities," the lawyer "of necessity may become an obstacle to truthfinding." Chief Justice Warren, too, has recognized that when the criminal defense attorney successfully obstructs efforts by the government to elicit truthful evidence in ways that violate constitutional rights, the attorney is "merely exercising . . . good professional judgment," and "carrying out what he is sworn to do under his oath—to protect to the extent of his ability the rights of his client." Chief Justice Warren concluded: "In fulfilling this responsibility the attorney plays a vital role in the administration of criminal justice under our Constitution."

Obviously, such eminent jurists would not arrive lightly at the conclusion that an officer of the court has a professional obligation to place obstacles in the path of truth. Their reasons, again, go back to the nature of our system of criminal justice and to the fundamentals of our system of government. Before we will permit the state to deprive any person of life, liberty, or property, we require that certain processes be duly followed which ensure regard for the dignity of the individual, irrespective of the impact of those processes upon the determination of truth.

By emphasizing that the adversary process has its foundations in respect for human dignity, even at the expense of the search for truth, I do not mean to deprecate the search for truth or to suggest that the adversary system is not concerned with it. On the contrary, truth is a basic value, and the adversary system is one of the most efficient and fair methods designed for determining it. That system proceeds on the assumption that the best way to ascertain the truth is to present to an impartial judge or jury a confrontation between the proponents of conflicting views, assigning to each the task of marshaling and presenting the evidence in as thorough and persuasive a way as possible. The truth-seeking techniques used by the advocates on each side include investigation, pretrial discovery, cross-examination of opposing witnesses, and a marshaling of the evidence in summation. Thus, the judge or jury is given the strongest possible view of each side, and is put in the best possible position to make an accurate and fair judgment. Nevertheless, the point that I now emphasize is that in a society that honors the dignity of the individual, the high value that we assign to truth-seeking is not an absolute, but may on occasion be subordinated to even higher values.

The concept of a right to counsel is one of the most significant manifestations of our regard for the dignity of the individual. No person is required to stand alone against the awesome power of the People of New York or the Government of the United States of America. Rather, every criminal defendant is guaranteed an advocate—a "champion" against a "hostile world," the "single voice on which he must rely with confidence that his interests will be protected to the fullest extent consistent with the rules of procedure and the standards of professional conduct." In addition, the attorney serves in significant part to assure equality before the law. Thus, the lawyer has been referred to as "the equalizer," who "places each litigant as nearly as possible on an equal footing under the substantive and procedural law under which he is tried."

The lawyer can serve effectively as advocate, however, "only if he knows all that his client knows" concerning the facts of the case. Nor is the client ordinarily competent to evaluate the relevance or significance of particular facts. What may seem incriminating to the client, may actually be exculpatory. For example, one client was reluctant to tell her lawyer that her husband had attacked her with a knife, because it tended to confirm that she had in fact shot him (contrary to what she had at first maintained). Having been persuaded by her attorney's insistence upon complete and candid disclosure, she finally "confessed all"—which permitted the lawyer to defend her properly and successfully on grounds of self-defense.

Obviously, however, the client cannot be expected to reveal to the lawyer all information that is potentially relevant, including that which may well be incriminating, unless the client can be assured that the lawyer will maintain all such information in the strictest confidence. "The purposes and necessities of the relation between client and his attorney" require "the fullest and freest disclosures" of the client's "objects, motives and acts." If the attorney were permitted to reveal such disclosures, it would be "not only a gross violation of a sacred trust upon his part," but it would "utterly destroy and prevent the usefulness and benefits to be derived from professional assistance." That "sacred trust" of confidentiality must "upon all occasions be inviolable," or else the client could not feel free "to repose [confidence] in the attorney to whom he resorts for legal advice and assistance." Destroy that confidence, and "a man would not venture to consult any skillful person, or would only dare to tell his counselor half his case." The result would be impairment of the "perfect freedom of consultation by client with attorney," which is "essential to the administration of justice." Accordingly, the new Code of Professional Responsibility provides that a lawyer shall not knowingly reveal a confidence or secret of the client, nor use a confidence or secret to the disadvantage of the client, or to the advantage of a third person, without the client's consent.

It must be obvious at this point that the adversary system, within which the lawyer functions, contemplates that the lawyer frequently will learn from the client information that is highly incriminating and may even learn, as in the Lake Pleasant case, that the client has in fact committed serious crimes. In such a case, if the attorney were required to divulge that information, the obligation of confidentiality would be destroyed, and with it, the adversary system itself. Even so, it is occasionally suggested that a lawyer who does not divulge a client's self-incriminatory information would be guilty of such crimes as obstruction of justice, misprision of a felony, or becoming an accomplice after the fact. Such statutes, however, cannot be understood as applying to lawyers who have learned incriminating information after the crime has already been committed. . . .

That is not to say, of course, that the attorney is privileged to go beyond the needs of confidentiality imposed by the adversary system, and actively participate in concealment of evidence or obstruction of justice. For example, in the Ryder case, which arose in Virginia several years ago, the attorney removed from his client's safe deposit box a sawed-off shotgun and the money from a bank robbery and put them, for greater safety, into the lawyer's own safe deposit box. The attorney, quite properly, was suspended from practice for 18 months. (The penalty might well have been heavier, except for the fact that Ryder sought advice from senior members of the bench and bar, and apparently acted more in ignorance than in venality.) The important difference between the Ryder case and the one in Lake Pleasant lies in the active role played by the attorney in Ryder to conceal evidence. There is no indication, for example, that the attorneys in Lake Pleasant attempted to hide the bodies more effectively. If they had done so, they would have gone beyond maintaining confidentiality and into active participation in the concealment of evidence.

The distinction should also be noted between the attorney's knowledge of a past crime (which is what we have been discussing so far) and knowledge of a crime to be committed in the future. Thus, a major exception to the strict rule of confidentiality is the "intention of his client to commit a crime, and information necessary to prevent the crime." Significantly, however, even in that exceptional circumstance, disclosure of the confidence is only permissible, not mandatory. . . .

In summary, the Constitution has committed us to an adversary system for the administration of criminal justice. The essentially humanitarian reason for such a system is that it preserves the dignity of the individual, even though that may occasionally require significant frustration of the search for truth and the will of the state. An essential element of that system is the right to counsel, a right that would be meaningless if the defendant were not able to communicate freely and fully with the attorney.

In order to protect that communication—and, ultimately, the adversary system itself—we impose upon attorneys what has been called the "sacred trust" of confidentiality. It was pursuant to that high trust that the lawyers acted in Lake Pleasant, New York, when they refrained from divulging their knowledge of where the bodies were buried.

QUESTIONS

1. *Why does Freedman believe that it was acceptable for the lawyers to withhold evidence in the Lake Pleasant case?*

2. *Do you accept his responses? Why or why not?*

3. *There are other ways of handling justice beside the adversarial system. Freedman briefly mentions the system that is used in communist countries. What sort of system do they have? Why does Freedman think our system is better? What do you think are the advantages and disadvantages of their system?*

4. *In the time since this was written, it has become much harder for lawyers legally to withhold evidence that is potentially significant to a case. Is this a healthy trend in your opinion? Why or why not?*

Professional Ethics in Law

The ethical principles of the adversarial justice system can be clarified by looking at the Code of Professional Responsibility of the American Bar Association. The document outlines the ethical duties of an attorney in America. As one might expect, this work is complex and subject to various interpretations; no lawyer's work would be complete without a few loopholes. However, by looking at it, one can get a good feeling for the type of things a lawyer is supposed to do and one can certainly see how a lawyer could get into the type of situation described in the Lake Pleasant case.

We have included the following sections of the Code of Professional Responsibility:

1. The Table of Contents

2. The Preamble, which underscores the ethical philosophy of the adversarial justice system

3. A section from the disciplinary rules of Canon 7, which outlines what a lawyer should do to be a "zealous advocate" for his client.

"ABA Code of Professional Responsibility"

CONTENTS[2]

CANON 1. A LAWYER SHOULD ASSIST IN MAINTAINING THE INTEGRITY AND COMPETENCE OF THE LEGAL PROFESSION

Disciplinary Rules

DR 1-101 Maintaining Integrity and Competence of the Legal Profession

DR 1-102 Misconduct

DR 1-103 Disclosure of Information to Authorities

CANON 2. A LAWYER SHOULD ASSIST THE LEGAL PROFESSION IN FULFILLING ITS DUTY TO MAKE LEGAL COUNSEL AVAILABLE

Ethical Considerations

Recognition of Legal Problems
Selection of a Lawyer: Generally
Selection of a Lawyer: Professional Notices and Listings
Financial Ability to Employ Counsel: Generally
Financial Ability to Employ Counsel: Persons Able to Pay Reasonable Fees
Financial Ability to Employ Counsel: Persons Unable to Pay Reasonable Fees
Acceptance and Retention of Employment

Disciplinary Rules

DR 2-101 Publicity in General

DR 2-102 Professional Notices, Letterheads, Offices, and Law Lists

DR 2-103 Recommendation of Professional Employment

DR 2-104 Suggestion of Need of Legal Services

DR 2-105 Limitation of Practice

DR 2-106 Fees for Legal Services

DR 2-107 Division of Fees Among Lawyers

DR 2-108 Agreements Restricting the Practice of a Lawyer

DR 2-109 Acceptance of Employment

DR 2-110 Withdrawal from Employment

QUESTIONS

1. *What do you think is meant by the phrase "maintaining the integrity and competence of the legal profession"?*

2. *Canon 2 deals with questions relating to making legal counsel available. Why is the availability of legal counsel an ethical question?*

3. *Canons 4 through 7 deal with similar issues. What do they have in common?*

4. *Why do you think the* appearance *of impropriety is emphasized in Canon 9?*

PREAMBLE

The Preamble explains the philosophical basis of the legal profession. Canon 7 deals with the most controversial idea in the legal system, the question of zealous advocacy. Read these documents and answer the questions that follow them.

> The continued existence of a free and democratic society depends upon recognition of the concept that justice is based upon the rule of law grounded in respect for the dignity of the individual and his capacity through reason for enlightened self-government. Law so grounded makes justice possible, for only through such law does the dignity of the individual attain respect and protection. Without it, individual rights become subject to unrestrained power, respect for law is destroyed, and rational self-government is impossible.
>
> Lawyers, as guardians of the law, play a vital role in the preservation of society. The fulfillment of this role requires an understanding by lawyers of their relationship with and function in our legal system. A consequent obligation of lawyers is to maintain the highest standards of ethical conduct.
>
> In fulfilling his professional responsibilities, a lawyer necessarily assumes various roles that require the performance of many difficult tasks. Not every situation which he may encounter can be foreseen, but fundamental ethical principles are always present to guide him. Within the framework of these principles, a lawyer must with courage and foresight be able and ready to shape the body of the law to the ever-changing relationships of society.

DR [Disciplinary Rule] 7-101. Representing a Client Zealously.

(A) A lawyer shall not intentionally:

(1) Fail to seek the lawful objectives of his client through reasonably available means permitted by law and the Disciplinary Rules, except as provided by DR 7-101(B). A lawyer does not violate this Disciplinary Rule, however, by acceding to reasonable requests of opposing counsel which do not prejudice the rights of his clients, by being punctual in fulfilling all professional commitments, by avoiding offensive tactics, or by treating with courtesy and consideration all persons involved in the legal process.

(2) Fail to carry out a contract of employment entered into with a client for professional services, but he may withdraw as permitted under DR 2-110, DR 5-102, and DR 5-105.

(3) Prejudice or damage his client during the course of the professional relationship, except as required under DR 7-102(B).

(B) In his representation of a client, a lawyer may:

(1) Where permissible, exercise his professional judgment to waive or fail to assert a right or position of his client.

(2) Refuse to aid or participate in conduct that he believes to be unlawful, even though there is some support for an argument that the conduct is legal.

DR 7-102. Representing a Client Within the Bounds of the Law.

(A) In his representation of a client, a lawyer shall not:

(1) File a suit, assert a position, conduct a defense, delay a trial, or take other action on behalf of his client when he knows or when it is obvious that such action would serve merely to harass or maliciously injure another.

(2) Knowingly advance a claim or defense that is unwarranted under existing law, except that he may advance such claim or defense if it can be supported by good faith argument for an extension, modification, or reversal of existing law.

(3) Conceal or knowingly fail to disclose that which he is required by law to reveal.

(4) Use perjured testimony or false evidence.

(5) Knowingly make a false statement of law or fact.

(6) Participate in the creation or preservation of evidence when he knows or it is obvious that the evidence is false.

(7) Counsel or assist his client in conduct that the lawyer knows to be illegal or fraudulent.

(8) Knowingly engage in other illegal conduct or conduct contrary to a Disciplinary Rule.

(B) A lawyer who receives information clearly establishing that:

(1) His client has, in the course of the representation, perpetrated a fraud upon a person or tribunal shall promptly call upon his client to rectify the same, and if his client refuses or is unable to do so, he shall reveal the fraud to the affected person or tribunal.

(2) A person other than his client has perpetrated a fraud upon a tribunal shall promptly reveal the fraud to the tribunal.

QUESTIONS

1. *What does it mean to say that "justice is based upon the rule of law grounded in respect for the dignity of the individual and his capacity through reason for enlightened self-government"?*

2. *Why do you think the writers of this preamble believe that individual rights are so important to justice in a democracy?*

3. *Why do you think it was necessary to include the statement in DR 7–101 that "a lawyer does not violate this Disciplinary Rule . . . by acceding to reasonable requests of opposing counsel"? What does it say about lawyers and our legal system that such a statement was not self-evident?*

4. *What does statement DR 7–102 say? Read it carefully. In what way does it restrict the lawyer's behavior? In what way does it leave the lawyer free?*

5. *Does statement DR 7–102 interfere with a lawyer's ability to be a zealous advocate? Why or why not?*

6. *Is there anything that you have read from the Code of Professional Responsibility that you think undermines Professor Freedman's position in the Lake Pleasant case? Why or why not?*

Case Studies in Legal Ethics

Do I Have to Tell Them?[3]

Now that we have some idea of what a lawyer's ethical duties are under the adversarial justice system, we can look at a case study in legal ethics and see how lawyers wrestle with their own ethical problems. The case study presented describes a situation in which a professor of legal ethics advises a student on how to handle an ethical problem that comes up. The problem challenges the student's ability to be both a zealous advocate and an officer of the court.

> A young woman bought a used car in San Francisco for $2500. She ran it a week and it conked-out on her, so she brought it back to the dealer who made some repairs. She took it out and again it wasn't working right. Again, the dealer repaired it, but now he wanted $1000 for the work before releasing the car to her. She didn't have the money. A lawyer-friend had told her she had no effective legal recourse.
> She went to another friend connected with San Francisco Consumer Action who told her she was being ripped-off and that the group would be glad to do something for her. They wrote a polite letter to the auto dealer to get her money back. The dealer didn't answer. The consumer group now checked and found that

it was okay to picket the dealer, provided they didn't block exits and entrances and used truthful, non-libelous signs. The placards the pickets used simply said that So and So Motors had sold a car to Ms. . . . . for $2500 and then tried to charge her another $1000 to make the car run right. Two days after the picketing began, the auto dealer's lawyer brought suit to enjoin the picketing and collect $6 million for libel and extortion.

At this point Consumer Action, which had no real funds, came to us for legal help. I assigned it to Mark Bessemer, a very bright but almost obnoxiously aggressive student. He was fantastically motivated to win, not just because he had once been taken by a used car dealer but because he saw it as a great injustice that had to be righted.

The judge in the case had already enjoined the picketing. Mark worked hard on an appeal and we got a reversal. By this time the case was attracting a lot of press coverage as the picketing continued.

Now Mark researched the case for *demurrer*[4] and decided there was no cause for action on the dealer's part. There were several problems here: were the placards libelous per se? Mark was convinced they weren't. And what about their crazy charge of extortion in a civil case? How could you bring extortion, a criminal charge, into a civil case? His research convinced him that it couldn't be done. If it couldn't be done, obviously their whole case wasn't worth a dime. There was no libel and the extortion charges, if any, would have to be brought by the prosecutor, not the auto dealer's lawyer.

As it happened, I had just finished doing a chapter for a California State Bar Continuing Legal Education booklet. I urged Mark to read it and then discuss it with me. The next day when he came in for our conference, he was white-lipped. His first question was, "My God, do I have to show them this?"

In the chapter I showed how it was possible to convert what was a criminal charge into a civil case. The possibility had arisen out of several California cases in the 1970–71 period. One special case had involved another used car dealer who had turned back an odometer. Ordinarily, that would be a fraud case but under the new doctrine once you showed that the odometer had been turned back and that you were damaged—as you were indeed, if you bought a car with only 12,000 miles showing when, in fact, it had been run 60,000 miles—why then you could pursue a fine civil case against the dealer.

And so when Mark exclaimed, "Do we have to show them

this? We'll lose the whole thing if we do," he had placed the ethical dilemma on my shoulders. And it was a peculiar dilemma, one that made me feel a little schizophrenic. If I were back in private practice in Los Angeles, as I had been for several years, and a young associate has come to me with a similar problem, I *probably* would have told him the functional truth: "Nobody tells opposing counsel anything like this in normal practice." But I was no longer in private practice. I was now a law teacher and supervisor of third-year clinical law students finding out about the law, about ethics and professional responsibilities. Further, I was responsible for them. I was pretty sure what the Code of Professional Responsibility said we had to do, but still it had been some time since I looked at it. So Mark and I both went over the Code carefully looking for an out. There wasn't any. The Code was miserably unambiguous: *We had to reveal.*

It might be one thing if you had to reveal when the chances were that opposing counsel would have hit on it anyway. That wouldn't be much of a revelation. But in this case the new doctrine was still quite exotic. Few lawyers knew about it. For one thing, my little chapter was still at the printers. To make the mandate for disclosure even crueler in this case was the near certainty that *if one did not disclose there was no way of getting caught.*

Reluctantly, I must admit, we did agree that at the hearing Mark *would* disclose. Still, there are disclosures and disclosures. Surely, what was called for here was minimal disclosure. Mark argued in a brief, non-argumentative and courteous way. He did cite the detrimental line of cases, but the judge and opposing counsel, hearing the concept for the first time at oral argument, simply did not pick up the importance of the cases.

The court sustained the demurrer. After it was over, the judge told Mark, "If you do as good a job as a lawyer as you did today, you will be an excellent lawyer." He didn't, of course, know of the temptations that Mark had been subjected to. Perhaps the loftiest comment on it came 2,300 years ago from Aristotle, in the Nicomachean Ethics: "Virtue, like art, constantly deals with what is hard to do, and the harder the task the better the success."

QUESTIONS

1. *What happened to the woman who bought the car that caused her to go to Legal Aid?*

2. *What did she do after Legal Aid looked at her case?*

3. *Why did Mark think at first that the used-car dealer had no case?*

4. *What made Mark think the dealer had a case?*

5. *How did Mark reveal the cases that could have jeopardized his position?*

6. *How did the court decide the case?*

7. *Write a summary of the case described.*

The following three commentators are attorneys who have been asked to determine whether Mark Bessemer and his teacher, Professor Kayne, behaved ethically. You will notice that the commentators focus on very different aspects of the case.

Comments from the Experts

JAMES D. FELLERS

Was the law student required to reveal to the court an article by Professor Kayne detrimental to the position being espoused in court by the student? Or even the cases discussed therein, which were pertinent to the issue in the student's case?

The Code of Professional Responsibility, in EC 7-23, provides: "Where a lawyer knows of legal authority in the controlling jurisdiction directly adverse to the position of his client, he should inform the tribunal of its existence unless his adversary has done so; but, having made such disclosure, he may challenge its soundness in whole or in part." DR 7-106 (B) states: "In presenting a matter to a tribunal, a lawyer shall disclose legal authority in the controlling jurisdiction known to him to be directly adverse to the position of his client and which is not disclosed by opposing counsel."

The decision reached by Professor Kayne in the example was a correct one. It was not necessary to disclose the Kayne article but it was necessary to inform the court of the detrimental cases. The student did so in a non-argumentative way. He properly could have attempted to distinguish those cases from his, and he also could have challenged the soundness of the legal conclusion in those cases. However, this is a matter of trial tactics, and the student seems to have made the proper tactical decision. . . .

The duty to disclose adverse legal authority is a departure from, and inconsistent with, the concept that our legal system is an adversary system. The Canons espouse that each side is to be represented zealously; the system permits a more able lawyer, or better prepared lawyer, to win. The duty to disclose contained in EC 7-23 goes counter to the adversary concept; in fact, it punishes the diligent researcher and rewards the lazy one. Most trial lawyers do not like the rule, but realize that, in addition to being an advocate, the lawyer is an officer of the court and disclosure of adverse authority is part of his duty to the court to see that justice is done.

There is general adherence to EC 7-23. A skillful lawyer can distinguish his case from the prior ones; after all, the facts of his case are different.

BRUCE S. ROGOW

One difficulty with commenting on these cases is that you have to take the facts as presented. You cannot pursue questioning to clarify a point. The point I have in mind here is a legal one: Do the California "criminal into civil" cases really apply to a consumer group's First Amendment fair comment? The odometer case is a good example of a criminal fraud law enacted for the benefit of the general public, which should be (and in many states such laws have always been) *tortious*[5] per se. My initial reaction is that the arguments are so strongly against applying those cases to the facts of this case that disclosure is not an issue. Certainly, one does not have to disclose every tortured theory which could be argued.

The problem really arises when, in *shephardizing*[6] a case which supports your position, you come upon an advance-sheet opinion slightly eroding your argument. Or, just prior to the hearing, while you are taking a quick glance at *Law Week*, you find a decision from another state or circuit which goes directly against you. I use those examples because they present the gray area in which disclosure problems arise. There is no doubt that an applicable Supreme Court case, decided the day before, must be disclosed, just as there is no doubt in my mind about the lack of need to disclose the "tortured theory" case.

The test is, I think, "applicability." If knowledge of a decision may actually influence the outcome of a case, then it must be disclosed to the court. I say "to the court" for a good reason. First, I want the court to know of my candor. The judge might be more inclined to believe my arguments distinguishing the case, if he or she knows I disclosed it. Secondly, why should I let my adversary look erudite from my work? When you inform the court by memo, or letter, a copy of course, goes to opposing counsel. If done orally, because you *just* found the case, you tell opposing counsel prior to the hearing.

Disclosure actually benefits your client. If you win in the lower court only because that court did not have the benefit of a new decision, the appeal will cost your client time or money in a losing cause. Even if disclosure causes you to lose a close case initially and on appeal, I think you have benefited the client. While winning is important, justice is more important, even for your client who (I assume) hopes to live in a civilized society. While I do not enjoy having to explain this philosophy to a client who has seen his case lost because he has an honest lawyer, it is a small price to pay for integrity.

Another benefit extends to future clients. When a lawyer achieves a reputation for fairness and candor, judges respond affirmatively to him or her. To the extent that trust enters into the decision-making process, that lawyer has a decided advantage over a sneaky adversary.

Going back to the case, I am troubled by the statement, "surely what was called for here was minimal disclosure." Giving minimal disclosure is like being "a little pregnant." Minimal disclosure connotes surreptitiousness to me. I agree that one does not have to belabor the opposing cases, but neither should one drop them into the argument while the judge is tying his shoelace. In brief or memorandum, a footnote briefly distinguishing the case is an effective way to disclose them.

HOWARD R. SACKS

The lawyer obviously did the right thing in this case. Section 7-106 (B) (1) of the Code of Professional Responsibility requires the lawyer to cite opposing authority.

It is, however, a sad commentary on private practice, at least in Los Angeles, that the lawyer apparently would not have done this had the case arisen in the context of private practice.

In talking with Mark, it might have been helpful to have

discussed with him the reasons underlying the ethical rule. It could have been pointed out that the adversary system will not work effectively unless the court is acquainted with *all* the relevant legal principles in the case before it. It might also have been noted that, if lawyers generally begin to adhere to this standard, Mark himself might someday benefit from the rule, i.e., opposing counsel digs up a case that Mark had overlooked. The lesson that Mark learned in this case might have been learned at a deeper level had he obtained a fuller understanding of the reasons underlying the rule, and the possible future benefits to him of complying with the rule.

QUESTIONS

1. *Does James Fellers think Professor Kayne handled the situation correctly?*

2. *What does Fellers think of EC-7-23? Why? Is this rule adhered to?*

3. *Why does Bruce Rogow think that it is likely that the odometer case may have little to do with the case being discussed here?*

4. *Why does Rogow think that disclosure benefits the client?*

5. *Does Rogow think the case discussed here was well handled?*

6. *How does Howard Sacks think that Professor Kayne could have handled the case better?*

7. *Write summaries of the three commentaries.*

ACTIVITIES

❶   Having read and discussed this case thoroughly, what are your opinions? Was it ethical for the student to use this "minimal disclosure" tactic? Discuss the case, making reference to the commentaries provided by the legal experts. Use the experts to bolster your own position. Argue against the experts when you believe they are wrong. Your essay should be 500–750 words long.

John Stuart Mill

Individual Rights and the Legal System

Throughout this discussion of the adversarial justice system, there has been an assumption made by all those who believe in the system. This is the idea that the rights of the individual must be respected, and that our justice system must serve to protect these rights. They are never exactly spelled out, but one assumes that they include the right to live freely without interference from the law unless one has committed a grievous crime against society. This leads us to a further question—and one that must illuminate our entire concept of the place of law in our society. The question is: Where do the rights of an individual end and those of society begin?

The justice system must perform a balancing act between protecting the individual and serving the needs of society. We have a justice system that claims to protect the individual from unfair harassment by laws or by society, and we have laws to protect society. And yet the question remains: at what point does an individual's actions become society's concern?

To answer this, it is appropriate to turn to the work of a philosopher and social critic, a man thoroughly familiar with the ways of the adversarial justice system, a man whose thinking embraced a passionate concern for both the individual and society. This man was John Stuart Mill. In looking at the work of Mill, we are trying to go one step beyond the ethical problems created by the adversarial system, to the ethical problems created by the whole concept of British and American law. We also weigh the potential conflict between an ethical belief in the sanctity of the individual (as is professed by most Americans and enshrined in the Constitution) and an ethical belief that the interests of society must be served.

Mill's Life

At the age of three, John Stuart Mill began the study of ancient Greek; by the age of seven he had studied Latin and Hebrew as well and, at twelve, had apparently mastered large areas of mathematics, political science, and philosophy. He was, quite simply, one of the greatest intellectual prodigies in history. He never attended school, having been solely educated under the close supervision of his father. He was, in fact, a guinea pig in his father's experiment on the intellectual potential of a child.

His father was a member of a group of English thinkers who were committed to the idea of *utilitarianism*. This was a philosophy that had as its basic premise the idea that the greatest good comes from creating happiness for the greatest number of people. They believed that you could quantify happiness, and that by simply adding up the total amount of happiness, created by any act, and subtracting whatever unhappiness the act may cause, one could determine whether or not the act was worth doing. There was a widespread belief that, ultimately, all ethical problems could be solved simply by an application to every situation of this formula. (As you can guess, this problem turned out to be a little harder than the early utilitarians suspected. Although many philosophers to this day consider themselves to be utilitarians, their beliefs differ quite markedly from these early ideas.)

Young John Stuart Mill was being groomed for the role of the great utilitarian philosopher; it was hoped that he would be the one to apply his extraordinary intellect to the solution of all ethical problems. This was more of a burden than any man could bear and, predictably enough, at the age of twenty, Mill suffered a "crisis of faith" when he questioned all of his education and all the ideas that he had been taught. He went into a long depression, believing that he was incapable of feeling anything. The serious lack of artistic and poetic sensibility in his life began to seem oppressive. He emerged from the crisis with a sense of the limitations of his education and even of utilitarianism as a principle. Although a good part of his adult life was dedicated to the defense of utilitarianism, he developed another side to his thought; he became very interested in personal liberty and individual freedom.

On Liberty

Although Mill paid lip service to utilitarianism in *On Liberty*, the main thesis of the book concerns the rights and liberties of individuals in society.

One can immediately sense the conflict between utilitarianism and individualism. How can promoting the greatest good for the greatest number of people be compatible with preserving the rights of the individual? Mill answers this question by stating that, ultimately, whatever best serves the rights of the individual also serves the interests of society. Without respect for individual freedoms, there is no way that society, as a whole, can secure happiness for a majority of its citizens.

Mill states the aims of *On Liberty* in a succinct phrase in his first chapter. It is "to assert one very simple principle . . . that the sole end for which mankind are warranted . . . in interfering with . . . liberty of action . . . is self-protection." In other words, you can only stop someone from doing something if he or she is going to hurt you. You can't stop a man for his own good, or stop a woman because you don't like what she is doing. The question remains: what does it mean to say that someone is hurting you? This is not an easy question. If I don't like rock 'n' roll and someone is blasting it on his stereo, should I have the right to force him to stop? Is he interfering with my rights or is he just expressing his individuality? In his fourth chapter, Mill gives some guidelines that will help us understand what he means by hurting others.

On Liberty has been a very influential book. In America, politicians of every political persuasion have felt that it is important to defend the rights of a person's private action that may be eccentric but harmless. Many of these politicians have not read the book, but its profound influence on the intellectual community in America has led to its ideas seeping down to all levels of society.

The writing style that Mill uses is both archaic and opaque to the modern layman, although philosophers consider him to be a model of clarity. After sifting through a welter of subordinate clauses in a 500-word sentence, you are unlikely to agree with them. In reading this selection, then, we will follow a procedure designed to get you through the thicket of words to the ideas beneath them.

ACTIVITIES

Look for the main clause of a sentence, which will usually have the important idea behind it.

❶ Mill loves to qualify his statements, but most of them are of little concern to nonprofessionals. They also make for long, unwieldy sentences that are hard to understand. Note the following sentence: "Though society is not founded on a contract, and though no good purpose is answered by inventing a contract to deduce social obligations from it, everyone who receives the protection of society owes a return for the benefit, and the fact of living in society renders it indispensable that each should be bound to observe a certain line of conduct towards the rest." In this sentence, there is one important phrase: "everyone who receives the protection of society owes a return for the benefit." The first part of the sentence tells us that Mill does not believe that society is based on a contract, a fact that is not of much interest to those not versed in the history of philosophy. The last part of the sentence elaborates on the idea of our obligation to society. But the meat of the sentence is in that one clause, and it is there that you should focus your attention.

❷ What is easiest to understand is usually most important. Mill was usually clear when it was important to be. With this in mind list the main ideas.

❸ Look for lists. Sometimes, Mill lists several ideas in succession, divided by numbering devices, semicolons, or commas. These lists are easy to understand and can give a clue to the general meaning of his theoretical positions.

❹ Keep a dictionary handy, but try to guess at the meanings. You will be surprised to see how often you are right.

❺ Keep in mind that you may need to read a passage more than once in order to understand it.

"Of the Limits to the Authority of Society over the Individual"[7]

EXCERPT 1

What, then, is the rightful limit to the sovereignty of the individual over himself? Where does the authority of society begin? How much of human life should be assigned to individuality, and how much to society?

Each will receive its proper share if each has that which more particularly concerns it. To individuality should belong the part of life in which it is chiefly the individual that is interested; to society, the part which chiefly interests society.

Though society is not founded on a contract, and though no good purpose is answered by inventing a contract in order to deduce social obligations from it, everyone who receives the protection of society owes a return for the benefit, and the fact of living in society renders it indispensable that each should be bound to observe a certain line of conduct towards the rest. This conduct consists, first, in not injuring the interests of one another, or rather certain interests which, either by express legal provision or by tacit understanding, ought to be considered as rights; and secondly, in each person's bearing his share (to be fixed on some equitable principle) of the labours and sacrifices incurred for defending the society or its members from injury and molestation. These conditions society is justified in enforcing at all costs on those who endeavour to withhold fulfillment. Nor is this all that society may do. The acts of an individual may be hurtful to others or wanting in due consideration for their welfare, without going to the length of violating any of their constitutional rights. The offender may then be justly punished by opinion, though not by law. As soon as any part of a person's conduct affects prejudicially the interests of others, society has jurisdiction over it, and the question whether the general welfare will or will not be promoted by interfering with it becomes open to discussion. But there is no room for entertaining any such question when a person's conduct affects the interests of no persons besides himself, or needs not affect them unless they like (all the persons concerned being of full age and the ordinary amount of understanding). In all such cases, there should be perfect freedom, legal and social, to do the action and stand the consequences.

ACTIVITIES

❶ Skim through Excerpt 1 to get a feeling for what Mill is saying.

❷ Now read the first two paragraphs more carefully. Then write what you think they mean.

❸ In the first two paragraphs you have just read, Mill argues that the individual should be concerned with matters that primarily concern the individual, and that society should concern itself with things that matter more to society. Can you think of some examples that only concern individuals? Can you think of instances that might only concern society?

❹ Read the third paragraph and write a summary of it.

❺ According to Mill, if you receive the protection of society, what is the line of conduct you should observe towards other members of society?

❻ In what two ways may society punish people? Under what circumstances should each punishment be used?

❼ What may society do when individuals hurt only themselves?

❽ Reread paragraphs 1–3 again with your summaries in hand.

❾ Keeping in mind the hints given above, check and rewrite each summary as you reread each paragraph. Eliminate extraneous details. Although Mill's writing will still be difficult, it should seem easier than it did the first time through. Take the time to write good paragraph summaries.

EXCERPT 2

It would be a great misunderstanding of this doctrine to suppose that it is one of selfish indifference which pretends that human beings have no business with each other's conduct in life, and that they should not concern themselves about the well-doing or well-being of one another, unless their own interest is involved. Instead of any diminution, there is need of a great increase of disinterested exertion to promote the good of others. But disinterested benevolence can find other instruments to persuade people of their good than whips and scourges, either of the literal or the metaphorical sort. I am the last person to undervalue the self-regarding virtues; they are only second in importance, if even second, to the social. It is equally the business of education to cultivate both. But even education works by conviction and persuasion as well as by compulsion, and it is by the former only that, when the period of education is passed, the self-regarding virtues should be inculcated. Human beings owe to each other help to distinguish the better from the worse, and encouragement to choose the former and avoid the latter. They should be forever stimulating each other to increased exercise of their higher faculties and increased direction of their feelings and aims towards wise instead of foolish, elevating instead of degrading, objects and contemplations. But neither one person, nor any number of persons, is warranted in saying to another human creature of ripe years that he shall not do with his life for his own benefit what he chooses to do with it. He is the person most interested in his own well-being: the interest which any other person, except in cases of strong personal attachment, can have in it is trifling compared with that which he himself has; the interest which society has in him individually (except as to his conduct to others) is fractional and altogether indirect, while with respect to his own feelings and circumstances the most ordinary man or woman has means of knowledge immeasurably surpassing those that can be possessed by anyone else. The interference of society to overrule his judgment and purposes in what only regards himself must be grounded on general presumptions which may be altogether wrong and, even if right, are as likely as not to be misapplied to individual cases, by persons no better acquainted with the circumstances of such cases than those are who look at them merely from without. In this department, therefore, of human affairs, individuality has its proper field of action. In the conduct of human beings towards one another it is necessary that general rules should for the most part be observed in order that people may know what they have to expect; but in each person's own concerns his individual spontaneity is entitled to free exercise. Considerations to aid his judgment, exhortations to strengthen his will, may be offered to him, even obtruded on him, by others; but he himself is the final judge. All errors which he is likely to commit against advice and warning are far outweighed by the evil of allowing others to constrain him to what they deem his good. . . .

ACTIVITIES

❶ Skim through Excerpt 2. In this paragraph, Mill first distinguishes his view from one of "selfish indifference" to others, and then goes on to argue that no one has the right to tell another adult what to do if the latter is not violating someone's rights.

❷ Read the paragraph carefully. Stop when you come to the sentence found about halfway through the paragraph, beginning with: "But neither one person, nor any number of persons, is warranted . . ."

❸ What is Mill saying up to this point? How does he think we should encourage the self-regarding virtues?

❹ Read the rest of the paragraph, and then answer the questions in Activities 5 and 6.

❺ Why should society not interfere with a person in matters that only concern the individual?

❻ What can society, or its members, do to influence a person in matters that only concern that person?

❼ Write a summary of Excerpt 2. Your summary should incorporate the information in Activities 3–6.

EXCERPT 3

We have a right, also, in various ways, to act upon our unfavourable opinion of anyone, not to the oppression of his individuality, but in the exercise of ours. We are not bound, for example, to seek his *society*; we have a right to avoid it (though not to parade the avoidance), for we have a right to choose the society most acceptable to us. We have a right, and it may be our duty, to caution others against him if we think his example or conversation likely to have a *pernicious* effect on those with whom he associates. We may give others a preference over him in optional good offices, except those which tend to his improvement. In these various modes a person may suffer very severe penalties at the hands of others for faults which directly concern only himself; but he suffers these penalties only in so far as they are the natural and, as it were, the spontaneous consequences of the faults themselves, not because they are purposely inflicted on him for the sake of punishment. A person who shows rashness, obstinacy, self-conceit—who cannot live within moderate means; who cannot restrain himself from hurtful indulgence; who pursues *animal pleasures* at the expense of those of feeling and intellect—must expect to be lowered in the opinion of others, and to have a less share of their favourable sentiments; but of this he has no right to complain unless he has merited their favour by special excellence in his social relations and has thus established a title to their good offices, which is not affected by his demerits towards himself. . . .

QUESTIONS

Here Mill shows how we can act on our unfavorable opinion of someone, and he gives some examples of behavior that he considers objectionable, but not hurtful to others.

1. *How may we act on our unfavorable opinion of someone who is not hurting others?*

2. *What are some of the behaviors Mill considers objectionable but not hurtful to others?*

ACTIVITIES

❶ Write a summary of Excerpt 3, which should include answers to the preceding questions, but not your opinions or views.

EXCERPT 4

Acts injurious to others require a totally different treatment. Encroachment on their rights, infliction on them of any loss or damage not justified by his own rights; falsehood or duplicity in dealing with them; unfair or ungenerous use of advantages over them; even selfish abstinence from defending them against injury—these are fit objects of moral reprobation and, in grave cases, of moral retribution and punishment. And not only these acts, but the dispositions which lead to them, are properly immoral and fit subjects of disapprobation which may rise to abhorrence. Cruelty of disposition; malice and ill-nature; that most antisocial and odious of all passions, envy; dissimulation and insincerity, irascibility on insufficient cause, and resentment disproportioned to the provocation; the love of domineering over others; the desire to engross more than one's share of advantages . . . , the pride which derives gratification from the abasement of others; the egotism which thinks self and its concerns more important than everything else, and decides all doubtful questions in its own favour—these are moral vices and constitute a bad and odious moral character, unlike the self-regarding faults previously mentioned, which are not properly immoralities and, to whatever pitch they may be carried, do not constitute wickedness. They may be proofs of any amount of folly or want of personal dignity and self-respect, but they are only a subject of moral reprobation when they involve a breach of duty to others, for whose sake the individual is bound to have care for himself. What are called duties to ourselves are not socially obligatory unless circumstances render them at the same time duties to others. The term duty to oneself, when it means anything more than prudence, means self-respect or self-development, and for none of these is anyone accountable to his fellow creatures, because for none of them is it for the good of mankind that he be held accountable to them.

QUESTIONS

Here Mill lists the qualities that are subject to moral reprobation, retribution, and punishment. He distinguishes these from the self-regarding faults listed previously under Excerpt 3.

1. *What examples does Mill give of "acts injurious to others"?*

2. *What are the dispositions that Mill considers "immoral and fit subjects of disapprobation"?*

3. *According to Mill, what is the difference between a self-regarding vice and a moral vice?*

ACTIVITIES

❶ Write a summary of Excerpt 4, which should incorporate the information in the answers to the preceding questions.

EXCERPT 5

The distinction between the loss of consideration which a person may rightly incur by defect of prudence or of personal dignity, and the reprobation which is due to him for an offence against the rights of others, is not a merely nominal distinction. It makes a vast difference both in our feelings and in our conduct towards him whether he displeases us in things in which we think we have a right to control him or in things in which we know that we have not. If he displeases us, we may express our distaste, and we may stand aloof from a person as well as from a thing that displeases us; but we shall not therefore feel called on to make his life uncomfortable. We shall reflect that he already bears, or will bear, the whole penalty of his error; if he spoils his life by mismanagement, we shall not, for that reason, desire to spoil it still further; instead of wishing to punish him, we shall rather endeavour to alleviate his punishment by showing him how he may avoid or cure the evils his conduct tends to bring upon him. He may be to us an object of pity, perhaps of dislike, but not of anger or resentment; we shall not treat him like an enemy of society; the worst we shall think ourselves justified in doing is leaving him to himself, if we do not interfere benevolently by showing interest or concern for him. It is far otherwise if he has infringed the rules necessary for the protection of his fellow creatures, individually or collectively. The evil consequences of his acts do not then fall on himself, but on others; and society, as the protector of all its members, must retaliate on him, must inflict pain on him for the express purpose of punishment, and must take care that it be sufficiently severe. In the one case, he is an offender at our bar, and we are called on not only to sit in judgment on him, but, in one shape or another, to execute our own sentence; in the other case, it is not our part to inflict any suffering on him except what may incidentally follow from our using the same liberty in the regulation of our own affairs which we allow to him in his.

QUESTIONS

Here, Mill outlines the difference in treatment that he recommends towards those who indulge in self-regarding vices and those who commit acts injurious to others.

1. *How should we treat those who incur "loss of consideration . . . by defect of prudence or of personal dignity" but do not commit any "offense against the rights of others"?*

2. *How should we treat one who has "infringed the rules necessary for the protection of his fellow creatures"?*

ACTIVITIES

❶ Write a summary of Excerpt 5, which should include answers to the preceding questions.

EXCERPT 6

The distinction here pointed out between the part of a person's life which concerns only himself and that which concerns others, many persons will refuse to admit. How (it may be asked) can any part of the conduct of a member of society be a matter of indifference to the other members? No person is an entirely isolated being; it is impossible for a person to do anything seriously or permanently hurtful to himself without mischief reaching at least to his near connections, and often far beyond them. If he injures his property, he does harm to those who directly or indirectly derived support from it, and usually diminishes, by a greater or less amount, the general resources of the community. If he deteriorates his bodily or mental faculties, he not only brings evil upon all who depended on him for any portion of their happiness, but disqualifies himself for rendering the services which he owes to his fellow creatures generally, perhaps becomes a burden on their affection or benevolence; and if such conduct were very frequent, hardly any offence that is committed would detract more from the general sum of good. Finally, if by his vices or follies a person does no direct harm to others, he is nevertheless (it may be said) injurious by his example, and ought to be compelled to control himself for the sake of those whom the sight or knowledge of his conduct might corrupt or mislead.

And even (it will be added) if the consequences of misconduct could be confined to the vicious or thoughtless individual, ought society to abandon to their own guidance those who are manifestly unfit for it? If protection against themselves is confessedly due to children and persons under age, is not society equally bound to afford it to persons of mature years who are equally incapable of self-government? If gambling, or drunkenness, or incontinence, or idleness, or uncleanliness are as injurious to happiness, and as great a hindrance to improvement, as many or most of the acts prohibited by law, why (it may be asked) should not law, so far as is consistent with practicability and social convenience, endeavour to repress these also? And as a supplement to the unavoidable imperfections of law, ought not opinion at least to organize a powerful police against these vices and visit rigidly with social penalties those who are known to practise them? There is no question here (it may be said) about restricting individuality, or impeding the trial of new and original experiments in living. The only things it is sought to prevent are things which have been tried and condemned from the beginning of the world until now—things which experience has shown not to be useful or suitable to any person's individuality. There must be some length of time and amount of experience after which a moral or prudential truth may be regarded as established; and it is merely desired to prevent generation after generation from falling over the same precipice which has been fatal to their predecessors.

QUESTIONS

Here, Mill anticipates an argument against his point of view. What he does is to present, as clearly as possible, an objection to his position. Later, he will show what is wrong *with this objection. But, for now, he is arguing* against *himself.*

1. *How could it be argued that one's vices really concern only oneself?*

2. *Even if the consequences of misconduct only concern one person, how could it be argued that society is still justified in restricting certain obnoxious behaviors?*

A C T I V I T I E S

❶ Write a summary of Excerpt 6, which should include the information in the answers to the preceding questions. Remember that Mill is expressing opinions that he disagrees with; be sure to make that point clear in your summary.

EXCERPT 7

I fully admit that the mischief which a person does to himself may seriously affect, both through their sympathies and their interests, those nearly connected with him and, in a minor degree, society at large. When, by conduct of this sort, a person is led to violate a distinct and assignable obligation to any other person or persons, the case is taken out of the self-regarding class and becomes amenable to moral disapprobation in the proper sense of the term. If, for example, a man, through intemperance or extravagance, becomes unable to pay his debts, or, having undertaken the moral responsibility of a family, becomes from the same cause incapable of supporting or educating them, he is deservedly reprobated and might be justly punished but it is for the breach of duty to his family or creditor, not for the extravagance. If the resources which ought to have been devoted to them had been diverted from them for the most prudent investment, the moral culpability would have been the same. . . .

In like manner, when a person disables himself, by conduct purely self-regarding, from the performance of some definite duty incumbent on him to the public, he is guilty of a social offence. No person ought to be punished simply for being drunk; but a soldier or a policeman should be punished for being drunk on duty. Whenever, in short, there is a definite damage, or a definite risk of damage, either to an individual or to the public, the case is taken out of the province of liberty and placed in that morality or law.

QUESTIONS

Mill now answers the criticism given in Excerpts 5 and 6. What he does is to draw attention to the different reasons one can have for punishing a person. He thinks it is crucial that you only punish for a breach of social duty.

1. When someone through "intemperance or extravagance" is unable to pay personal debts, what should he or she be punished for? Why?

2. What is the difference between a private citizen being drunk and a soldier or policeman being drunk on duty?

3. From Mill's standpoint, should a person who is driving while drunk be punished?

ACTIVITIES

❶ Write a summary of Excerpt 7, which should include answers to the preceding questions.

EXCERPT 8

But the strongest of all the arguments against the interference of the public with purely personal conduct is that, when it does interfere, the odds are that it interferes wrongly and in the wrong place. On questions of social morality, of duty to others, the opinion of the public, that is, of an overruling majority, though often wrong, is likely to be still oftener right, because on such questions they are only required to judge of their own interests, of the manner in which some mode of conduct, if allowed to be practised, would affect themselves. But the opinion of a similar majority, imposed as a law on the minority, on questions of self-regarding conduct is quite as likely to be wrong as right, for in these cases public opinion means, at the best, some people's opinion of what is good or bad for other people, while very often it does not even mean that—the public, with the most perfect indifference, passing over the pleasure or convenience of those whose conduct they censure and considering only their own preference. There are many who consider as an injury to themselves any conduct which they have a distaste for, and resent it as an outrage to their feelings; as a religious bigot, when charged with disregarding the religious feelings of others, has been known to retort that they disregard his feelings by persisting in their abominable worship or creed. But there is no parity between the feeling of a person for his own opinion and the feeling of another who is offended at his holding it, no more than between the desire of a thief to take a purse and the desire of the right owner to keep it. And a person's taste is as much his own peculiar concern as his opinion or his purse. It is easy for anyone to imagine an ideal public which leaves the freedom and choice of individuals in all uncertain matters undisturbed and only requires them to abstain from modes of conduct which universal experience has condemned. But where has there been seen a public which set any such limit to its censorship?

QUESTIONS

Mill answers an objection he raised earlier, where it was suggested that society can regulate things that we know from long practice are no good, even if they only affect the individual. He distinguishes between one's personal feelings and those that society has for the individual.

1. *What is the strongest objection Mill can offer to the idea of public interference in private concerns?*

2. *Why is public opinion likely to be wrong in matters of private concern? Why is it more likely to be right in matters of public concern?*

3. *What is wrong with the position of the religious bigot who says that others disregard his/her feelings by persisting in their offensive beliefs? What analogy does Mill make to demonstrate his point?*

ACTIVITIES

❶   Write a summary of Excerpt 8, which should include answers to the preceding questions.

Further Remarks on Mill

Mill goes on to suggest that no government or society, if given the right to legislate private morality, shows sufficient restraint. He gives examples of the unrestrained behavior of some societies. Religious persecution, widely practiced, is commonly done on the grounds that the persecutors know the true religion and thus have an obligation to persuade, by force if necessary, all those who hold incorrect and personally harmful beliefs. Mill considers this an abomination, interfering with a personal liberty of belief that cannot harm anyone except the person involved, and then only on the highly debatable premise that these persecutors *are* totally correct about the hell-fire that awaits those who profess other beliefs. He also cites the examples of the prohibition of dancing, games, and other entertainment that were put into law by the Puritans.

Mill argues that, at the time he was writing, there were further attempts to curtail personal liberties that would punish people who were willingly engaged in activity that harmed no one. He cites three examples: one is legislation that prohibits the sale of liquor, the second is legislation that forbids work on the Sabbath, and the third is persecution of Mormons on the ground that they practiced polygamy. He argues that although he personally objects to polygamy, we must remember that the women thus polygamously wedded did so voluntarily.

From these examples, we can get a fairly clear picture of the type of activities that Mill wants to keep outside of legislation. They are called, in modern parlance, *victimless crimes*. This means that, although the activities are considered wrong, no one is really hurt by them.

QUESTIONS

1. *Can you think of other examples of victimless crimes?*

2. *Do you agree with Mill that victimless crimes should not be subject*

to legislation? If you agree, restate Mill's reasons for not making them matters of legislation. If you disagree, state why such matters should be legislated, opposing the position that Mill holds.

ACTIVITIES

❶ Assemble all your notes and summaries on Mill. Rewrite them as one summary. Eliminate redundancies and clarify points that you understand better now. This rewriting exercise will help you solidify your ideas.

Adversarial Justice and the Price of Freedom

The ideas of Mill, regarding individual liberty and the ideas embodied in the adversarial justice system, have a great deal in common. Both stem from a deep regard for the rights of the individual, and from a distrust of the power of the state. The long history of the abuse of power carried out in the name of the state shows the ease with which states that have the legal means to impose their will on people do so. Moreover, the horrible tortures that have been perpetuated in the name of public morality give one a healthy respect for the skepticism about the "benevolence" of the state that Mill expresses and that the Adversarial Justice System embodies.

Nevertheless, it is clear that this concern for individual freedom has its down side. It requires one to tolerate a certain lack of efficiency in the conduct of life and business. Trials in communist countries are much quicker; criminals found guilty of capital crimes may be taken out and executed the same day, without the endless appeals that can keep an American on death row for years. We must tolerate, in the name of individual liberty, the rantings of various lunatics and are helpless to arrest someone who might commit a crime.

Adversarial justice does not guarantee true justice. Mill's concept of individual liberty does not guarantee that people's rights will be respected, nor does it lead to the most effective way to run a society. No one would claim that these ideas are perfect, but most Americans are inclined to think that the benefits outweigh the disadvantages.

Nevertheless, one must not underestimate the inconvenience our justice system and legal philosophy impose on us. In Singapore, you need never worry about seeing a person whose long hair or whose filthy appearance you might find offensive. In Saudi Arabia, you need not wait for the wheels of justice to grind into motion slowly to punish a thief. The punishment is swift and sure. And no lawyer in China would take pictures of bodies and not report them to the authorities. But it happens and it is legal here. This is the price we pay when we consider individual liberty.

ACTIVITIES

❶ Give some examples of the inconveniences caused by a respect for individual liberties. Do you think these inconveniences are worth the price for individual liberties? Why or why not?

❷ J. Edgar Hoover once said: "Justice has nothing to do with law and order." What do you think this quote means?

Endnotes for Chapter 1

1. "Where the Bodies are Buried: The Adversary System and the Obligation of Confidentiality." Reprinted with the permission of Macmillan Publishing Company from *Lawyer's Ethics in an Adversarial System*, by Monroe H. Freedman. The Bobbs–Merrill Company, Inc., 1975.

2. Reprinted with the permission of the American Bar Association, from *ABA Code of Professional Responsibility*, pp. iii–iv, 1, 36–37. The American Bar Association, 1980.

3. Reprinted with permission of Murray Teigh Bloom from *Case Studies in Legal Ethics* by Marvin S. Kayne with Murray Teigh Bloom. Meilan Press, 1974.

4. *demurrer*: in law, an argument which claims that even if the facts of a case are as alleged by the opposing party, they do not sustain the claim based upon them.

5. *tortious*: a legal term relating to a *tort*, or a wrongful act which damages another person's property or reputation, and for which the damaged party deserves compensation.

6. *shephardizing*: gathering together.

7. "Of the Limits to the Authority of Society over the Individual" from *On Liberty*, by John Stuart Mill. John W. Parker and Son, 1859.

CHAPTER 2

ETHICS AND BUSINESS:
Profits and
Principles

The natural conflict between business ethics and the precepts of the golden rule[1] are explored in this chapter. In an essay by the author we consider the general problem of lying in business. We look at a case study in which a businessman obviously put profits above principles. We deliberate on the point at which devious business practices are no longer acceptable. We then consider the ethical philosophy of Immanuel Kant, who argues that lying is never justifiable.

The Principles of Capitalism: A Natural Conflict

A conflict between business and ethics is implied in the very principles of capitalism, for in Adam Smith's idealized state of perfect *laissez-faire*,[2] each person is looking out for his own interests, trying to maximize his advantage. The miracle of capitalism, as Smith sees it, is that the best means to insure a price fair to both buyer and seller is for each individual to act in an apparently selfish way. This principle thus suggests that a moral virtue, such as fairness, can be achieved through apparently amoral action on the part of all the participants in the transaction. Thus, the amoral stance of business, whose sole end is to make money, is sanctioned in the very principles of our economic system. Furthermore, it is suggested that everything will work out morally for the best in the end, so there is no real reason for the businessperson to worry about moral principles.

There is, of course, a fundamental level on which the Adam Smith model does not really operate. Smith assumes a relative equality between buyer and seller. In Smith's mythically perfect capitalist marketplace there are no monopolies, no government regulations of industry, no protective tariffs, no unionized workers; that is, none of the many interfering factors that actually occur in the world and make prices more than mere market transactions. It must be conceded that these factors will never be totally eliminated, and so the perfect market transaction will never be the norm in the world. If this state of pure amorality, leading to fairness, is not achieved, we cannot expect business to disassociate itself completely from moral questions.

It is very clear, in fact, that business and business people do concern themselves with morals, as the proliferation of materials on business ethics assures us. Some of these works are simpleminded, self-congratulatory essays written by successful business people and composed, one assumes, to assure others that one need not be a crook to be rich. Others are dull and pompous analytical tomes by professional philosophers that either criticize or justify some business behavior in the arcane jargon of the university. We assume that these writers attach some practical significance to their work, but few business people have the time or the inclination to decipher these views. Other works are attempts by either business people or religious figures to show that making money is compatible with biblical precepts. And a few of their views are lucid and straightforward attempts to show what business is really like, and to determine if there really is any connection between business practice and ethical behavior, as we usually conceive it.

But the conflict between making money and doing right still exists; and there is no doubt that in business, behavior that looks ethical is practiced not because of the moral principles involved, but because ethics is often compatible with the bottom line. Frequently, a company that makes a big show of its principles, in certain areas, is not so scrupulous when pressed to the wall in some other way.

This conflict is the subject of this chapter. Ultimately, the question becomes: can a businessperson be truly ethical? Or are business people fooling themselves when they piously proclaim their principles?

Is It Ethical to Lie in Business?

It is interesting to see the perspective of business people towards the whole issue of lying. Most business people who have been questioned about the issue have been aware that a certain amount of deception and exaggeration is involved in business, but most also think that being ethical is good business practice.

Perhaps the most provocative position offered on the relationship of business to ethics was in an article by Albert Z. Carr in *Harvard Business Review* (Jan./Feb. 1968). In this article, Mr. Carr argues that lying in business is analogous to bluffing in poker. Both are strategies that are perfectly acceptable because they are permissible within the rules of the game. The rules of poker permit bluffing, and everyone understands that this will be done. The rules of the business game permit exaggeration, and the promotion of products that are obsolete, as well as intensive lobbying of public officials to look after one's interests. Business people pretend that they are motivated by public concern when they are actually trying to prevent public hostility. Such activities, Carr argues, are expected of business people, and should be accepted as a normal part of business practice.

Carr's article is attractively presented and well-written, and it probably represents an accurate assessment of what really happens in many situations. However, it brings up a number of problems and also exposes, perhaps inadvertently, some of the weaknesses of the business perspective.

One notices, for example, that Carr suggests that business is a game, much like poker, in which the so-called honest player is not one who does not lie (or, in the terminology of poker, "bluffs"), but simply the person who abides by the rules of the game. This analogy depends, however, on the assumption that all those playing the game understand the rules and are, in fact, playing by the same rules. This may well be true when talking of the relationship between one business and another, but does it hold equally well for the relationship between business and the consumer? Are consumers aware that business is a game wherein bluffing is allowed, with the only constraints being whether or not business people can get away with it? There is a concerted effort on the part of businesses to give the impression to the public that they are constrained by real concern for principles: for example, look at the self-congratulatory ads run by oil companies that focus on their support for the arts and various environmental projects. We can conclude that their aim may be to keep the public unaware of how the oil companies really think. This gives the business an advantage in dealing with the consumers. Thus, the relationship is not quite that of two players in a game playing by the same rules; the relationship is more like one partner deliberately concealing from the other certain rules of the game in order to stack the deck in his or her favor.

A second problem with Carr's argument stems from the idea that a business person is ethical if the law is obeyed. This seems to contradict what Carr says at another point, which is that ethics has nothing to do with business. What seems to be happening, here, is that Carr has two ideas about ethics, and he is switching from one concept to another. When he states that a business person who obeys the law is ethical, he maintains that he is following the rules of the business game, as conceived by the business community. Furthermore, he is making an assumption about the nature of ethics, which is that the only way we can call a person ethical is by examining the motives for the action. If the person is not motivated by ethical concerns, then we cannot say that he is ethical. This "motivist" approach to ethics is one that we will consider, in some depth, later in this chapter. What is clear is that Carr is switching approaches to ethics in midstream, which leads him to apparently contradictory positions.

From a purely practical perspective, Carr's approach is problematic as well. In the next section, we will look at a case in which a businessman, without breaking any laws, got himself involved in a project that would be almost universally condemned as evidence of the most cynical disregard for basic moral precepts. And yet, if we accept Carr's idea that an honest businessperson is one who does not break any laws, then Dr. Barbouti's behavior is within the bounds of acceptability. Does Mr. Carr really suggest that building chemical-weapon plants is morally acceptable? If he does not, then he must make his precepts more rigid. For there is little doubt that, even in the business community, the person who turns down an offer to develop chemical warfare is regarded more highly than one who regards nerve gas as a simple business opportunity, rather than as an abomination.

Business in Action

"The Mysterious Dr. B."[3]

The following story illustrates the amoral behavior that Carr claims is typical of business. Although chemical weapons have been banned since 1925, in a universal reaction to the horrible effects these weapons had on their victims in World War I, it is still possible for a business person, operating legally, to set up a plant capable of producing them. Dr. Barbouti's carefully evasive statements and the rationalizations of his behavior seem to bear out Carr's understanding of the way business works.

Spring 1984: Rolf Kiefer, owner of a small metal-construction firm in Wiesbaden, West Germany, receives a request to bid on the construction of a technology park in North Africa. The man soliciting the bids calls it a "big contract." Kiefer is intrigued, but as he says later, "when someone comes in with a suitcase full of money, you feel wary." When Kiefer learns that the "park" is to be built in Libya, he bows out. "I assumed from the outset that the man was talking about a weapons factory," claims Kiefer, "and we didn't want to get involved."

February 1985: Imhausen-Chemie, a major West German chemical-supply company, contracts with a Frankfurt firm called IBI to supply certain materials for the technology park.

December 1987: The press reports that the U.S. has evidence that Libya is building a chemical-warfare weapons facility.

August 1988: IBI closes down its Frankfurt office.

September 1988: The U.S. State Department declares that Libya "has established a chemical-warfare production capability" at Rabta, 40 miles south of Tripoli. Colonel Muammar Gaddafi protests that Rabta is designed to manufacture only pharmaceuticals.

February 1989: The Bonn government discloses that its intelligence services warned nine years earlier that Gaddafi could be preparing to make chemical weapons "with the help from unknown East and West German firms." This admission comes several weeks after authorities, prodded by the U.S., begin an official investigation and seize twelve boxes of IBI documents. Among them are letters of agreement between Imhausen-Chemie and the mysterious IBI-Ihsan Barbouti International.

Question: Who is Ihsan Barbouti?

Seated in the coffee shop of a London hotel, the stocky, goateed 61-year-old Iraqi businessman tortures his well-worn black worry beads. "I don't want to lie to you," Ihsan Barbouti tells the interviewer in his charmingly imperfect English, then adds disconcertingly, "and I don't want to tell you the truth also at the same time." Asked whether he ever dealt in deadly weapons, he says "I have done nothing bad. I don't deal with arms. Arms dealing is the opposite of my character. But I don't deal with something else. I don't deal with cigarettes, because I feel cigarettes is against the health."

What may be even more "against the health" is Libya's chemical-weapons plant, which U.S. intelligence officials say was masterminded by Barbouti. In an interview with a TIME correspondent, the amiable Dr. Barbouti, as he prefers to be called, readily admits he was the designer and prime contractor for the entire Rabta complex—with the exception of what he describes as the "pharmaceutical" plant. Barbouti insists that his only involvement with this facility was to sell building materials to the Libyans and that he had no inkling the plant might be used for sinister purposes.

Western intelligence sources scoff, saying that they have clear evidence that Barbouti was the key broker for the chemical factory. Though they have yet to find proof that he knew the Libyans planned to make nerve gas there, at least one official flatly labels Barbouti "the central villain" of the plot and "the subject of intense scrutiny for some time." In fact, both the Swiss and West German governments are conducting criminal investigations of his role in the Libyan project, and tax authorities in England and Scotland are looking into his Byzantine business affairs.

What is known about this nimble entrepreneur is that he is a rich man, with a fortune of perhaps $100 million. He claims to own companies in Switzerland, Greece, the Middle East and Thailand, as well as ten or 15 firms in England. "There's many people behind me," he says expansively. "If I phone now for $40 million, tomorrow I see the $40 million in my pocket. From friends—Saudi, Gulf, Iraqi. That's all like a consortium. I am a front man." He is also a man gifted in the ways of global deal-making, Swiss bank accounts and multimillion-dollar real estate enterprises in a number of countries, including the U.S.

Since, as Barbouti explains, he wants neither to lie nor to tell the truth, the details of the story he relates may be subject to considerable refinement. He says he was born to a wealthy Iraqi family, studied architecture in Zurich and Vienna and received a doctorate in West Berlin (hence "Doctor"). He taught architecture at Baghdad University in Iraq, ran a private consulting business there, invested in banking, insurance and industry, and served as a sometime government adviser. In 1969, a year after the Baath Party came to power, Barbouti fled the country, fearing that he might be arrested as a spy because he had built a headquarters for a foreign-owned petroleum group. For nearly a decade he moved around the Middle East and Europe, finally settling in London with his wife and three children. Along the way, he picked up a multimillion-dollar fee as a broker in a Saudi crude-oil deal. That was just the beginning of his good fortune.

Early in 1984, he says, the Libyan government offered him a consultancy, and in June he signed a five-year contract with the energy ministry. His salary was $200,000 a year, plus periodic raises, bonuses and a commodious house in Tripoli. "I am working 365 days for them, any time they need me," he says. "And I have to make this Rabta project. I saw it as a nice object, very clean, a big one. And I say, "why not? And I start planning with them the technology center." What Barbouti may not have known was that the Libyans had sought a chemical-weapons capability as early as 1978; by 1984 they had already bought the compounds needed to produce such weapons in bulk. Now Barbouti was about to help Gaddafi realize his dream.

Over a period of four years, Barbouti spent two or three days a month in Libya, designing and supervising construction of the "technology center." As prime contractor and chief procurement agent, he traveled the globe recruiting expertise and labor. For Rabta he provided Japanese-designed desalinization and electrical equipment, as well as plastic molding and precision machining plants, a foundry from a Danish firm, a metal-working plant, a power station, a water-treatment facility, a maintenance workshop and three warehouses. He had plenty of money to spend; one Rabta contract, he boasted to a friend, was worth nearly $2 billion.

By 1985 Barbouti's IBI had set up a network of offices stretching from Europe to Asia. In West Germany, where export-license rules have been hopelessly lax (but now, belatedly, are undergoing revision), he signed up Imhausen-Chemie as chief subcontractor for the project. Intelligence officials say Barbouti's newly opened offices in Hong Kong helped arrange a complex scheme by which material was sent to Imhausen's representative in Hong Kong and transshipped to Rabta. In this way, they ex-

ETHICS AND BUSINESS

plain, Barbouti managed to avoid arousing suspicions about Gaddafi's real intent.

While Barbouti acknowledges that he was aware of the chemical plant, he says he is sure it was not designed to turn out chemical weapons. "In four years, sitting with the engineers and technical people on committees, nobody has mentioned or hinted that something secret is there," he says. In fact, he argues, one Rabta building, code-named Pharma 150 and reportedly the center for poison-gas manufacture, was not even included in his original design. "I draw the site plan myself—my hand," declares Barbouti, adding that Pharma 150 was built sometime in 1987, after he completed his work at Rabta.

Intelligence sources are more than skeptical about Barbouti's claim. They have reconnaissance photos showing that construction of Pharma 150 began at the same time as the rest of Rabta's buildings, and was "well along" by 1986, when Barbouti was still deeply involved in the project. Nor do Barbouti's protestations square with the fact that his company arranged for the supply of protective equipment for handling toxic chemicals at the plant and remained active in the project, according to one official, "well into 1988." Barbouti's case is not helped, moreover, by the fact that he shuttered his Frankfurt office shortly after the U.S. first informed Bonn that Imhausen-Chemie was implicated in the Rabta affair. Barbouti dismisses that as mere coincidence and not an attempt to hide his tracks.

To be sure, there are no hidden tracks. If intelligence authorities want to interrogate Barbouti, they will find him in London, fingering his worry beads. It is unlikely they will discover that he broke any laws. He was, after all, a legitimate Iraqi businessman who happened to be Libya's middleman and who knew nothing about the manufacture of chemical weapons. He won't lie, but he may not want to tell the truth either.

QUESTIONS

1. *Why do you think the writer mentioned Rolf Kiefer at the outset?*

2. *What does Barbouti claim his involvement was in the Rabta project?*

3. *What do western intelligence sources think he did?*

4. *According to intelligence officials, why did Barbouti run materials through his Hong Kong offices?*

5. *What makes intelligence sources suspicious of Barbouti's claims that he knew of no attempt to build a chemical weapons plant?*

6. *Is it possible that Barbouti is not really lying, but that the intelligence sources are still correct about those activities? How could he be both not lying and not telling the truth?*

Further Remarks on the Barbouti Case

Reading the foregoing, one is struck by the fact that Dr. Barbouti probably believes, at some level, that he is a legitimate businessman who has done no wrong. How can he rationalize his behavior? Can he seriously think that it is acceptable business practice to help Libya develop chemical weapons?

Barbouti probably does have some doubts about his actions. He knows that he will be widely condemned. He also knows that many other businessmen (like Rolf Kiefer) would balk at the thought of dealing in such matters; and that Libya's role as a supporter of international terrorism will make the prospect of that country having chemical weapons rather frightening. He must be aware that chemical weapons were banned after World War I because of the hideous deaths that they brought to those exposed to them. Moreover, the survivors of these attacks suffered as nobody should suffer.

But Dr. Barbouti must also know that the self-righteous indignation of Americans and Russians is sheer hypocrisy, for both nations have chemical-weapons capability, and both have used chemical weapons in recent wars. He also knows that someone else will be making the chemicals, so he can absolve himself of the responsibility for the actual creation of these weapons. Barbouti must realize that, although Rolf Kiefer may not be willing to design the Libyan plant, he is not alone in seeing a business opportunity here. Whether or not Dr. Barbouti designs the plant, if the Libyans want it, it will be built. Such beliefs allow a businessperson to continue the free flow of profits with a minimum of psychic pain.

Of course, it can be argued that the people involved in chemical-weapons development are at the sleaziest end of the business community. Their work, by its nature, involves them in the most horrible decisions. Most business people, however, do not have to decide whether or not to produce agents of death. In Carr's article, he cited a number of examples of business decisions made by ordinary people that could easily be done with a clear conscience, and yet involved deceptive practices. Should a person who looks younger than his years lie about his age to get a job in a field where youth is valued? Should an industry representative omit significant facts when discussing the business with representatives of a government regulatory agency? Should the produce manager of a store try to sell half-rotten tomatoes by including one, with its good side exposed, in every tomato six-pack? Such decisions may seem more acceptable than developing chemical weapons, but they still involve deception.

Additionally, Carr makes the point that if businessmen do the honest thing, they do so not for the sake of honesty but because they gain something by the appearance of honesty. If you tell the truth about your age, it is because the consequences of being caught in the lie are worse than the advantages of lying. But if the consequences of being caught are not sufficiently severe, then business people would feel no compunction to tell the truth.

The Ethical Theories of Immanuel Kant

After reading about the morass of rationalizations, justifications, cynical manipulations, and plain lying involved in business, one wishes for an ethical perspective of simplicity and clarity. Can one undercut the convoluted logic of the businessperson who wants to claim both ethical virtue and business acumen? Is there a philosophical perspective that can, if taken seriously, force such a person to see that this conduct is stripped of ethical pretense?

Among modern philosophers, the one whose ideas present the greatest challenge toward ethical rationalizers is Immanuel

Kant. Although his ideas are expressed in the language of academic thought, the basic principles that he elucidates are simple. What he was attempting to do in some of his ethical writing is to provide a justification for commonly held moral beliefs. So he seeks, by means of a philosophical analysis, to justify the belief in the "golden rule," to satisfy the feeling that lying, cheating, and stealing are wrong. Although one may disagree with both his conclusions and his way of reaching them, there is no doubt that his analysis is brilliant and illuminating, and the arguments he presents are bound to make even the most convinced rationalizer uncomfortable.

Kant himself led a life that morally was virtually blameless, a situation made easier by the fact that he followed the quiet routine of a disciplined scholar and professor. His own habits were so regular that it was said that the townspeople of Königsberg, where he lived all his life, could set their watches by the time he passed their houses on his daily walk. Despite a constitution so frail that he was not expected to survive childhood, he lived eighty years. He attributed his powers of survival to his regular habits, the absence of strain in his life, and the careful attention he paid to his health. It was a life as far removed from the world of business as one could imagine, and it could be suggested that his rectitude was the consequence of a lack of moral conflict. Having few difficult moral decisions to face, it was easy for him to lead a moral life.

One must consider, however, that people choose the lifestyle with which they feel comfortable. Kant chose the life of a professor because he believed it would afford him the serenity he wanted. When someone decides to deal in weapon sales, it affirms a willingness to put up with the attendant moral problems that go along with that business. One is generally not born into the weapons business, but, rather, one chooses to be in it. In cases of extreme poverty or oppression, the issue of choice may not really be there, but that is not the issue when we are citing the choices made by the average legitimate businessperson. Those who choose a business fraught with moral problems are saying something about themselves in that choice. They, too, could benefit from the discomfort caused by Kant's uncompromising and carefully argued perspective.

The following selections are from Kant's *Groundwork of the*

Metaphysics of Morals. Despite the imposing title, he meant the book to be a popular work for general consumption, not a work for professional philosophers. Nevertheless, it is still very difficult in spots. Remember that the point of reading a passage is to grasp the general thrust of Kant's argument, not to understand every little phrase. Fortunately, the general thrust of the argument is really fairly simple. Some operating principles may be in order to help you through. One characteristic of Kant's writing is that he makes a point rather simply, then elaborates on it in a way that confuses more than it clarifies. Obviously, the thing to do here is not to worry too much about the elaboration, but to make a special point of the main idea. Generally, each excerpt has one or two main ideas. If something seems important, but you cannot figure it out, read the passage over several times and try to translate the passage into simple English and short sentences. If this is impossible, after a few tries, just go on. Kant repeats ideas that are important, so you may well catch the same thought later.

As you read, take notes, writing down the important ideas. Most significant ideas are covered in the questions at the end of each excerpt. If you can answer those questions, you will learn fairly well all you need to know.

The Metaphysics of Morals[4]

EXCERPT 1

Nothing can possibly be conceived in the world, or even out of it, which can be called good, without qualification, except a Good Will. Intelligence, wit, judgment, and the other *talents* of the mind, however they may be named, or courage, resolution, perseverance, as qualities of temperament, are undoubtedly good and desirable in many respects; but these gifts of nature may also become extremely bad and mischievous if the will which is to make use of them, and which, therefore, constitutes what is called *character*, is not good. It is the same with the *gifts of fortune*. Power, riches, honour, even health, and the general well-being and contentment with one's condition which is called *happiness*, inspire pride, and often presumption, if there is not a good will to correct the influence of these on the mind, and with this also to rectify the whole principle of acting, and adapt it to its end. The sight of a being who is not adorned with a single feature of a pure and good will, enjoying unbroken prosperity, can never give pleasure to an impartial rational spectator. Thus a good will appears to constitute the indispensable condition even of being worthy of happiness.

There are even some qualities which are of service to this good will itself, and may facilitate its action, yet which have no intrinsic unconditional value, but always presuppose a good will, and this qualifies the esteem that we justly have for them, and does not permit us to regard them as absolutely good. Moderation in the affections and passions, self-control, and calm deliberation are not only good in many respects, but even seem to constitute part of the intrinsic worth of the person; but they are far from deserving to be called good without qualification, although they have been so unconditionally praised by the ancients. For without the principles of a good will, they may become extremely bad; and the coolness of a villain not only makes him far more dangerous, but also directly makes him more abominable in our eyes than he would have been without it.

A good will is good not because of what it performs or effects, not by its aptness for the attainment of some proposed end, but simply by virtue of the volition, that is, it is good in itself, and considered by itself is to be esteemed much higher than all that can be brought about by it in favour of any inclination, nay, even of the sum-total of all inclinations. Even if it should happen that, owing to special disfavour of fortune, or the niggardly provision of a step-motherly nature, this will should wholly lack power to accomplish its purpose, if with its greatest efforts it should yet achieve nothing, and there should remain only the good will (not, to be sure, a mere wish, but the summoning of all means in our power), then, like a jewel, it would still shine by its own light, as a thing which has its whole value in itself. Its usefulness or fruitlessness can neither add to nor take away anything from this value. It would be, as it were, only the setting to enable us to handle it the more conveniently in common commerce, or to attract to it the attention of those who are not yet connoisseurs, but not to recommend it to true connoisseurs, or to determine its value.

QUESTIONS

1. *What is the only good without qualification?*

2. *Why cannot qualities of temperament or gifts of fortune be unqualified goods?*

3. *What are some qualities that can aid good will and are nevertheless not unqualified goods?*

4. *Does it matter whether good will is able to achieve its goal?*

EXCERPT 2

I omit here all actions which are already recognized as inconsistent with duty, although they may be useful for this or that purpose, for with these the question whether they are done *from duty* cannot arise at all, since they even conflict with it. I also set aside those actions which really conform to duty, but to which men have *no* direct *inclination*, performing them because they are impelled thereto by some other inclination. For in this case we can readily distinguish whether the action which agrees with duty is done *from duty*, or from a selfish view. It is much harder to make this distinction when the action accords with duty, and the subject has besides a *direct* inclination to it. For example, it is always a matter of duty that a dealer should not overcharge an inexperienced purchaser; and wherever there is much commerce the prudent tradesman does not overcharge, but keeps a fixed price for everyone, so that a child buys of him as well as any other. Men are thus *honestly* served; but this is not enough to make us believe that the tradesman has so acted from duty and from principles of honesty; his own advantage required it; it is out of the question in this case to suppose that he might besides have a direct inclination in favour of the buyers, so that, as it were, from love he should give no advantage to one over another. Accordingly the action was done neither from duty nor from direct inclination, but merely with a selfish view.

QUESTIONS

1. *What is the difference between an action done from duty and an action done from self-interest?*

EXCERPT 3

On the other hand, it is a duty to maintain one's life; and, in addition, everyone has also a direct inclination to do so. But on this account the often anxious care which most men take for it has no intrinsic worth, and their maxim has no moral import. They preserve their life *as duty requires*, no doubt, but not *because duty requires*. On the other hand, if adversity and hopeless sorrow have completely taken away the relish for life; if the unfortunate one, strong in mind, indignant at his fate rather than desponding or dejected, wishes for death, and yet preserves his life without loving it—not from inclination or fear, but from duty—then his maxim has a moral worth.

To be beneficent when we can is a duty; and besides this, there are many minds so sympathetically constituted that, without any other motive of vanity or self-interest, they find a pleasure in spreading joy around them, and can take delight in the satisfaction of others so far as it is their own work. But I maintain that in such a case an action of this kind, however proper, however amiable it may be, has nevertheless no true moral worth, but is on a level with other inclinations, *e.g.* the inclination to honour, which, if it is happily directed to that which is in fact of public utility and accordant with duty, and consequently honourable, deserves praise and encouragement, but not esteem. For the maxim lacks the moral import, namely, that such actions be done *from duty*, not from inclination. Put the case that the mind of that philanthropist was clouded by sorrow of his own, extinguishing all sympathy with the lot of others, and that while he still has the power to benefit others in distress, he is not touched by their trouble because he is absorbed with his own; and now suppose that he tears himself out of this dead insensibility, and performs the action without any inclination to it, but simply from duty, then first has his action its genuine moral worth. Further still; if nature has put little sympathy in the heart of this or that man; if he, supposed to be an upright man, is by temperament cold and indifferent to the sufferings of others, perhaps because in respect of his own he is provided with the special gift of patience and fortitude, and supposes, or even requires, that others should have the same—and such a man would certainly not be the meanest product of nature—but if nature had not specially framed him for a philanthropist, would he not still find in himself a source from whence to give himself a far higher worth than that of a good-natured temperament could be? Unquestionably. It is just in this that the moral worth of the character is brought out which is incomparably the highest of all, namely, that he is beneficent, not from inclination, but from duty.

It is in this manner, undoubtedly, that we are to understand those passages of Scripture also in which we are commanded to love our neighbour, even our enemy. For love, as an affection, cannot be commanded, but beneficence for duty's sake may; even though we are not impelled to it by any inclination—nay, are even repelled by a natural and unconquerable aversion. This is *practical* love, and not *pathological*—a love which is seated in the will, and not in the propensions of sense—in principles of action and not of tender sympathy; and it is this love alone which can be commanded.

QUESTIONS

1. *Under what circumstances does preserving one's life have moral worth? Why does life preservation have moral worth under these circumstances and no other?*

2. *Why does Kant believe that there is no genuine moral worth in spreading happiness if one finds pleasure in doing so?*

3. *What does Kant think the Bible means when it states: "Love thy neighbor"?*

EXCERPT 4

The second proposition is:[5] That an action done from duty derives its moral worth, *not from the purpose* which is to be attained by it, but from the *maxim*[6] by which it is determined, and therefore does not depend on the realization of the object of the action, but merely on the *principle of volition*[7] by which the action has taken place, without regard to any object of desire. It is clear from what precedes that the purposes which we may have in view in our actions, or their effects regarded as ends and springs of the will, cannot give to actions any unconditional or moral worth. In what, then, can their worth lie, if it is not to consist in the will and in reference to its expected effect? It cannot lie anywhere but in the *principle of the will* without regard to the ends which can be attained by the action. For the will stands between its *a priori*[8] principle, which is formal, and its *a posteriori*[9] spring, which is material, as between two roads, and as it must be determined by something, it follows that it must be determined by the formal principle of volition when an action is done from duty, in which case every material principle has been withdrawn from it.

QUESTIONS

1. *How does an action done from duty gain its moral worth?*

EXCERPT 5

The third proposition, which is a consequence of the two preceding, I would express thus: *Duty is the necessity of acting from respect for the law.*[10] I may have *inclination* for an object as the effect of my proposed action, but I cannot have *respect* for it, just for this reason, that it is an effect and not an energy of will. Similarly, I cannot have respect for inclination, whether my own or another's; I can at most, if my own, approve it; if another's, sometimes even love it; *i.e.* look on it as favourable to my own interest. It is only what is connected with my will as a principle, by no means as an effect—what does not subserve my inclination, but overpowers it, or at least in case of choice excludes it from its calculation—in other words, simply the law of itself, which can be an object of respect, and hence a command. Now an action done from duty must wholly exclude the influence of inclination, and with it every object of the will, so that nothing remains which can determine the will except objectively the *law*, and subjectively *pure respect* for this practical law, and consequently the maxim that I should follow this law even to the thwarting of all my inclinations.

ETHICS AND BUSINESS

Thus the moral worth of an action does not lie in the effect expected from it, nor in any principle of action which requires to borrow its motive from this expected effect. For all these effects—[agreeableness of one's condition, and even the promotion of the happiness of others]—could have been also brought about by other causes, so that for this there would have been no need of the will of a rational being; whereas it is in this alone that the supreme and unconditional good can be found. The pre-eminent good which we call moral can therefore consist in nothing else than *the conception of law* in itself, *which certainly is only possible in a rational being*, in so far as this conception, and not the expected effect, determines the will. This is a good which is already present in the person who acts accordingly, and we have not to wait for it to appear first in the result.

QUESTIONS

1. *Why does Kant think we can never have reverence for an inclination?*

2. *Why does Kant say that moral worth cannot depend on the result expected of an action?*

EXCERPT 6

But what sort of law can that be, the conception of which must determine the will, even without paying any regard to the effect expected from it, in order that this will may be called good absolutely and without qualification? As I have deprived the will of every impulse which could arise to it from obedience to any law, there remains nothing but the universal conformity of its actions to law in general, which alone is to serve the will as a principle, *i.e.* I am never to act otherwise than *so that I could also will that my maxim should become a universal law*. Here, now, it is the simple conformity to law in general, without assuming any particular law applicable to certain actions, that serves the will as its principle, and must so serve it, if duty is not to be a vain delusion and a chimerical notion. The common reason of men in its practical judgments perfectly coincides with this, and always has in view the principle here suggested.

QUESTIONS

1. *What kind of law can determine good will?*
2. *How ought one act in order to have good will?*

EXCERPT 7

Let the question be, for example: May I when in distress make a promise with the intention not to keep it? I readily distinguish here between the two significations which the question may have: Whether it is prudent, or whether it is right, to make a false promise? The former may undoubtedly often be the case. I see clearly indeed that it is not enough to extricate myself from a present difficulty by means of this subterfuge, but it must be well considered whether there may not hereafter spring from this lie much greater inconvenience than that from which I now free myself, and as, with all my supposed *cunning*, the consequences cannot be so easily foreseen but that credit once lost may be much more injurious to me than any mischief which I seek to avoid at present, it should be considered whether it would not be more *prudent* to act herein according to a universal maxim, and to make it a habit to promise nothing except with the intention of keeping it. But it is soon clear to me that such a maxim will still only be based on the fear of consequences. Now it is a wholly different thing to be truthful from duty, and to be so from apprehension of injurious consequences. In the first case, the very notion of the action already implies a law for me; in the second case, I must first look about elsewhere to see what results may be combined with it which would affect myself. For to deviate from the principle of duty is beyond all doubt wicked; but to be unfaithful to my maxim of prudence may often be very advantageous to me, although to abide by it is certainly safer. The shortest way, however, and an unerring one, to discover the answer to this question whether a lying promise is consistent with duty, is to ask myself, Should I be content that my maxim (to extricate myself from difficulty by a false promise) should hold good as a universal law, for myself as well as for others? and should I be able to say to myself, "Every one may make a deceitful promise when he finds himself in a difficulty from which he cannot otherwise extricate himself"? Then I presently become aware that while I can will the lie, I can by no means will that lying should be a universal law. For with such a law there would be no promises at all, since it would be in vain to allege my intention in regard to my future actions to those who would not believe this allegation, or if they over-hastily did so, would pay me back in my own coin. Hence my maxim, as soon as it should be made a universal law, would necessarily destroy itself.

I do not, therefore, need any far-reaching penetration to discern what I have to do in order that my will may be morally good. Inexperienced in the course of the world, incapable of being prepared for all its contingencies, I only ask myself: Canst thou also will that thy maxim should be a universal law? If not, then it must be rejected, and that not because of a disadvantage accruing from it to myself or even to others, but because it cannot enter as a principle into a possible universal legislation, and reason extorts from me immediate respect for such legislation. I do not indeed as yet *discern* on what this respect is based (this the philosopher may inquire), but at least I understand this, that it is an estimation of the worth which far outweighs all worth of what is recommended by inclination, and that the necessity of acting from *pure* respect for the practical law is what constitutes duty, to which every other motive must give place, because it is the condition of a will being good *in itself*, and the worth of such a will is above everything.

QUESTIONS

1. *What is the difference between telling the truth out of a sense of duty and telling the truth out of a concern for inconvenient results?*

2. *How can one determine if lying accords with duty?*

3. *What is the logical problem involved in making a lying promise a universal law?*

4. *How can you have good will if you are totally ignorant?*

5. *Here are some of the duties that Kant says we must follow if we are to have a will that acts in conformity to the universal law; i.e., the categorical imperative: One must not lie, steal, commit suicide, or neglect one's talents. He argues that one cannot make any of these activities into universal laws; therefore, they must be rejected. Can you figure out why he thinks they cannot be turned into universal laws? What would happen if these activities became universal laws?*

6. *What do you see as the strong points in Kant's ethics? What do you see as the weaknesses? Justify your answers.*

ACTIVITIES

❶ Assemble the answers to the questions following all the excerpts. Reread the excerpts to see if there is any more material you would like to add. Then write a summary of all seven excerpts.

Kantian Ethics and Business

Kant saw his task as giving rational justifications for commonly held ethical beliefs. He took it for granted that most people instinctively feel that lying is wrong. He also thought that by using a motivist approach to ethics, he would be putting ethics on a more solid, rational ground. It certainly does make sense to say that good will is the only unqualified good. But it has been argued that Kant's philosophy really has very little to do with real life and the necessities of survival. In the business world, it is argued by Carr and many others, rigid honesty would lead to financial suicide.

There are several questions that the Kantian philosophers could put to business people. The first is to ask them where total honesty would lead them. Do they really know that it is impossible, or are they just assuming that the foreseeable short-term losses will lead to financial ruin? The second question is whether it might be better to get into a line of work that requires fewer ethical compromises. Certain businesses are far less ethically compromising than others. Why choose munitions as your line of work when you can open a restaurant? Does not your very choice of business reflect on you as a person? Can you be a moral, upright dealer in munitions or chemical weapons? Or can we pass moral judgment on those whose values are so skewed and whose personal greed is so deep that they would enter into contracts to develop materials to kill people?

Kant's philosophy can serve as a valuable reminder that certain things are clearly wrong, whatever may be gained by doing them. If it seems depressing to be told to do your duty and not to think of your self-interest, you should also remember that Kant was not oblivious to the value of self-interest. He stated that behaviors that are in accord with both duty and self-interest should be cultivated. He even professed that it is a duty to try to be happy, but not to be happy at the expense of others or at the expense of duty.

Perhaps the best way to look at the interaction of duty, happiness, and self-interest is to consider an idea from a philosopher of an even more rigorous turn of mind than Kant. Benedict de Spinoza's *Ethics* looks, on paper, like a series of geometrical theorems. From this basis he develops an extraordinary philosophical perspective. One of his ideas is that people are primarily motivated by an interest in self-preservation. But he also observed that if one truly grasps the larger picture of things, one sees that small-minded, selfish behavior does not really serve your own interests. In the larger sense, you must do what is best for everyone, for in so doing you also do what is best for yourself. The Ihsan Barboutis of this world hurt themselves, as well as others, in their short-sighted greed. If they could see *sub specie eternitatis*, under the form of eternity, they could not persist in their sordid behavior.

QUESTIONS

1. *What effect would a wholesale adoption of Kantian ethics have on the business community? Give examples of conflicts that a business person may have between a desire to stay in business and a strict application of Kantian morality to life.*

Endnotes for Chapter 2

1. *golden rule*: an ethical rule which is generally phrased "Do unto others as you would have them do unto you." It can be found in the New Testament as part of Jesus's Sermon on the Mount, Matthew 7:12, Luke 6:31.

2. *laissez-faire*: a theory of economics which claims that the government should interfere as little as possible with the economic affairs of the state.

3. Reprinted with the permission of Time, Inc., from "The Mysterious Dr. B.," *Time*, February 27, 1989, pp. 40–41. Copyright 1989, Time, Inc.

4. Selections from the *Fundamental Principles of the Metaphysic of Morals* by Immanuel Kant, translated by Thomas Kingsmill Abbott, Third Edition. Longmans, Green and Co., 1873.

5. The first proposition is that in order to have moral worth an action must be done from duty.

6. *maxim*: a principle upon which we act.

7. *principle of volition*: the reason for the action.

8. *a priori*: not based on prior study or examination; nonanalytic.

9. *a posteriori*: derived from actual observation or experimental data.

10. Law here means something more like "a law of nature" than the law of the land. It is a principle of action that must be obeyed if one is to avoid being self-contradictory.

CHAPTER 3

ETHICS AND MEDICINE:
The Power of the Practitioner

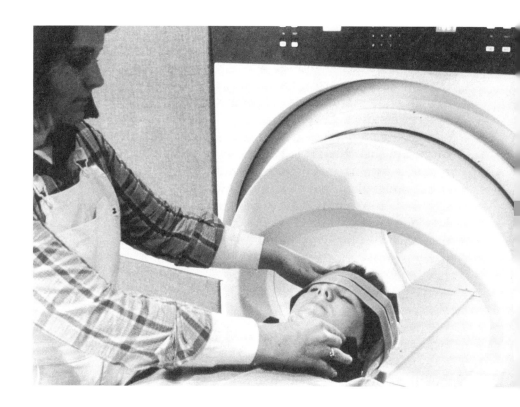

This chapter begins with three essays that explore the historical factors that have contributed to the contemporary doctor's self-image and the justifications of modern medical procedures. Some case studies from the experience of a physician illustrate the world-view of the doctor and also show the poignancy of the tragedies practitioners face on a daily basis. The ethical obligations of doctors are considered within the context of American law in an essay by Thomas Szasz from his book, The Theology of Medicine. *Dr. Szasz considers the difficulties that doctors face in accepting these limitations in the light of the historical powers granted to doctors.*

A Historical Perspective

This unit deals with origins. It is an attempt to delve into the history of medicine and see where the present–day doctor comes from, to see the reasons for the way medicine operates today, and to view contemporary ethical perspectives in medicine in the light of these historical factors.

Doctors possess extraordinary power. People permit them to violate their bodies with needles and catheters. A doctor can render a person unconscious, perform surgery, and remove part of the body, plant materials, attach tubes and wires to the patient, and force immobility. Given this power, the moral responsibility of a doctor is awesome. And as most of the procedures are not only invasive, but very painful, it puts in an ironic light the primary rule of codes of medical ethics—*primum non nocere*, that is, first, do no harm.

It is easy enough to ascribe these procedures to necessity. We can say that invasive and painful procedures are necessary for the health of the patient. But no choices are ever that simple. The use of needles, catheters, surgery, drugs, and huge machines, such as x–ray and CAT scan devices are not simply rooted in necessity, but in the historical position of doctors in society, in their training, and in their own sense of mission and importance. To ignore these factors is not only naive but misleading. It reduces medical ethics to a series of prescriptive pronouncements that show neither respect nor understanding for the problems doctors face. Before we can decide if extended chemotherapy, often with hideous side effects, should be tried on patients who have not long to live, we should understand why such treatment would even be contemplated.

To gain a better grasp of the historical position of doctors, read the Hippocratic oath. This ancient Greek's work is still relevant in the medical profession. There are three essays on historical aspects of medicine that will help illuminate present-day medical practice. When we read case studies and opinions of practicing doctors, we encounter cautionary voices who warn of the dangers inherent in the power we give doctors.

The Hippocratic Oath

The Hippocratic oath is traditionally taken by doctors upon their graduation from medical school. Fewer schools ask doctors to take this oath today because they realize that a modern doctor would be hard pressed to follow it explicitly. It lives on as a tradition, and it also reinforces the idea that there is a sort of fraternity among doctors; they are bound together in their practice of the healing arts. Among doctors, there is still a strong sense of loyalty to the profession. Many cases have surfaced when doctors protected incompetent practitioners in their ranks. About twenty years ago, a doctor wrote a book complaining about the greed and incompetence of many fellow doctors. He did not use his own name or the real names of the alleged crooks and butchers he discussed. In the medical fraternity, he explained, one simply did not reveal such facts.

In reading the oath itself, try to notice which parts of it are relevant to contemporary medicine and which parts no longer apply. The prohibition against using the knife was a reference to a division of labor between physicians and surgeons. Surgeons were not "real doctors" in Hippocrates' day. In fact, it is only recently that the training of a surgeon is largely undertaken at the same institutions as the training of other doctors.

Commentary on Hippocrates[1]

Hippocrates—the "father of Medicine"—is mentioned by Plato as "A professional trainer of medical students." There are three ancient biographies of Hippocrates which state that he was born on Cos in 460 B.C., that he belonged to the guild of physicians called Asclepiadae, that he traveled all over Greece, that he stayed the plague at Athens and at other places, that his life was long but of uncertain length, tradition making him 85 to 109 at his death. There is a good deal of fable in these accounts, and modern scholarship is inclined to be skeptical as to whether Hippocrates was really an actual person, or whether from vague beginnings the name came to be applied to all the writings of the Corpus, the product of numerous disciples of a school of thought. Still, Plato's evidence is usually reliable, and would indicate Hippocrates was a living man. There is nothing improbable about the accounts except the reference to staying the plague at Athens: Thucydides says that medical treatment was unavailing.

Whether the Asclepiadae were priests in the temples of Aesculapius, or a guild bound by rules, whose members swore the Hippocratic Oath, is debatable.

The works of Hippocrates are varied: they are a library of medical practice probably written by a school rather than one man. "Airs, Waters and Places," "Epidemics," "Regimen," "Prognostics," "The Sacred Disease" (refutation of the idea that disease was sent by a god), "Aphorisms," "Ancient Medicine," are some of the books in the Corpus.

The Hippocratic Oath is traditionally the obligation which Hippocrates imposed upon his pupils. Actually its origin is unknown. From internal evidence it can be dated as originating between the fifth century B.C. and the first century A.D.: Aesculapius was not invoked as a god before the fifth century B.C. and Apollo would not have been invoked as a god after the first century A.D. Again studying from internal evidence, it is not an oath but an indenture between master and pupil. That it was widely used in this way up to the Middle Ages is assumed, since there is a Christian and an Arabic form of the Oath; in these, in the invocation, the names of the pagan deities are replaced by Christian and Moslem gods. Galen wrote that ancient physicians comprised "a clan of Aesclepiadae, who taught their sons anatomy, who, in turn, transmitted their learning to the next generation." Many believe the Oath was the pledge required of all who were admitted to this clan of the Aesclepiadae.

There are many puzzling clauses in the Oath: (1) The prohibition against cutting for the stone: this is omitted from the Christian oath: it is suggested that cutting for the stone involved castration, which was abhorrent to the pagan Greeks, acceptable to Christians with their notions of celibacy. (2) The prohibition against giving poisons—the words are really *pharmacon oudeni*—deadly drugs: in modern practice this would prevent the giving of any drug with a lethal range.

THE OATH

I swear by Apollo Physician, by Asclepius, by Health, by Panacea and by all the gods and goddesses, making them my witnesses, that I will carry out, according to my ability and judgement, this oath and this indenture. To hold my teacher in this art equal to my own parents; to make him partner in my livelihood; when he is in need of money to share mine with him; to consider his family as my own brothers, and to teach them this art, if they want to learn it, without fee or indenture; to impart precept, oral instruction, and all other instruction to my own sons, the sons of my teacher, and to indentured pupils who have taken the physician's oath, but to nobody else. I will use treatment to help the sick according to my ability and judgement, but never with a view to injury and wrong-doing. Neither will I administer a poison to anybody when asked to do so, nor will I suggest such a course. Similarly I will not give a woman a pessary to cause abortion. But I will keep pure and holy both my life and my art. I will not use the knife, not even, verily, on sufferers from stone, but I will give place to such as are craftsmen therein. Into whatsoever houses I enter, I will enter to help the sick, and I will abstain from all intentional wrong-doing and harm, especially from abusing the bodies of man or woman, bond or free. And whatsoever I shall see or hear in the course of my profession, as well as outside my profession in my intercourse with men, if it be what should not be published abroad, I will never divulge, holding such things to be holy secrets. Now if I carry out this oath, and break it not, may I gain for ever reputation among all men for my life and for my art; but if I transgress it and forswear myself, may the opposite befall me.

1. *In what ways can today's doctors follow the oath of Hippocrates? In what ways would this be impossible?*

2. *In your opinion, do doctors today seem to be as much of a secret society as Hippocrates suggests they were in ancient Greece?*

3. *Why do you think the oath specifically forbids abortion?*

Medical Attitudes

The Hippocratic oath gave us an introduction to the doctor's world. It showed us that some of the ideas of present-day doctors were around in antiquity, even though much has changed. Although today's doctor is not required to treat teachers of medicine like family members, there is still a strong fraternal sense in the medical profession. Doctors may no longer belong to a religious order, but they do undergo a painful initiation into the profession, and they have maintained a sense of their own exclusivity and importance.

The following essays look at factors that have tied doctors together historically and have led to their feelings of exclusivity and superiority. Sometimes, however, these factors led them to falter in their mission. The falterings have been due to very human factors, but they must be acknowledged. Later, we will look at doctors grappling with some of the traditional problems of "medical ethics," but first we will set the background against which these problems occur.

Romantic Visions and the Practice of Medicine

Imagine this scene:

Once upon a time there was a land of beautiful valleys and green forests, where people lived in simplicity and comfort. They were healthy and happy. They lived long lives on a simple diet. Old men of ninety climbed mountains with their great-grandchildren. They had little, but they wanted nothing. The greed, neuroses, and illnesses of civilization were unknown to them.

Now imagine this scene:

The time—the future. The place—Earth. The miracles of science have conquered the last great barrier—disease. People live into their old age beautiful and healthy. Life spans of 120 years are common. Infections are insignificant; cancer has been eliminated. Genetic engineering has reduced birth defects to the occasional mistake. People are happier and healthier than ever before.

These two scenes, so alike in their romantic idealism, so unlike anything that we see in the world today, are recurrent visions in the history of man. They appear across cultures and time, with the characters changed but the theme remaining the same. The Chinese Taoists spoke of a golden age where people regularly lived for 100 years. Hesiod, the ancient Greek writer, spoke of a time when the Gods roamed among men. Perhaps the clearest vision of the perfect past is the Garden of Eden. The idealization of a past that cannot be remembered but that can be imagined seems to fulfill a deep human need, as though we want to believe that happiness was once achieved in a world that now seems so full of pain and suffering.

Visions of the perfect future Utopia are as powerful as pictures of an idealized past. How do we recapture this perfection? We use magical powers. The magical powers can be those of religious miracle, as in the Second Coming; or they can be through political miracle, as in the Communist Utopia; or they can be through scientific miracle, which will transform us, through magical potions encased in implausibly small pills, into close relations to the Immortals.

To many, the last means to perfection offers the most attractive possibility. The leap of faith required to accept the theological doctrines of Christianity or Marxism is difficult, for it demands that we believe that the world will change in ways that are completely outside of our experience. The Christian "Day of Judgment" will be the most unusual day indeed; and the Marxist notion of the state withering away sounds ludicrous in a world where governments everywhere turn into vast Leviathans that swallow people whole, particularly in the Communist world. But Science! We see the march of Science before our eyes. We see new technology bring convenience into our lives. We are bombarded with stories of the latest medical miracles in drug therapy, surgical techniques, and genetic research. In a world where life can be created in a test tube, can immortality be far behind?

When thinking about medicine today, some people have a vision of a perfect past in which the friendly family doctor made house calls. Others have a similarly Utopian picture of the lives of their ancestors, who they imagine living in perfect health on a diet of natural foods. Visions of the future are populated with genetically altered humans who have stopped the aging process; more modest Utopians see a world without cancer or infectious disease. The pictures of the past, ridiculous as they are, probably do no harm. The unrealistic visions of the future can unfortunately raise people's expectations, and then make them very disappointed when these expectations are not fulfilled. The most negative effect of the pictures of the past is that they are perpetuated rather cynically in soft-focus television commercials to peddle life insurance. The most negative effect of the promised future that does not materialize is that the medical profession finds itself in big trouble. Tired of the arrogance of doctors who have promised but not delivered, people take to suing them for trivial reasons, leading to a major crisis in the cost of malpractice insurance. (Prices have become so high in recent years that many doctors are paying one-third of their incomes in malpractice-insurance fees.) People also begin to doubt that medical science has all the answers, which means that many of them go to alternative practitioners for their medical salvation. This may be a very healthy trend; but it is bad for the business of traditional doctors because so many prospective patients, who have bitter feelings toward physicians for promising so much and delivering so little, go to acupuncturists, faith healers, and chiropractors.

Where does medical arrogance come from? Why do doctors think that scientific medicine has all the answers? This attitude is not new. Renaissance doctors thought that cures for all ills were just around the corner. Both the modern doctor and his Renaissance forebear believed that they had found the theoretical key to the

ETHICS AND MEDICINE

problem of disease. They believed that by the application of the theory to treatment, they could discover cures.

From this base, they developed pictures of a perfect future, and in so doing tapped into a deep human desire. But theories have been notoriously unreliable guides to reality, and the reliance on theory has had some tragic consequences in the history of medicine, as we shall see. Besides, there is no reason to think that today's Utopian visionaries have the "right" theory, any more than their predecessors did.

ACTIVITIES

❶ There are materials, quite easy to find, that show either the nostalgia for an earlier and healthier time, or a vision of a scientifically enhanced healthy future. Magazines like *East-West* give us a picture of the perfect past; magazines like *Longevity* give us our scientifically enhanced future. If you go into any fair-sized library, you will find materials on Alternative Health Strategies and Nutritional Therapy that will make you feel that everything we eat today is garbage, compared to the pure foods our ancestors enjoyed. There will also be materials on Life-Extension that deal with various means available now (or soon to be available) that will help us live to one hundred years. Either through magazine articles or a selected passage in a book, find an example of the perfect past or the perfect future. Write a 500-word description of the reference you have chosen, remembering not to take the prospect too seriously. Attach a copy of the article to your essay.

Theories and Medicine

Human beings want certainty in a world that is fraught with uncertainty. When they find a system of thought that gives them answers that they like, they try to fit all their experiences into that system. Things become good or bad, right or wrong, insofar as they fit into the system. A believer in democracy will look at an authoritarian government and say: "That is bad because it is authoritarian." The implication is that the only good government is a democratic one. A religious person may consider an atheist bad purely because he is an atheist, and not even consider that person's behavior in a particular situation. Marxists in political science or philosophy may condemn a theory because it is incompatible with Marxism, rather than judging its internal coherence or intelligibility.

A system of thoughts or ideas is very convenient. It gives one a framework to deal with each new idea or situation. However, systematic thinking can easily be lazy thinking and it can even be dangerous, as the history of medicine shows us.

The most significant system in early Western medical history was the humoral theory, first developed in ancient Greece, and later written in stone by Galen, a Rome-based physician in the second century. This system was only discarded in the seventeenth century. The basic tenet of the system was that disease was due to an imbalance of the four "humors" or elements of the body. The blood was used as a basis for the humors, and four parts of the blood formed the basis of the analysis. What we call blood serum today was called "yellow bile." Black sediment was called "black bile." Fibrin, the substance responsible for blood clotting, was called "phlegm." The fourth part was blood itself. The four humors corresponded with the four elements of the universe, with certain qualities, certain organs of the body, and with certain temperaments in a person. Yellow bile was associated with fire, of a hot and dry quality, with the liver, and with a choleric or fiery temper. Black bile was associated with the element earth, with a cold and dry quality, with the spleen, and with a melancholy temperament. Phlegm was associated with the element water, with a cold and wet quality, with the brain, and with a phlegmatic temperament—slow moving and sluggish. Blood was associated with air, with a hot and wet quality, with the heart, and with a sanguine and optimistic temperament.

Through this system, man was linked to the universe, and the various parts of the world were linked to each other. Man's internal system reflected the balance of the universe, and disease was created by an imbalance of these elements. The cure was to restore the balance. Each disease had a quality of its own, linked to the temperament of the person, and the treatment represented a quality that counteracted the particular disease. If a condition could be described as an excess of yellow bile, which was hot and dry, then the treatment would involve a concoction that was cold and wet.

It was Galen, physician to five Roman emperors, who classified and established a great number of the cures, based on the humoral theory. His writings served as the major medical texts for over fifteen hundred years. He tried to link all diseases to his particular version of the humoral system, and his impressively authoritarian dogmas were unquestioningly accepted in most medical practice. So powerful was the influence of Galen that the fact that he made some glaring errors in his description of the human body went unnoticed or ignored until the seventeenth century. When his errors were noted by Paracelsus, Michael Servetus, and others, there were cries of blasphemy from the medical establishment. How dare you criticize Galen! When Servetus clearly revealed the faults in Galen's theory concerning the circulation of blood, the reaction was not to honor him, but instead, to burn him at the stake. Treatments that did not agree with the humoral system were ignored or ridiculed, not because they were shown to be ineffective, but because they were ideologically incorrect. If it did not fit into the system, it could not be true.

When the Galenic system collapsed—and it fell not with a bang but with a whimper—slowly phased out in the seventeenth century, it did not mean the end of medical practice that was based on an authoritarian theory. To be sure, in a good deal of the eighteenth and nineteenth centuries, there was no universally accepted medical system. Towards the end of this period, one of the great tragedies of medical history occurred, one that vividly showed the powerful pull of theoretical doctrine over practical experience.

Hospitals in the early nineteenth century were repositories of filth and disease. Doctors would not even wash their hands, as they went from patient to patient. They would deal with corpses at one moment and sick people the next. A doctor's gown was caked with old blood, and the dirtier it was, the better, because the filth was evidence of hard work. In such an environment, it is not surprising that giving birth in a hospital was frequently a death sentence for mother, child, or both. One in four mothers giving birth in a hospital died.

In the middle of the nineteenth century, Ignaz Semmelweis had the perceptivity to notice that a mother had a much better chance of living if she went to a midwife. He also had the sense to ask why this was so. He noticed that there was one basic difference between doctors and midwives: doctors attended post-mortems, midwives did not. If doctors would wash their hands in the interval between handling corpses and handling women in labor, perhaps the death rate would drop. He instructed his staff to clean themselves before delivering a baby. In no time the death rate in his ward dropped from one in four to one in a hundred.

Did doctors all over the world rush to wash their hands? No! They felt insulted that Semmelweis had implicated them in the deaths of women giving birth. No one likes to be told that they are killing people, least of all those who are supposed to be saving lives. Besides, at this point in history, there was no reason for them to believe in cleanliness. There was no theory to justify it. The relationship between filth and disease had no theoretical basis.

Semmelweis was appalled. He called his opponents in the medical profession murderers. This did not win him any popularity contests. His colleagues waged a vicious campaign against him and finally ran him out of the medical practice. The number of mothers and babies eventually saved through his efforts is incalculable; it has been suggested that no one person in history ever did more to raise general life expectancy. Unfortunately, his career and eventually his life were destroyed. He died in an insane asylum, driven mad by the insanity around him.

There are many reasons for this black episode in the history of medicine. But a comparison of the behavior of the medical profession towards Semmelweis and the behavior towards Lister will demonstrate how large a part theory played in this tragedy.

Less than 20 years separated the work of Semmelweis from that of Lister. Joseph Lister read about the work of Louis Pasteur and the germ theory of disease. This theory stated that disease is carried by airborne particles that lodge themselves in the body and cause illness. Colds supposedly were caused by "germs," passing from one person to another through the air or through physical contact. If disease could be passed in this way, doesn't it make sense to say that doctors could pass germs from one patient to another through their hands or instruments? Lister recommended soaking instruments in carbolic acid to destroy all germs, and demanded meticulous cleanliness on the part of the hospital staff. An extraordinary drop in hospital–related infections followed almost immediately in institutions that heeded Lister's recommendations. Rather rapidly, cleanliness in hospitals became the rule rather than the exception. The empirical evidence in favor of Semmelweis' work was as dramatic as that which accompanied Lister's. Their discoveries were along the same lines. And yet one man was ruined while the other was feted. What was the difference between these two discoveries? One was based on empirical observation; the other was based on an established theory.

Once the germ theory was accepted, it had an enormous impact on the standards of cleanliness everywhere. Cities cleaned their streets, and sewage systems were introduced in western Europe and America. Standards of personal hygiene were encouraged and were avidly taken up by the emerging middle class. By the turn of the century, urban cleanliness had reached levels that had not been seen since the days of ancient Rome.

As a result, the incidence of cholera and typhus dropped quickly. Tuberculosis, the most feared disease of the nineteenth century, declined. The greatest gains in life expectancy in history occurred between 1880 and 1930, and these gains were a direct consequence of cleaning up people, hospitals, and cities.

What is sadly ironic is that cleanliness was recognized as important by some people long before the germ theory was formulated. Pliny the Elder attributed the generally good health of the natives of Rome to their level of sanitation. In the early Renaissance, many doctors maintained scrupulously clean hands and instruments. But it took 1,500 years, after the fall of Rome, to find a city as clean as the ancient capital, and early nineteenth-century doctors laughed at the lavation habits of their predecessors. They knew no theoretical reason for washing, so why should they do so?

We should not be so blind as to imagine that the unthinking reliance on theory rather than on empirical evidence that was demonstrated by the doctors who crucified Servetus and Semmelweis no longer exists. Today, the belief in "scientific medicine," and all that this implies, has led many doctors to ignore or ridicule possibly efficacious treatments that do not conform to medical orthodoxy. While scientific medicine floundered in its attempts to develop a cure for certain cancers, it viciously persecuted people who looked for alternative treatments. Reputations were ruined, practitioners were run out of the country, people were sometimes imprisoned for daring to treat cancer by means other than radiation, drugs, or surgery—the only acceptable approaches to cancer treatment according to the American Cancer Society (ACS). Patients were warned to beware of "quacks" who suggested that nutritional or emotional factors could be causes of cancer and that nutrition and psychological therapy could be part of the treatment. It was ironic that, in 1984, the ACS conceded that nutrition and mental status might play a role in the development of cancer. Books came out with the approval of ACS that made noises about an anticancer diet which included such staples of unorthodox nutritional therapy as carrots and cabbages. The modern day Semmelweises and Servetuses, who have had their careers and reputations sacrificed to the altar of scientific medicine, may yet be vindicated.

This belief in the tools and methods of scientific medicine has also led doctors to be guilty of reckless prescriptions of harmful drugs and treatments. The development of the wonder drugs of modern medicine has been a double-edged sword. On the one hand, antibiotics have made the treatment of infections and certain acute infectious diseases possible, where once treatment was uncertain and survival doubtful. Pneumonia rarely kills basically healthy people today, as it often did in the days before antibiotics. But the irony of these miracles is that they come at a horrible price, for they have created a whole new range of diseases that are purely associated with their use. They also have encouraged the development of new bacteria and viruses that are resistant to antibiotics. As a result, scientists spend a good deal of time developing new antibiotics to counter infectious agents that have become resistant to the previous generation of drugs. Side effects of some treatments are so horrible that they seem worse than the disease. Too frequent use of antibiotics can ruin people's immune systems as well, making them more likely to get sick in the future. It may be that some future generation will regard the chemotherapy given to cancer patients today with the same horror that we look at bloodletting, leeches, and other staples of seventeenth-century medicine.

We must remember that modern doctors have a serious vested interest in following the dictates of orthodox medicine in the United States. They must go through approximately sixteen years of schooling between entering medical school and being able to set up a practice in their specialty. During those years, they are bombarded with facts to be memorized, many of which will do little good in their practice as doctors. They undergo the terrors of internship, during which they may have to stay awake for as long as thirty hours at a stretch while they are "on call." They are subject to the whims of older doctors, often doing a great deal of work for them without getting much credit. The entire process is a lengthy and sadistic initiation into the profession. After having undergone such hardships to become a doctor, it is not surprising that physicians are so reluctant to consider any treatments that do not accord with their training. "All that we suffered for must be worth something," one can imagine them saying.

Doctors look down on chiropractors and acupuncturists not because their methods do not work (not having studied them, they have no idea if their methods have any validity or not), but because they are "healers" who have not yet suffered as they did. In addition, their theories and approaches radically differ from that of a modern medical doctor and, what is worse, these approaches might undermine some of the training so heavily invested in by older doctors.

This is not to imply that these alternative approaches are superior to modern medicine, nor am I saying that medical advances of the past half century have not been significant. The development of antibiotics was an extraordinary achievement; the advances in the treatment of trauma cases in the past ten years have been astounding, allowing people to recover from injuries that in earlier times would have killed them or left them permanently disabled. Microsurgery has made possible operations that were previously impossible. The very real achievements of modern medicine must be acknowledged—but with a caveat, for success in some areas does not mean success in all areas, and it behooves the modern doctor to be cautious about the treatments used, and to be skeptical of extreme claims within the profession, just as he or she would be skeptical of the claims of nondoctors. This skepticism must also be tempered with a willingness to accept occasionally that certain treatments may work which the doctor cannot fully understand.

Ironically, the greatest doctors in history, the same ones who advocated simplicity in medical treatment, also respected open-mindedness in medical practice. Hippocrates warned doctors not to disdain folk cures. Paracelsus laughed at Galen, and told his students to read patients rather than books. Sydenham considered the needs of the patient to be more important than any theory. William Osler, writing at the height of belief in the germ theory, boldly held that the nature of the patient matters more than the nature of the disease. Medical theory has been a crutch for mediocrities in the field since the earliest days of medicine. The good and ethical doctor has always been able to see beyond the theories he or she knows, beyond training and vested interests, to the needs of those to be healed.

QUESTIONS

1. *What were the four humors of the body, according to the humoral theory? What were some of the associations with each humor?*

2. *How was disease treated, according to the precepts of the humoral theory?*

3. *What were conditions like for women giving birth in hospitals early in the nineteenth century? How did Semmelweis change these conditions? What were the reactions of his medical colleagues to his work?*

4. *How do the differing stories of Semmelweis and Lister illustrate the impact that a theory can have on people's perceptions of a situation?*

5. *What are some of the dangers of an unthinking reliance on scientific medicine?*

6. *Why are doctors likely to follow the dictates of orthodox medical practice?*

Why Is Medicine So Complicated?

Previously, we touched on the issues of simplicity and complication in medical practice. One of the curious facts about the history of medicine is that it does not represent a consistent evolution towards increasingly accurate diagnoses and effective remedies. In fact, one can look at the history of medicine as a series of degenerations. It seems that, in Western civilization, each society has gone from periods of comparative medical simplicity, in which the remedies proposed and diagnostic tools were fairly straight-forward and at least did not hurt the patient, to increasingly intrusive, more harmful and forbiddingly complex treatments.

For example, the ancient Sumerian and Babylonian civilizations were the first to develop a systematic approach to health and disease. They believed that disease could either have a natural or supernatural cause. If the disease had a supernatural origin, they would call in a priest; if the disease had a natural origin, they would call in a physician who would suggest either drugs or surgery. What is curious is that, in looking at the earliest writings, we find that prescribed remedies were simple, commonsensical, and only rarely required the use of supernatural props to advance their natural cures. Later writings, on the other hand, were full of hocus-pocus and complex mixtures of herbs to be administered in conjunction with certain magical incantations.

The Egyptians, who inherited the Sumerian ideas, show a similar pattern. The early writings display a taste for simple remedies, based on a study of the human body and on empirical observation of disease. In time, however, their medicine too became a cornucopia of magical incantations and complicated drug formulas that had to be mixed in precise quantities and in special ways. Doctors found it necessary to specialize, so that patients could end up going to one physician for throat problems and another one for stomach ailments.

This tendency toward complexity was not confined to the ancient world. Complex pharmacopoeias, developed by the physician Galen during a declining period in ancient Roman medicine, continued to be used well into the seventeenth century. Shortly after the Galenic system fell apart, an Age of Heroic Medicine took place. There were extraordinary medical treatments, during which traumatic and apparently sadistic practices were the norm. The following gruesome tale about the last illness of Charles II of England is typical.

SIXTEEN OUNCES OF BLOOD . . .[2]

Sixteen ounces of blood were removed from a vein in his right arm with immediate good effect. As was the approved practice at this time, the King was allowed to remain in the chair in which the convulsions seized him; his teeth were held forcibly open to prevent him biting his tongue; the regimen was, as Roger North pithily describes it, 'first to get him to wake, and then to keep him from sleeping'. Urgent messages had been dispatched to the King's numerous personal physicians, who quickly came flocking to his assistance: they were summoned regardless of distinctions of creed and politics, and they came. They ordered cupping-glasses to be applied to his shoulders forthwith, and deep scarification to be carried out, by which they succeeded in removing another eight ounces of blood. A strong antimonial emetic was administered, but as the King could be got to swallow only a small portion of it, they determined to render assurance doubly sure by a full dose of Sulphate of Zinc. Strong purgatives were given, and supplemented by a succession of *clysters*.[3] The hair was shorn close and pungent blistering agents were applied all over his head; and as though this were not enough, the red-hot cautery was requisitioned as well. So severe were the convulsions that the physicians at first despaired of his life, but in some two hours consciousness was completely restored.

The practices mentioned here continued for some days, with thirteen doctors trying their hand at healing the king. When he died a few days later, one could only wonder whether it was the disease or the doctors who killed him. These practices continued in use until well into the nineteenth century. But in noting their barbarity, we should not be blind to the fact that the same temptation to use complex, heroic measures that are fundamentally useless exists even today. Patients are subjected to delicate heart operations that are very unlikely to improve their condition; drug therapies with grotesque side effects are given to cancer patients for types of cancer that are not particularly helped by these treatments. For years, many people were given dangerous operations for disc problems in their backs, a procedure that usually aggravated the condition. Intrusive and painful tests are still given to determine illness, and few doctors even think to look into ancient Chinese methods of diagnosis that seek to determine the same illnesses by far simpler and less harmful means. In the most bizarre instance, AIDS patients are given drugs which suppress the immune system because the diseases that develop due to the

ETHICS AND MEDICINE

virus are traditionally treated in this way. Their already weakened immune systems then become further weakened, making them likely to get sick again—this time helped along by the "treatment" they are getting.

Why has medical practice tended to prefer the complex and harmful treatment to the simple one? Why has medicine, time and again, slipped into needless complexity, with the full support of a large segment of the population? It is significant that the greatest doctors in history have often been quite opposed to this tendency, as we have already observed.

With so many of the most respected medical practitioners opposed to this tendency, we must conclude that there is a deep and powerful need that allows this mindless complexity to continue to reassert itself. The depth of this need becomes especially apparent when we see that reckless prescriptions contradict one of the fundamental precepts of medical ethics, a precept that all codes of medical ethics at least pay lip service to—*primum non nocere*—first, do no harm.

Explanations of this apparent paradox are necessarily speculative. Several possibilities come to mind, however, that can at least make some sense of the situation. One explanation can spring from an understanding of the nature of the relationship between doctor and patient. Patients come to a doctor because of weakness, aware that they have a problem. They want the doctor to take on some of the burden and respond to their difficulties. They want a show of strength and confidence, an effort to do something positive for them. The patient feels weak in the presence of the doctor, and looks up to the doctor as an authority figure. This impression is reinforced by the props of the medical profession— the white lab coat, suggesting both the priest and science, the medical paraphernalia, the prescriptions written in an ancient language.

All this suggests that the doctor is privy to some esoteric knowledge beyond the ken of ordinary mortals. The doctor reinforces this image and the sense of power over the patient by suggesting cures. If a patient comes into a doctor's office feeling ill, and is told merely to go home and rest, the patient will feel disappointed. If, worse, the doctor suggests that he or she does not know what is wrong, the patient may well feel cheated. The patient wants the doctor to demonstrate extraordinary knowledge and control. Simple remedies and professed ignorance do not enhance this image. Complex treatments and elaborate explanations do. Furthermore, if the doctor really does not know what is wrong with a patient, which happens a lot more often than most people realize, there is the temptation to try several approaches to the illness in the hope that one of them will work. Complex drug treatments can easily develop in this way.

A factor related to the ones mentioned above is that people's ability to be cured is strongly influenced by the faith that they have in their doctor. If they believe the treatment will work, it is more likely to do so. Although a complex and useless remedy may not be effective in itself, it may, in conjunction with the patient's faith in the omnipotence of the doctor, allow him or her to rally natural defenses more efficiently. This is a risky business, however, for complex drugs are also more likely to contain elements that are dangerous to the patient. Perhaps a better solution would be for the doctor to say that the patient is receiving some exotic potion, but actually to prescribe a placebo. This is quite a common practice, although one may conclude that there are glaring moral problems suggested by such wholesale lying.

The effectiveness of placebos leads us to yet another reason why these complex remedies develop, namely, the fickle nature of disease. Two people with identical symptoms can have vastly different diseases. Two people with identical viruses can have totally different symptoms. A virus that can kill one person will be harmless in another. A disease that seems to be terminal can suddenly reverse its course, never to reappear. A harmless bug can suddenly turn lethal. As for treatments, it is notorious that the same treatment can cure one person and kill another. It is, furthermore, extremely difficult to determine exactly what causes one patient to get better in any particular case. Was it really the drug that cured the patient? A complex drug, it is figured, is more likely to have some effective ingredient in it. A cautious doctor might be loath to alter a remedy that seems to be working, even though he or she may suspect that it has many extraneous parts.

Another factor might well be greed. A prominent doctor wrote a book on the medical profession, about twenty years ago, in which he suggested that doctors performed unnecessary surgery and devised uselessly complex treatments because they wanted to make money. An honest doctor is not going to become as rich as a crooked one. The easiest way to be dishonest in the medical profession is to schedule useless surgery and meaningless treatments. Because of people's trust in doctors, and their respect for esoteric complexity, it is an easy thing to do and tempting to a doctor who suffered through years of impecunity in medical school.

Thus, we can see that for many reasons, some quite justifiable and others somewhat more dubious, why doctors have been tempted to choose elaborate and useless treatment over simple, effective ones. This is only one of the factors in the history of medicine that have created the moral perspective of the contemporary doctor.

QUESTIONS

1. *What factors may have led to the tendency of medicine to become increasingly complex? Can you think of any other possible factors that were not listed in the essay?*

2. *Has there been any pressure within medicine to counteract the trend towards complexity? Why do you think these pressures have not been sufficient to overcome the trend toward complexity?*

3. *What ethical problems can you see that a doctor would face, when confronted with a patient, that would call for a more complex remedy? What psychological factors would facilitate the use of such a remedy?*

A Doctor Faces the Issues

We have examined some of the pressures that face the contemporary doctor by looking at historical and human factors that influence thinking and acting in the medical profession. Let us now read an article by a physician, Dr. Donald Hayes of the University of North Carolina Medical Center, who discusses a number of ethical problems he has faced in the course of his practice. While reading, keep in mind both his perspective as a contemporary medical practitioner and the inherited tradition.

Note the principles followed in each case. They show the pragmatism of a man dealing with real ethical situations on a daily basis.

"Ethical Issues in Modern Medicine"[4]

Some of the perplexing problems encountered in medicine today are new, some are old, and others are merely old problems in new guises or contexts. Among the old concerns are decision making related to death and dying, euthanasia, suicide, and psychosurgery. Some new concerns are presented by the ability to transplant organs, and by the ability to detect fetal abnormalities prior to birth. Promising to be even more complex are the problems presented by our ability to perform various feats of genetic engineering. Perhaps the oldest set of problems appearing in new forms is that group of concerns surrounding our social welfare practices. My own experiences have exposed me to several decision-making situations involving these subjects.

EUTHANASIA

One of my college classmates was W.S. He was known as a serious-minded fellow who was like Joe Bltfszk in Li'l Abner. W. walked around under that same dark cloud. If anything bad was going to happen, it would always happen to W. All his life he had aspired to physicianhood. He had studied hard to get into college and worked his way through when he did get there. All his dreams seemed to be coming true when he was accepted into medical school and was married to a lovely young woman in the same year.

Through medical school, internship, and three years of specialty training, W. continued to be the "hard luck kid." It became a standing joke among us that, if someone were going to die, he would do so on W.'s night on call. This meant that he worked harder and longer than anyone else, often with more disappointments. Despite this, he and his wife managed to have two lovely children during this time.

After completing his training, W. went into practice in a small North Carolina town. For a year his practice thrived; he bought a new car and house, and he and his wife decided to enlarge their family. When she was three months pregnant, they decided to take their first vacation ever. While lying on the beach one day enjoying the unaccustomed luxury, W. felt strange discomfort in his left flank and shoulder. He discounted this as being related to the unusual activities of playing with children and swimming in the surf. However, the next day he felt a fullness and hardness in the left side of his abdomen. Recognizing that he had an enlarged spleen, W. returned to his *alma mater*, this time as a patient.

Examination of the patient, his blood and bone marrow, showed that he had leukemia. Contrary to W.'s usual bad luck, he did not appear to have one of the acute forms, but rather chronic granulocytic leukemia, which carries with it a survival time of over 3 years in 95% of instances. He was begun on therapy with busulfan, and we all heaved a collective sigh of relief as he left the hospital with his disease under apparent control.

After a few months, it became obvious that W. had not lost his propensity for "hard luck". In spite of the apparent diagnosis of chronic granulocytic leukemia, he was back in the hospital. It fell my lot to care for him while there, one of the most difficult experiences in my life.

When he entered the hospital, W.'s predominant problems were weakness and anemia. Although blood transfusions relieved his symptoms rapidly, diffuse bone pain soon occurred. This worsened rapidly and was only partially relieved by large doses of narcotic analgesic drugs. A few days later, weakness of the legs appeared, which was followed rapidly by paraplegia due to spinal cord compression from leukemic infiltrates. As if this were not enough of a problem, *thrombocytopenia*[5] developed and W. became blind overnight due to intracranial hemorrhage. The next morning I was confronted by a dying friend, 32 years old, the father of two children, husband of a young woman carrying his third child. This man stopped between screams of pain to stare at me with sightless eyes, grasped my hand, and begged me to help him die. "If you can't hurry it up for me, Don, at least let me die as quickly as you can," he said. My decision: whether to stop all supportive measures except the narcotics or whether to continue drugs and blood transfusions in an almost vain effort to achieve a remission of the leukemia.

Although I do not believe I could have done so, I was grateful to W. for not burdening me by asking me to kill him. It was relatively easy for me to decide to stop transfusions, antibiotics, and other such measures. It was also easy for me to order as much narcotic as necessary to keep him comfortable. I am happy to note that he lived only a few hours more after this. My problems with this case were really worse after W.'s death.

This experience forced me to examine my beliefs and practices about death and dying. As a result of this examination, I was able to evolve certain working principles:

1. There is a difference between prolonging life and prolonging the act of dying. The physician is pledged to the former and not the latter.

2. There is a difference between allowing someone a "good death" (agathanasia or benemortasia) and killing him (euthanasia). The former is often desirable, the latter is never permissible.

3. The patient suffering from a fatal disease often suffers great pain. Many physicians and nurses are reluctant to give amounts of narcotic analgesic drugs sufficient to relieve pain. The reasons given for this reluctance are: fear of inducing narcotic addiction and fear of the patient's pain becoming unresponsive to narcotics. The former reason is foolish, the latter specious. The patient experiencing pain from fatal disease should receive as little narcotic as possible but as much as required to relieve that pain short of fatal dosages.

4. The dying person needs most an attitude of sympathetic helpfulness from attending health professionals, plus a commitment on their part to absolute truthfulness. I should point out here that truthfulness need not be equated with bluntness or insensitivity.

5. The thing all dying persons fear most is abandonment by individuals who are significant to them. This fear should be recognized by all concerned and the occurrence prevented.

6. Many problems related to death and dying arise from a failure of health professionals to recognize that someone must make a critical decision at a critical time for each person. Health professionals should be trained to accept this responsibility and not pass it on to other professionals, to family, or, even worse, to

an insensate machine. The following poem describing the experience of a nine-year-old boy who underwent open heart surgery describes most poignantly this failure of assumption of responsibility:

Billy Smith is dead.
His mind got the message first and
Stopped thinking.
His lungs got the message next, and
Quit breathing, so they
Put him on a pump, and
Pumped him.
I got the message when I
shined a light in Billy's eyes.
He looked, owl-like, back.
He didn't blink; his
Pupils stayed wide.
"Dead," I said,
But his heart
(or, rather, myocardium)
Didn't get the message.
It kept making blips-on-the-monitor
So we stood around and watched blips,
And watched each other shine lights
In Billy's owl-eyes.
Hoping they *wouldn't* be owly *this* time
But they always were, and we all
Got the message.
Billy's parents got the message, and
Quit coming.
Special nurses got the message, and
Got bored.
Medical students got the message, and
Got mad when called, early a.m.
To draw bloods, et cetera.
Crippled Children's Fund got the message, and
Paid, big; but
Billy's myocardium just kept blipping,
Artificial breather kept breathing,
Finally Billy's myocardium perked up its ears,
Got the message,
And let Billy die

A. French, first-year resident, M.D.
Sacramento Medical Center. 1967

SUICIDE

Every physician-in-training encounters at least one instance in which, given another chance, he would do something differently. Mine involved an episode which occurred as I worked a busy night in the emergency room of a large city hospital. After putting countless sutures in the lacerated skins of children, thugs, and assorted alcoholics, applying casts to fractured extremities, tussling with violent inebriates and assorted other unpleasant tasks, I looked up to see the police bringing in G.

G. was well known to all emergency room crews. He had a chart which was two inches thick with emergency room records accumulated over several years. Most of these visits followed the same pattern: he would come in or be brought in by the police, his breath heavy with alcohol fumes; he would be tearful, sometimes abusive, and complaining of abdominal pain.

On several occasions, he had been admitted to the hospital and studied intensively to determine the origin of his symptoms. At none of these times was an organic basis for these symptoms found. The front of the chart showed "abdominal pain of undetermined origin" and "inadequate personality" as the final diagnoses.

Every emergency room visit followed the same sequence: G. would complain bitterly and tearfully of pain; the examining physician, finding no significant abnormality, would give him a mild analgesic. G. would then depart, still complaining bitterly and often threatening to harm himself. The intervals between visits varied but each visit seemed to be associated with or preceded by several days of depression and alcohol ingestion.

On the night in question, I examined G. rather perfunctorily and sent him on his way. As he left the emergency room he turned to me and asked dramatically: "Which way is the river?" Short on both patience and sympathy, I responded by mutely pointing the way.

I will never forget the sinking feeling I had as I looked up a few hours later and saw the ambulance driver wheel in a sheet-covered body. Somehow I knew who was under that sheet. My fears were confirmed when I lifted the covering and looked into G.'s face. I felt an even greater impact as I lifted the cover further and saw his hands. Even though he had been dead for a few hours, clutched tightly in his right hand was the envelope full of APC tablets I had given him, and clutched equally tightly in his left hand was the clinic appointment slip I had filled out for him.

The waves of guilt which swept over me were indescribable. Had I made the ethical decision in this case?

Of course the obvious answer was: "No!" But the reason for the answer is not so obvious. In fact, I believe that an individual may elect to commit suicide and be making an appropriate decision. My own experience has shown me many instances in which I could see that an individual might very well be better off dead than to continue to live in his circumstances. W., the physician with leukemia, is a good case in point.

Why, then, did I say that my response was the wrong one? The reason lies in one of the conditions I attach to the belief that suicide may be an acceptable course of action. This is that the individual choosing suicide should do so in full possession of two things: 1. his own faculties for rational decision making, and 2. a full exposition of all possible options open to him. I not only did not know whether these things were true for G., I made no effort to find out.

Another element of my performance in this case, which I continue to criticize, is my failure to do the most loving and reasonable thing possible under the circumstances. . . . I can conceive of a situation in which allowing someone to commit suicide might be the most loving and reasonable thing possible. However, I cannot convince myself that this was the case with G.

Finally, I believe in this situation I failed to recognize one more thing. In assuming the role of physician, one renounces the right to treat patients on the basis of personal preference or moralistic judgment, but must provide his best treatment on the basis of human rights and dignity.

PSYCHOSURGERY

Although psychosurgery was out of favor for several years, it has recently been widely discussed. Genetic research has suggested the possibility of spotting potentially aggressive offenders by chromosome studies. In view of this possibility, it has been suggested that such surgery on the potentially aggressive XYY chromosome bearer might render him less threatening to society. These considerations led me to examine my own performance in one instance involving psychosurgery.

E. was a 32 year old white female whom I first saw when she was admitted to the hospital where I was serving as a resident in psychiatry. She had been treated for seven or eight years with several psychotic episodes. On these occasions, she had been diagnosed as a paranoid schizophrenic. She had always been very immature and highly impulsive. During her psychotic episodes she was shamelessly exhibitionistic, aggressive, hostile, and self-destructive. At one time, she slashed her wrists.

Because of her hostile, uninhibited behavior which was not improved by other treatments, we considered *prefrontal leukotomy*.[6] Following a conservative bent, we operated only on one side. After this she was almost immediately improved.

She was certain a miracle had occurred and said: "I couldn't stand that suffering any longer, I was going to kill myself . . . Now I am going to be the real person I always wanted to be." Four weeks later she went into the worst psychotic episode she ever had.

After four months, we repeated the operation on the other side. She then became shy, quiet, colorless, placid, almost apathetic, but friendly and mildly affectionate, stereotyped, and very correct. Previously, especially in her more active periods, she had been hypercritical, vitriolic, colorful, and extremely shocking in her crude but clever humor. People laughed, but withdrew. After surgery, everyone was drawn to her as to a fragile, passive child.

Prior to her operations, her room was as chaotic as her behavior, with pin-up girls and men, flaming orange drapes, scattered books and clothes. After her surgery, her room was bare and uninviting, not at all from necessity. Except for her few little possessions arranged neatly on the dresser, there was nothing to distinguish it from any institutional "cell" anywhere.

Before the operations, she had violent crushes and quarrels with nurses and female patients and was wantonly promiscuous with men.

Previously she often spoke of herself as being two people in one—"a devil and a saint, Dr. Jekyll and Mr. Hyde." After surgery she said: "I am just myself."

In retrospect, I still wonder if the decisions made in this case were ethical. Obnoxious and reprehensible as the behavior of this patient was, did we (society) have the right to change it by this means? Which of the persons we saw here was the *real* one with all her natural attributes—the presurgical, between operations, or postsurgical one? How "bad" or deviant does one's behavior have to be before a physician can ethically change him or her into another person by surgical means?

I include this case in this account because it is one about

which I am not yet sure even though years have passed. There are so many questions left unanswered in our society that I am not sure we can assume the right of destruction of personhood implied by psychosurgical procedures.

Another brief case history makes this point of concern well. At one time I was the responsible physician in a unit caring for psychiatric patients who were violent or potentially so. The terror of the unit was a young man who was kept constantly in a padded cell because he was so violent. No one dared approach him to care for him. His food was slid under the door to him. He was bathed by "hosing him down" periodically.

Since this was in the days before tranquilizers, he was the first subject all the staff thought of when a study of the first tranquilizer, chlorpromazine, was instituted. Unbeknownst to us, the study was a double blind one.

When our obstreperous patient was placed on study, we assumed we could tell rapidly which substance he was getting. Within hours after he was started on the study, he became approachable. In a few days, he was absolutely docile and rational. The nurse and attendants found that he could be fed, bathed and attended to in normal fashion. The physicians found he could be examined and conversed with just as with any other patient. Only after several weeks, during which we marvelled about the efficacy of the new tranquilizers, did we find that this patient had been receiving a placebo. The ingredient which had caused the remarkable change in this violent man was the fact that we began treating him as a human being. In how many cases of "mental illness" in our society could we achieve the same result with the same method?

ABORTION AND PRENATAL DIAGNOSIS

E.A., now aged 15, was well-known in the sixth grade for her lush, mature figure. This made her an object of ridicule to her classmates, but gave her a considerable status in the eyes of older students, particularly boys. To gain acceptance among them she made herself readily available for sexual "fun and games." By the time she was in the eighth grade her promiscuity was familiar to all the students in her school, and she had no real friends. Being an outcast herself, she sought the company of outcasts, the members of the local drug subculture. Although she was not using drugs herself, her parents took her to their family physician for a "check-up." He opined to them that she was probably a drug user and advised them to "put their foot down" with her. Her reaction to the subsequent behavior of her parents was then to begin using drugs intentionally. In a period of two years, she ran the gamut of drugs from marijuana to psychedelics to stimulants. She became known as a "garbage head" whose 15-year old body was available to anyone with the price of a "hit" of anything.

I first saw E.A. in a community crisis intervention center because she "crashed" after a "speed run." In the course of her evaluation we found not surprisingly, that she had gonorrhea. We also found that she was ten weeks pregnant. E.A. had no idea who the father was. She gradually began to feel that an abortion was the most practical solution to this problem for her. Added weight was given to this feeling by the history of multiple-drug use and finding of chromosome breakage in amniocentesis. She was doing better in other respects and felt that termination of the pregnancy would allow her to make a "fresh start." Unfortunately, life was not to be that simple. Her mother felt that she should bear her child in "payment for her sin." Her father was uncertain. The relationship which existed between E.A. and me was such that she and her family turned to me for help with this decision.

In analyzing my response to E.A.'s plight, I found that I leaned most heavily on the thinking of Dr. Albert Schweitzer. It was he who enunciated the ethic of Reverence for Life. Among his writing I found the following: "A man is ethical only when life, as such, is sacred to him—and when he devotes himself helpfully to all life that is in need of help. To the man who is truly ethical all life is sacred, including that which from the human point of view seems lower in the scale. He makes distinctions only as each case comes before him, and under the pressure of necessity, as, for example, when it falls to him to decide which of two lives he must sacrifice in order to preserve the other."

The first things I had to accept was the fact that someone was going to be hurt no matter what decision was made. Secondly, I had to accept that abortion, no matter how it is dressed up in euphemisms and rationalizations, is still the destruction of life.

Finally, I was able to boil this question down to its simplest alternatives: If E.A. were to carry this baby full term and delivery, who would be hurt? If she had an abortion, who would be hurt? Since the answers to both questions were the same, I then thought of the degrees to which each individual would be hurt and helped the family reach their decision that an abortion was the better option.

Of course, there is no way of knowing the long-term consequences of an abortion. Likewise, there is no way of knowing this was the "right" decision in this case, but it seemed to draw this previously disturbed and estranged family together. Like Dr. Schweitzer, no one was happy with this decision to take a life. But it was made on the basis of the best judgement available at that time in those circumstances.

Also in keeping with Dr. Schweitzer's ethic, I am unable to say that I am categorically in favor of or opposed to abortion. I, too, believe each case must be decided upon individually as it arises.

Recognizing that we cannot forecast the consequences of our moral decisions, we must commit ourselves to deal with the consequences with the same integrity with which we made the decision. Following this concept, I have maintained contact with this family and made it clear to them that I continue to share their concerns.

Discussion

Once embarked on an examination of this sort, it is hard to find a stopping point because of the absence of definitive answers to any of the perplexing questions which arise. In fact, the process of trying to answer such questions often simply leads to more questions.

The best synthesis of available information and the most acceptable set of basic conclusions is that of E. Mansell Pattison, which can be summarized as follow:

1. Specific religious/moral values couched in traditional religious systems have led us and our society to obscurity rather than enlightenment.

2. The process of moral decision making rests squarely with us, the members of this society.

3. Although we do have absolute moralistic/humanistic values to which we in our culture are committed, they provide us no substantive absolute answer in most situations.

4. We, along with the other members of our society, face competing and contradictory values.

5. Ethical medical decision making is a process. We are involved in a process of reaching the best possible social consensus at this time in history regarding a number of complex issues.

6. We should continue to evaluate, examine, and assess the effects of these problems and our attempted solutions of them on our society.

QUESTIONS

1. *Look at the principles Dr. Hayes developed concerning treatment of dying patients. Rephrase these principles in your own words.*

2. *What reasons does Dr. Hayes give for saying that he mishandled the case of "G." (the man who committed suicide)? Do you feel that Dr. Hayes should be as hard on himself as he was in this case? Why or why not?*

3. *Do you think the doctors were justified in performing a leukotomy on "E."? Why or why not?*

4. *How does the case of the violent patient, who became calm when given placebos, illustrate the danger of the blind acceptance of theories mentioned in the essay that opened this chapter?*

5. *Was an abortion a justified procedure in the case of "E.A."? Why or why not?*

6. *Why do you think Pattison says "specific religious/moral values . . . have led . . . to obscurity rather than enlightenment?*

Medicine and Human Freedom: The Work of Dr. Thomas Szasz

In looking at the psychosurgery issue, we are facing one of the most fundamental ethical problems for both doctors and patients. The question is one of freedom and responsibility. Does a doctor have the right to force the patient to undertake a certain course of treatment? How much right does a patient have to choose his or her own treatment? Can a patient be forced to undergo treatment at the insistence of family members? These questions are critical in medicine as a whole, but they become even more crucial in the area of psychiatric treatment.

As one learns from the history of medicine, in the medical community there is a tendency to attach tremendous importance to the opinions and theories of doctors. People, at large, ascribe semidivine status to doctors. This tendency gives doctors a great deal of responsibility, and makes patients feel less responsible for their own behavior and treatment. But, as we have also noted, the reliance on theories in medicine and the tendency to deify doctors can be very dangerous. Dr. Szasz addresses these dangers in this work.

Dr. Szasz (pronounced like "sauce") is a Hungarian-American psychiatrist who has written a number of works that harp on a few basic themes. He believes that the concept of mental illness is misleading, that psychiatry, as it is practiced today, is largely fraudulent, that consent is the basis for all relationships, including that between doctor and patient, and that many so-called scientific and medical problems are really political problems in disguise. He has been closely associated with the Libertarian party in the United States, a group that believes in minimal government. He has been a vocal advocate of some Libertarian programs—for example, the legalization of numerous drugs.

Dr. Szasz is concerned about the connection between medical theory and religion. In drawing this analogy, he is trying to make the point that there should be a separation of medicine (or, for that matter, science) and state, just as there is a separation of church and state.

Freedom and Responsibility[7]

The crucial moral characteristic of the human condition is the dual experience of freedom of the will and personal responsibility. Since freedom and responsibility are two aspects of the same phenomenon, they invite comparison with the proverbial knife that cuts both ways. One of its edges implies options: we call it freedom. The other implies obligations: we call it responsibility. People like freedom because it gives them mastery over things and people. They dislike responsibility because it constrains them from satisfying their wants. That is why one of the things that characterizes history is the unceasing human effort to maximize freedom and minimize responsibility. But to no avail, for each real increase in human freedom—whether in the Garden of Eden or in the Nevada desert, in the chemical laboratory or in the medical laboratory—brings with it a proportionate increase in responsibility. Each exhilaration with the power to do good is soon eclipsed by the guilt for having used it to do evil.

Confronted with this inexorable fact of life, human beings have sought to bend it to their own advantage, or at least to what they thought was their advantage. In the main, people have done so by ascribing their freedom and hence also their responsibility, to some agency outside themselves. They have thus projected their own moral qualities onto others—moralizing them and demoralizing themselves. In the process, they have made others into puppeteers and themselves into puppets.

Evidently, the oldest scheme for constructing such an arrangement is religion: only deities have free will and responsibility; people are mere puppets. Although most religions temper this imagery by attributing some measure of self-action to the puppets, the importance of the underlying world view can hardly be exaggerated. Indeed, people still often try to explain the behavior of certain self-sacrificing persons by saying that they are carrying out God's will; and, perhaps more important still, people often claim to be carrying out God's will when they sacrifice others, whether in a religious crusade or in a so-called psychotic episode. The important thing about this imagery is that it makes us witness to, and even participants in, a human drama in which the actors are seen as robots, their movements being directed by unseen, and indeed invisible, higher powers.

If stated so simply and starkly, many people nowadays might be inclined to dismiss this imagery as something only a religious fanatic would entertain. That would be a grave mistake, as it would blind us to the fact that it is precisely this imagery that animates much contemporary religious, political, medical, psychiatric, and scientific thought. How else are we to account for the systematic invocation of divinities by national leaders? Or the use of the Bible, the Talmud, the Koran, or other holy books as guides to the proper channeling of one's freedom to act in the world?

One of the universal solvents for guilt, engendered by the undesirable consequences of one's actions, is God. That is why religion used to be, and still is, an important social institution.

But the belief in deities as puppeteers and in people as puppets has diminished during the past few centuries. There has, however, been no corresponding increase in the human acceptance of, and tolerance for, personal responsibility and individual guilt. People still try to convince themselves that they are not responsible, or are responsible only to a very limited extent, for the undesirable consequences of their behavior. How else are we to account for the systematic invocation of Marx and Mao by national leaders? Or the use of the writings of Freud, Spock, and other ostensibly scientific works as guides to the proper channeling of one's freedom to act in the world? Today, the universal solvent for guilt is science. That is why medicine is such an important social institution.

For millennia, men and women escaped from responsibility by theologizing morals. Now they escape from it by medicalizing morals. Then, if God approved a particular conduct, it was good; and if He disapproved it, it was bad. How did people know what God approved and disapproved? The Bible—that is to say, the biblical experts, called priests—told them so. Today, if Medicine approves a particular conduct, it is good; and if it disapproves it, it is bad. And how do people know what (Medicine—that is to say, the medical experts, called physicians—tells them so.)

The extermination of heretics in Christian pyres was a theological matter. The extermination of Jews in Nazi gas chambers was a medical matter. The inquisitorial destruction of the traditional legal procedures of Continental courts was a theological matter. The psychiatric destruction of the rule of law in American courts is a medical matter. And so it goes.

QUESTIONS

1. What is the crucial moral characteristic of the human condition, according to Dr. Szasz?

2. Why do people embrace freedom and avoid responsibility? What have they tried to do about this condition? Have they succeeded? Why or why not?

3. *How does religion represent a way for people to bend to their own advantage the problem of freedom and responsibility?*

4. *What has taken over the role of religion in the past few centuries? How has it done this?*

Suffering and Salvation

Human life—that is, a life of consciousness and self-aware-ness—is unimaginable without suffering. Without pain and sorrow, there could be no pleasure and joy; just as without death, there could be no life; without illness, no health; without ugliness, no beauty; without poverty, no riches; and so on ad infinitum with the countless human experiences we categorize as undesirable and desirable.

All our exertions—moral and medical, political and personal—are directed toward minimizing undesirable experiences and maximizing desirable ones. However, if the calculus of personal conduct could be reduced to such a simple prudential principle, human life would be much less complicated than it is. What complicates it of course is the fact that many of the things we regard as desirable are opposed by, or can be secured only at the cost of, others that we regard as also desirable. There seems to be no limit to the internal conflicts and contradictions among the things we abstractly value and wish to maximize. For example, enjoyable eating or drinking often conflicts with good health, sexual pleasure often conflicts with dignity, liberty often conflicts with security, and so on. This is, quite simply, why the pursuit of relief from suffering, reasonable though it may seem, cannot be an unqualified personal or political goal. And if we make it such a goal, it is certain to result in more, not less, suffering. In the past, the greatest unhappiness for the greatest number was thus created by precisely those political programs whose goal was the most radical relief of suffering for the greatest number of human beings. While those campaigns against suffering were in progress, people viewed them with unqualified approval; now we look back at them as the most terrifying tyrannies.

In the absence of the perfect vision that comes only with

hindsight, let us at least try to look at our own age critically. If we do so we shall glimpse—or even see clearly enough—the contours of two contemporary ideologies that have set themselves as the same perennial goal—namely, the radical relief of suffering for the greatest numbers. One of these, holding the East in its grip, is the Marxist-Communist campaign against unhappiness: it promises total relief from suffering through victory over capitalism, the ultimate cause of all human misery. The other, holding the West in its grip, is the scientific-medical campaign against unhappiness: it promises total relief from suffering through victory over disease, the ultimate cause of all human misery.

In countries under Communist rule, where its efforts to relieve suffering are unchecked by any effective countervailing force, Communism has thus succeeded in being the greatest source of suffering; whereas in the so-called free West, where "therapeutism" has achieved a power unchecked by any effective countervailing force, Medicine has succeeded in becoming one of the greatest sources of suffering.

How medicine, the art of healing, has changed from man's ally into his adversary, and how it has done so during the very decades when its powers to heal have advanced the most momentously during its whole history—that is a story whose telling must await another occasion, perhaps even another narrator. It must suffice here to note that there is nothing new about the fact that in human affairs the power to do good is usually commensurate with, if not exceeded by, the power to do evil; that human ingenuity has created, especially in the institutions of Anglo-American law and politics, arrangements that have proved useful in dividing the power to do good into its two basic components— namely, *good* and *power*; and that these institutional arrangements, and the moral principles they embody, have sought to promote the good by depriving its producers and purveyors of power over those desiring to receive or reject their services. The most outstanding monument to that effort on the part of rulers to protect their subjects from those who would do them good, even if it meant doing them in, is the First Amendment clause guaranteeing that "Congress shall make no law respecting an establishment of religion, or prohibiting the free exercise thereof." Let me indicate briefly how I think that guarantee, and the moral and political principles it embodies, applies to our contemporary conditions.

QUESTIONS

1. *What is the difficulty with any attempt to minimize suffering?*

2. *What have been the results of recent attempts to minimize suffering? Why is this so?*

Medicine and the First Amendment

Everyone now recognizes the reality of spiritual suffering—that is, of the fact that men, women, and children may be, and often are, distressed because they can neither find nor give meaning to their lives, or because they can neither accept nor create satisfactory standards for regulating their personal conduct. Although these circumstances result in untold suffering, no one in the United States—certainly, no judicial or legal authorities—would contend that such unhappiness justifies the forcible imposition of certain religious beliefs and practices on the sufferers. Such an intervention, even if it proved "helpful" in relieving the suffering, would violate the First Amendment guarantee against the "establishment of religion."

I try to show that this principle applies, and ought to be applied, to medical or so-called therapeutic interventions as well. I maintain, in other words, that suffering caused by illness—regardless of whether it is actual bodily illness or alleged mental illness—cannot be the ground, in American law, for depriving a person of liberty, even if the incarceration is called *hospitalization*, and even if the intervention is called *treatment*. I contend that such use of state power—whether rationalized as the necessary deployment of the police power or as the therapeutic application of the principle of *paren patriae*[8]—is contrary to the ideas and ideals enshrined in the First Amendment to the Constitution.

How, then, has it come about that medicine has succeeded where religion has failed? How has therapy been able to breach the wall separating church and state where theology has been unable to do so? Briefly put, medicine has been able to achieve what religion has not, primarily by a radical violation of our vocabulary, of our conceptual categories; and secondarily, through the subversion of our ideals and institutions devoted to protecting us from reposing power in those who would help us whether we like it or not. We have done it before to the blacks. Now we are doing it to each other, regardless of creed, color, or race.

How was slavery justified and made possible? By calling blacks *chattel* rather than *persons*. If blacks had been recognized as persons, there could have been no selling and buying of slaves, no fugitive slave laws—in short, there could have been no American slavery. And if plantations could be called *farms*, and forcing blacks to work on them could be called guaranteeing them their *right to work*, then slavery might still be regarded as compatible with the Constitution. As it is, no term can now conceal that slavery is involuntary servitude. Nothing can. Whereas anything can now conceal the fact that institutional psychiatry is involuntary servitude.

How are involuntary psychiatric interventions—and the many other medical violations of individual freedom—justified and made possible? By calling people *patients*, imprisonment *hospitalization*, and torture *therapy*; and by calling uncomplaining individuals *sufferers*, medical and mental-health personnel who infringe on their liberty and dignity *therapists*, and the things the latter do to the former *treatments*. This is why such terms as mental health and the *right to treatment* now so effectively conceal that psychiatry is involuntary servitude.

It is at our own peril that we forget that language is our most important possession or tool; and that whereas in the language of science we explain events, in the language of morals we justify actions. We may thus explain abortion as a certain type of medical procedure but must justify permitting or prohibiting it by calling it *treatment* or the *murder of the unborn child* . . .

To be sure people do suffer. And that in fact—according to doctors and patients, lawyers and laymen—is now enough to justify calling and considering them patients. As in an earlier age through the universality of sin, so now through the universality of suffering, men, women, and children become—whether they like it or not, whether they want to or not—the patient-penitents of their physician-priests. And over both patient and doctor now stands the Church of Medicine, its theology defining their roles and the rules of the games they must play, and its canon laws, now called *public health* and *mental health* laws, enforcing conformity to the dominant medical ethic.

My views on medical ethics depend heavily on the analogy between religion and medicine—between our freedom or the lack of it, to accept or reject theological and therapeutic intervention. It seems obvious that in proportion as people value religion more highly than liberty, they will seek to ally religion with the state and support state-coerced theological practices; similarly, in proportion as they value medicine more highly than liberty, they will seek to ally medicine with the state and support state-coerced therapeutic practices. The point, simple but inexorable, is that when religion and liberty conflict, people must choose between theology and freedom; and that when medicine and liberty conflict, they must choose between therapy and freedom.

If Americans were confronted with this choice today, and if they regarded religion as highly as they regard medicine, they would no doubt try to reconcile what are irreconcilable—by calling incarceration in ecclesiastical institutions *the right to attend church* and torture on the rack *the right to practice the rituals of one's faith*. If the latter terms were accepted as the proper names of the former practices, coerced religious observance and religious persecution could be held to be constitutional. Those subjected to such practices could then be categorized as persons *guaranteed their right to religion*, and those who object to such violations of human rights could be dismissed as the subverters of a free society's commitment to the practice of *freedom of religion*. Americans could then look forward breathlessly to the next issues of *Time* and *Newsweek* celebrating the latest breakthrough in *religious research*.

And yet, perhaps it is still not too late to recall that it was respect for the cure of souls, embraced and practiced freely or not at all, that inspired the framers of the Constitution to deprive clerics of secular power. It was enough, I assume they reasoned, that theologians had spiritual power; they needed no other for the discharge of their duties. Similarly, it is respect for the cure of bodies (and "minds"), embraced and practiced freely or not at all, that inspires me to urge that we deprive clinicians of secular power. It is enough, I believe, that physicians have the power inherent in their scientific knowledge and technical skills; they need no other for the discharge of their duties. . . .

QUESTIONS

1. *What analogy does Dr. Szasz make between spiritual suffering and medical suffering? Why does he make this analogy?*

2. *How has medicine been able to become part of the state when the church has failed to do so?*

3. *How are the medical violations of individual freedom made possible?*

Priest and Physician

Let me hasten to say that I am not denying the scientific or technical aspects of medicine. On the contrary, I believe—and it is rather obvious—that the genuine diagnostic and therapeutic powers of medicine are much greater today than they have ever been in the history of mankind. That, precisely, is why its religious or magical powers are also much greater. Anyone who interprets my efforts to explain, and sometimes to reduce, the magical, religious, and political dimensions of medicine as an effort to cast aspersions on, or to belittle, its scientific and technical dimension does so at his own peril. This book is addressed to those persons who understand the difference between why a priest wears a cassock and a surgeon a sterile gown, between why an orthopedic surgeon uses a cast and psychoanalyst a couch. Unfortunately, many people don't.

Why don't they? Why indeed should they? Why should anyone want to distinguish between technical and ceremonial acts, roles, and words? There is probably only one reason—namely, the desire to be free and responsible. If a person longs to submit to authority, he will find it useful to bestow ceremonial powers on those who wield technical skills, and vice versa; it will make the authorities seem all the more useful as priests and physicians.

People who possess certain intellectual knowledge or technical skills are obviously superior, at least in those respects, to people who do not. Thus, unless people long for a dictatorship of technicians—say, of physicians—they ought to make sure that the expert's favorable social position due to his having special skills is not further enhanced by attributing ceremonial powers to him as well. Conversely, unless they long to be fooled by fakers—say, by psychiatrists—they ought to make sure that the expert's favorable social position due to his having special ceremonial skills, or to such skills being attributed to him by others, is not further enhanced by crediting him with technical powers he does not possess.

Formerly, people victimized themselves by attributing medical powers to their priests; now, they victimize themselves by attributing magical powers to their physicians. Faced with persons endowed with such superhuman powers—and, of course, benevolence—ordinary men and women are inclined to submit to them with that blind trust whose inexorable consequence is that they make slaves of themselves and tyrants of their "protectors." That is why the framers of the Constitution urged their fellow Americans to respect priests for their faith but to distrust them for their power. To enable them to do so, they erected a wall separating church and state.

I hold, similarly, that people should respect physicians for their skill but should distrust them for their power. But unless the people erect a wall separating medicine and the state, they will be unable to do so and will succumb precisely to that danger from which the First Amendment was supposed to protect them.

QUESTIONS

1. *What is the distinction between the ceremonial and scientific role of doctors that Dr. Szasz is making?*

2. *How does Dr. Szasz think we should regard physicians?*

ACTIVITIES

❶ Collect the answers to the questions following all four excerpts. Reread the excerpts. Then write a summary of all four excerpts, making sure you include all of Dr. Szasz's major contentions in your summary.

Further Remarks on Freedom and Responsibility in Medical Ethics

Dr. Szasz's position is based on the idea that people must take individual responsibility for their own actions. All attempts to pass responsibility onto others—either to the state, to religious leaders, or to scientists—are potentially dangerous, for people who are given power may be tempted to abuse that power. For this reason, he opposes involuntary psychiatric incarceration, laws restricting or prohibiting various drugs, and mandatory inoculation programs. In fact, these days, involuntary incarceration is much rarer, and it seems that battle, at least, has turned in Dr. Szasz's favor. Some people have noted that letting psychiatric patients out on the streets has exacerbated the already critical problem of homelessness in large American cities. Schizophrenics who would have been put away in the past are now wandering the streets, incapable of really adjusting to society. The evidence that schizophrenics are swelling the homeless ranks, however, is still largely anecdotal, but it has been used by some psychiatrists and politicians to justify a return to earlier policies of forced psychiatric detention.

Whether or not we agree with Dr. Szasz's position, and whether or not we accept his analogies between religion and medicine, he still provides us with a challenge that is hard to ignore. His questions cut into the very heart of doctor–patient ethics. They are provocative and central to our understanding of medical ethics.

QUESTIONS

1. *Who should decide what treatment to apply and who does the doctor serve?*

2. *How should we take a doctor's advice?*

3. *How does the Hippocratic oath underline the theological aspects of medicine that Dr. Szasz talks about?*

4. *How can people's romantic visions of the past and future make it easier for them to give their freedom to doctors?*

5. *From the perspective of the validity of medical theories, what is the danger of giving doctors too much political power?*

6. *How do you think Dr. Szasz would have evaluated Dr. Hayes' behavior in the psychosurgery case? Explain your answer.*

Endnotes for Chapter 3

1. Reprinted from *A Source Book of Medical History* by Logan Clending. Copyright 1943, Dover Publications, Inc.

2. Reprinted from *The Last Days of Charles II* by Raymond Crawford. London and Oxford: Oxford University Press, 1909.

3. *clysters*: enemas.

4. Reprinted with permission of C. Allen Haney, from "Ethical Issues in Modern Medicine" by Dr. Donald Hayes, in *Some Practical Aspects of Modern Medical Ethics*, proceedings of a symposium at the Bowman Gray School of Medicine, Wake Forest University, Feb 14–15, 1975. Copyright 1975, C. Allen Haney.

5. *thrombocytopenia*: an abormal decrease in the number of blood platelets, often associated with leukemia.

6. *prefrontal leukotomy*: a surgical procedure performed on the front part of the brain. Used to relieve mental illnesses.

7. Reprinted with the permission of Louisiana State University Press from *The Theology of Medicine: The Political-Philosophical Foundations of Medical Ethics* by Thomas Szasz. Copyright 1977, Thomas S. Szasz.

8. *paren patriae*: Latin term referring to the "fatherland."

CHAPTER 4

ETHICS, EXISTENTIALISM, AND ZEN:
Turning the World Topsy-Turvy

This chapter offers the reader a chance to clear the mind of the cobwebs of lazy thinking. Two selections from the writing of Sören Kierkegaard offer a variety of possible ways of looking at the world: the first selection is an argument against constancy in human relationships; the other presents the position of the ethical supremacy of universal laws by examining the behavior of Abraham in the Biblical story of Abraham and Isaac. Twentieth-century existential positions, particularly that of Jean-Paul Sartre, are considered in a brief essay by the author. A longer essay explores the relationshiop between religion and ethics. Afterward, we consider the rather original explorations of ethics and self-discovery of the Zen Buddhists, through some popular writings and Zen stories.

The Ethics of the Possible

"Supposing the truth is a woman—what then?" With this challenge, Friedrich Nietzsche began his book *Beyond Good and Evil*. Nietzsche was looking back on the history of philosophy, noting that philosophers have spent their time trying to find answers—clear-cut, dogmatic assertions that they could claim constituted the truth. But he asks: "Perhaps the gruesome seriousness, the clumsy obtrusiveness, with which they have approached truth so far have been awkward and improper methods for winning a woman's heart." If truth is not dogmatic—if it is playful, or changing, or uncertain, or even just not reducible to a formula, then philosophers have been barking up the wrong tree in trying to reduce the truth to a series of axioms.

Moral truth, expressed in a series of prescriptions and prohibitions, suffers from the same axiomatic quality. And if "truth is a woman," then this simplistic reduction of morality to a set of formulas is a laughable folly, however comfortable simple answers may be to those who prefer not to think for themselves, or to take responsibility for their actions.

The spirit of Nietzsche's challenge has been taken up by some of the greatest minds of the past one hundred fifty years.

Even in earlier times, some of the finest thinkers have been loath to reduce morality or truth to simplistic responses. Let us look at the works of two existential philosophers and at the thought of the Zen Buddhist school in an attempt to take our minds out of the dogmatic slumber that is so easy and comfortable to maintain.

The Existentialism of Sören Kierkegaard

Existentialism as Philosophy and Fad

If you had walked into a café in the student quarter of Paris in the late 1940s, it is likely that you would have come across groups of young people dressed in black, morosely staring at the wall, smoking cigarettes, and mumbling monosyllables. Of course, in every age, there have been groups of miserable youths with such affectations, but in the late '40s these people called themselves "existentialists." If you could get them to talk, you would hear words like "alienation," "inauthenticity," and "despair," as words that described both their own state of mind and their general impression of the world. They might speak of the "meaninglessness of existence" and would justify their morbidity and inaction by saying that nothing matters, anyway. True, these poses came not out of a careful reading of the great existential philosophers, but out of adherence to a fad. However, in the public imagination, for a number of years, the word "existentialism" was linked to a vision of the cultivated despair of these types.

By then, it had been almost a hundred years since the first philosopher whom we call an existentialist had died. In that hundred-year period, some of the greatest minds had been thinking along existential lines, as revealed in their writing. Certainly, the range of thought that we call existential is very great, but once one is attuned to this way of thinking, it is quite easy to recognize the existential signature on a work of philosophy or literature. For all existentialists, "truth is a woman"; she is human, subjective, fleeting, perhaps playful, always beyond the grasp of formulas or axioms, sometimes ridiculous, and never predictable. The existentialists look at a person's own experience to determine something of the truth. They do not see answers in rules or regulations but in each individual's experience of life. Often, the existential philosopher works from personal experience in order to develop a philosophy.

The first philosopher to work consistently in this way was the Danish thinker Sören Kierkegaard (1813–55). To emphasize the kaleidoscopic nature of truth, he wrote books under a variety of pseudonyms, each supposed author revealing a point of view that clarified some aspect of the truth, but at no time purporting to be "the truth." People often wonder which, if any, character of his imagination Kierkegaard agreed with. This is the wrong question. All the characters show us something of the truth but none show the complete truth. Kierkegaard does not agree or disagree with any of these positions. He merely presents them so that his readers will understand more of the different ways the world can be experienced. Nor does this imply that Kierkegaard was merely an observer, objectively looking at things from the outside. He clearly identified with some of these characters more than with others, and he clearly thought some positions more worthwhile than others. But none could lay exclusive claim to a complete understanding of any issue.

This concern with the individual experience of truth is shared by all existentialists, although the way they handle this subjective approach varies greatly. They are united, however, in seeing morality as a personal experience, and they all see laws and rules as inadequate in dealing with the complexities of moral decisions. In emphasizing this complexity, they all also place great responsibility on each individual for his or her own moral choices. To lend greater power to our understanding of individual responsibility, some existentialists use language that is harsh and negative. These words are familiar to readers of existential literature, and it was these buzzwords that were taken up by morose cafe dwellers of the late '40s, as part of their existential personas.

Other important existential thinkers after Kierkegaard include Friedrich Nietzsche (1844–1900), whose writings include a vast and brilliant expose of the hypocrisy of conventional morality and religion; Martin Heidegger (1889–1976), whose complex works emphasize the poetic nature of experience and the relations of our actions to our own morality; Gabriel Marcel (1889–1973), who ties existential thought to his own experience as a convert to Catholicism; Martin Buber (1878–1965), a thinker who tries to express the importance of deeply personal experiences; Karl Jaspers (1886–1971), who engages in a relentless reexamination of the history of philosophy in the light of his own thinking; Albert Camus (1913–60), who weaves themes of existential absurdity into his novels and essays, and Jean-Paul Sartre (1905–80), the most popular and visible of all the existentialists, whose work we will examine in more detail.

Q U E S T I O N S

1. *What does Nietzsche mean when he says "truth is a woman"?*

2. *What do existential philosophers have in common?*

A C T I V I T I E S

❶ Choose an event, an occasion, or a casual occurrence. The "event" can be as simple as a sports event, a movie, or a classroom activity.

❷ Write a 300-word description of the event from your point of view.

❸ Write another description of the event from the point of view of some participant in the event. For example, if you are describing a movie, describe it as it may have seemed to one of the actors.

❹ What do you learn by seeing these issues from different points of view?

Sören Kierkegaard

Brilliant, cruel, by turns elegant and incomprehensible, compulsively verbose and yet sometimes remarkably succinct, a man who hid behind multiple pseudonyms and yet made his own life the subject of his philosophy, Sören Kierkegaard is among the most fascinating and exasperating figures in the history of philosophy. The contradictions and multiple layers of his thinking were part of his attempt to undermine all philosophical systems of thought. However, his own thoughts do not neatly fit together and do not make a coherent whole. Sometimes, it is hard to know what he really thought, and that was precisely his point; there are no simple solutions to human problems.

His work is usually divided into two periods: the early "pseudonymous" works and, later, works that he published under his own name. The earlier works are intended to reveal a variety of perspectives on the truth. The later works are largely polemical tracts against corruption in the church and a plea for a greater emphasis on the individual's relationship with God, rather than filtering individual experience through ecclesiastical authority or doctrine.

Perhaps the most interesting idea that Kierkegaard had was his division of people into three categories: those whose life mainly consisted of a search for pleasure were in the aesthetic stage; those whose lives were primarily guided by a sense of duty were in the ethical stage, and those guided by their own relationship with God were in the religious stage. His early writings represent attempts to elucidate these perspectives by having his various pseudonymous personalities express the opinions that certain aesthetic or ethical people would possess.

Of the three perspectives, the most difficult to maintain would be the religious one. One can understand the aesthetic perspective, even if one disapproves of a life devoted to seeking pleasure. The ethical perspective is the most widely admired in our society; a person who is loyal, obedient, and does his duty is considered a model citizen. On the other hand, a religious person may be asked, in the course of his devotion to God, to perform acts that do not accord with what we normally call duty. At such times, the religious person may suffer extraordinary conflicts, for he can never be sure that what he thinks is a message from God really is so.

There have been countless madmen in history who have murdered people and committed other hideous crimes because "God told them to do it." The religious person can never be certain that he is not mad. In addition, because the relationship with God is a uniquely personal experience, it is not something that can be easily communicated to others. Hence, the religious person also suffers from the loneliness that his experience imposes on him.

This feeling of loneliness and insanity Kierkegaard called the "agony of Abraham." It is the experience Abraham had when God called on him to kill his only son. Could Abraham be sure that God really had called on him to commit such a heinous act? He could not, and yet his faith commanded him to obey the word of God. The experience of this agony is central to Kierkegaard's thought and the subject of continued reexamination in his writing.

The two selections from Kierkegaard, included here, are examples of his pseudonymous writing, and show both the range and variety of his thinking. The first represents an aesthetic perspective that turns conventional, moral ideas on their heads for fun. The second represents the perspective of an ethical writer who is trying to understand Abraham's action. The ethical thinker can admire Abraham, but he cannot understand him.

Remember that neither of these writings represent the "truth," as Kierkegaard saw it. They represent perspectives on truth that Kierkegaard presented for us to examine.

QUESTIONS

1. *What is the viewpoint of the aesthetic, the ethical, and the religious person?*

2. *Why is the religious view the most difficult to maintain?*

"Rotation of Crops"[1]

The following selection is from a chapter in Kierkegaard's book, *Either/Or*, a two-volume work that gives us examples of how, first, the aesthetic person (the "either") and, then, the ethical person (the "or") looks at the world. In this selection, the aesthetic writer (identified only as "A") is trying to show how you can increase pleasure by engaging in what is completely and deliberately arbitrary. The great worry the author has is that he is afraid that he will be bored. This then, is his recipe to stave off boredom. Previously, the author argued that one must abstain from friendship because the constancy that it demands could become tiresome.

Guard, then, against *friendship*. How is a *friend* defined? A friend is not what philosophy calls the necessary other but the superfluous third. What are the rituals of friendship? One drinks *dus*; one opens an artery, mingles one's blood with the friend's. Just when this moment arrives is difficult to determine, but it proclaims itself in a mysterious way; one feels it and can no longer say *De* to the other. Once this feeling is present, it can never turn out that one has made a mistake such as Gert Westphaler made when he drank *dus* with the executioner.—What are the sure signs of friendship? Antiquity answers: *idem velle, idem nolle, ea demum firma amicita* [agreement in likes and dislikes, this and this only is what constitutes true friendship]—and is also extremely boring. What is the meaning of friendship? Mutual assistance with counsel and action. Two friends form a close alliance in order to be everything to each other, even though no human being can be anything for another human being except to be in his way. Well, we can help each other with money, help each other into and out of our coats, be each other's humble servants, gather for a sincere New Year's congratulation, also for weddings, births, and funerals.

But just because one stays clear of friendship, one will not for that reason live without contact with people. On the contrary, these relationships can take a deeper turn now and then, provided that one always—even though keeping the same pace for a time—has enough reserve speed to run away from them. It may be thought that such conduct leaves unpleasant recollections, that the unpleasantness consists in the diminishing of a relationship from having been something to being nothing. This, however, is a misunderstanding. The unpleasantness is indeed a piquant ingredient in the perverseness of life. Moreover, the same relationship can regain significance in another way. One should be careful never to run aground and to that end always to have forgetting in mind. The experienced farmer lets his land lie fallow now and then; the theory of social prudence recommends the same thing. Everything will surely come again but in a different way; what has once been taken into the rotation process remains there but is varied by the method of cultivation. Therefore, one quite consistently hopes to meet one's old friends and acquaintances in a better world but does not share the crowd's fear that they may have changed so much that one could not recognize them again. One fears, instead, that they may be altogether unchanged. It is unbelievable what even the most insignificant person can gain by such sensible cultivation.

Never become involved in *marriage*. Married people pledge love for each other throughout eternity. Well, now, that is easy enough but does not mean very much, for if one is finished with time one is probably finished with eternity. If, instead of saying "throughout eternity," the couple would say "until Easter, until next May Day," then what they say would make some sense, for then they would be saying something and also something they perhaps could carry out. What happens in marriage? First, one of them detects after a short time that something is wrong, and then the other one complains and screams: Faithlessness! Faithlessness! After a while, the other one comes to the same conclusion and a state of neutrality is inaugurated through a balancing of accounts by mutual faithlessness, to their common satisfaction and gratification. But it is too late now, anyway, because a divorce involves all kinds of huge problems.

Since marriage is like that, it is not strange that attempts are made in many ways to shore it up with moral props. If a man wants to be separated from his wife, the cry goes up: He is a mean fellow, a scoundrel, etc. How ridiculous, and what an indirect assault upon marriage! Either marriage has intrinsic reality [*Realitet*], and then he is adequately punished by losing it, or it has no reality, and then it is unreasonable to vilify him because he is wiser than others. If someone became weary of his money and threw it out the window, no one would say he is a mean fellow, for either money has reality, and then he is adequately punished by not having it anymore, or it has no reality, and then, of course, he is indeed wise.

One must always guard against contracting a life relationship by which one can become many. That is why even friendship is dangerous, marriage even more so. They do say that marriage partners become one, but this is very obscure and mysterious talk. If an individual is many, he has lost his freedom and cannot order his riding boots when he wishes, cannot knock about according to whim. If he has a wife, it is difficult; if he has a wife and perhaps children, it is formidable; if he has a wife and children, it is impossible. Admittedly, there is the example of a gypsy woman who carried her husband on her back throughout life, but for one thing this is a great rarity and, for another, it is very tiring in the long run—for the husband. Moreover, through marriage one falls into a very deadly continuity with custom, and custom is like the wind and weather, something completely indeterminable. To the best of my knowledge, it is the custom in Japan for the husbands also to be confined during childbirth. Perhaps the time is coming when Europe will import the customs of foreign lands.

Even friendship is dangerous; marriage is still more dangerous, for the woman is and will be the man's ruination as soon as he contracts a continuing relationship with her. Take a young man, spirited as an Arabian horse; let him marry and he is lost. At the outset, the woman is proud, then she is weak, then she swoons, then he swoons, then the whole family swoons. A woman's love is only pretense and weakness.

Just because one does not become involved in marriage, one's life need not for that reason be devoid of the erotic. The erotic, too, ought to have infinity—but a poetic infinity that can just as well be limited to one hour as to a month. When two people fall in love with each other and sense that they are destined for each other, it is a question of having the courage to break it off, for by continuing there is only everything to lose and nothing to gain. It seems to be a paradox, and indeed it is, for the feelings, not for the understanding. In this domain it is primarily a matter of being able to use moods; if a person can do that, an inexhaustible variation of combinations can be achieved.

Never take any *official post*. If one does that, one becomes just a plain John Anyman, a tiny little cog in the machine of the body politic. The individual ceases to be himself the manager of the operation, and then theories can be of little help. One acquires a title, and implicit in that are all the consequences of sin and evil. The law under which one slaves is equally boring no matter whether advancement is swift or slow. A title can never be disposed of; it would take a criminal act for that, which would incur a public whipping, and even then one cannot be sure of not being pardoned by royal decree and acquiring the title again.

Even though one stays clear of official posts, one should nevertheless not be inactive but attach great importance to all the pursuits that are compatible with aimlessness; all kinds of unprofitable pursuits may be carried on. Yet in this regard one ought to develop not so much extensively as intensively and, although mature in years, demonstrate the validity of the old saying: It doesn't take much to amuse a child.

Just as one varies the soil somewhat, in accordance with the theory of social prudence (for if one were to live in relation to only one person, rotation of crops would turn out badly, as would be the case if a farmer had only one acre of land and therefore could never let it lie fallow, something that is extremely important), so also must one continually vary oneself, and this is the real secret. To that end, it is essential to have control over one's moods. To have them under control in the sense that one can produce them at will is an impossibility, but prudence teaches us to utilize the moment. Just as an experienced sailor always scans the sea and detects a squall far in advance, so one should always detect a mood a little in advance. Before entering into a mood, one should know its effect on oneself and its probable effect on others. The first strokes are for the purpose of evoking pure tones and seeing what is inside a person; later come the intermediate tones. The more practice one has, the more one is convinced that there is often much in a person that was never imagined. When sentimental people, who as such are very boring, become peevish, they are often amusing. Teasing in particular is an excellent means of exploration.

Arbitrariness is the whole secret. It is popularly believed that there is no art to being arbitrary, and yet it takes profound study to be arbitrary in such a way that a person does not himself run wild in it but himself has pleasure from it. One does not enjoy the immediate object but something else that one arbitrarily introduces. One sees the middle of a play; one reads the third section of a book. One thereby has enjoyment quite different from what the author so kindly intended. One enjoys something totally accidental; one considers the whole of existence [*Tilværelse*] from this standpoint; one lets its reality run aground on this. I shall give an example. There was a man whose chatter I was obliged to listen to because of the circumstances. On every occasion, he was ready with a little philosophical lecture that was extremely boring. On the verge of despair, I suddenly discovered that the man perspired exceptionally much when he spoke. This perspiration now absorbed my attention. I watched how the pearls of perspiration collected on his forehead, then united in a rivulet, slid down his nose, and ended in a quivering globule that remained suspended at the end of his nose. From that moment on, everything was changed; I could even have the delight of encouraging him to commence his philosophical instruction just in order to watch the perspiration on his brow and on his nose.

Baggesen tells somewhere that a certain man is no doubt a very honest fellow but that he has one thing against him: nothing rhymes with his name. It is very advantageous to let the realities of life be undifferentiated in an arbitrary interest like that. Something accidental is made into the absolute and as such into an object of absolute admiration. This is especially effective when the feelings are in motion. For many people, this method is an excellent means of stimulation. Everything in life is regarded as a wager etc. The more consistently a person knows how to sustain his arbitrariness, the more amusing the combinations become. The degree of consistency always makes manifest whether a person is an artist or a bungler, for up to a point everyone does the same. The eye with which one sees actuality must be changed continually. The Neoplatonists assumed that people who fell short of perfection on earth became after death more or less perfect animals according to their merits; those who, for example, had practiced social virtues on a minor scale (punctilious people) turned into social creatures—for example, bees. Such a view of life, which here in this world sees all human beings transformed into animals or plants (Plotinus also believed this—that some were changed into plants) offers a rich multiplicity of variation. The artist Tischbein has attempted to idealize every human being as an animal. His method has the defect that it is too serious and tries to discover an actual resemblance.

The accidental outside a person corresponds to the arbitrariness within him. Therefore he always ought to have his eyes open for the accidental, always ought to be *expeditus* [ready] if something should come up. The so-called social pleasures for which we prepare ourselves a week or a fortnight in advance are of little significance, whereas even the most insignificant thing can accidentally become a rich material for amusement. To go into detail here is not feasible—no theory can reach that far. Even the most elaborate theory is merely poverty compared with what genius in its ubiquity easily discovers.

QUESTIONS

1. *Why does the author claim that it is good for social relationships to change frequently?*

2. *Why is he opposed to marriage?*

3. *Why does he think it is silly to condemn a man for seeking a separation from his wife?*

4. *What does he think two people should do if they fall in love and start to feel that they are made for each other? Why?*

5. *Why does he feel that one should not engage in business?*

6. *What are some of the advantages that he notes of being arbitrary?*

Fear and Trembling[2]

Kierkegaard assigns the authorship of this book to "Johannes de Silentius," whose opinions represent that of a more-or-less typical ethical perspective. In the passage reproduced here, de Silentius is trying to explain the difference between the tragic hero of antiquity and Abraham. The tragic hero is someone who is forced, in the name of duty, to perform an act that he considers repugnant. The religious person, such as Abraham, does not follow ethical rules but instead follows the will of God.

When a son is forgetful of his duty,[3] when the state entrusts the father with the sword of justice, when the laws require punishment at the hand of the father, then will the father heroically forget that the guilty one is his son, he will magnanimously conceal his pain, but there will not be a single one among the people, not even the son, who will not admire the father, and whenever the law of Rome is interpreted, it will be remembered that many interpreted it more learnedly, but none so gloriously as Brutus.

. . . if Brutus had had a righteous son and yet would have ordered the lictors to execute him—who would have understood them? If these three men had replied to the query why they did it by saying, "It is a trial in which we are tested," would people have understood them better? . . .

The difference between the tragic hero and Abraham is clearly evident. The tragic hero still remains within the ethical. He lets one expression of the ethical find its *telos*[4] in a higher expression of the ethical; the ethical relation between father and son, or daughter and father, he reduces to a sentiment which has its *dialectic*[5] in the idea of morality. Here there can be no question of a *teleological suspension of the ethical.*[6]

With Abraham the situation was different. By his act he overstepped the ethical entirely and possessed a higher *telos* outside of it in relation to which he suspended the former. For I should very much like to know how one would bring Abraham's act into relation with the *universal*,[7] and whether it is possible to discover any connection whatever between what Abraham did and the universal—except the fact that he transgressed it. It was not for the sake of saving a people, not to maintain the idea of the state, that Abraham did this, and not in order to reconcile angry deities. If there could be a question of the deity being angry, he was angry only with Abraham, and Abraham's whole action stands in no relation to the universal; it is purely personal undertaking. Therefore, whereas the tragic hero is great by reason of his moral virtue, Abraham is great by reason of a personal virtue. In Abraham's life there is no higher expression for the ethical than this, that the father shall love his son. Of the ethical in the sense of morality there can be no question in this instance. Insofar as the universal was present, it was indeed cryptically present in Isaac, hidden as it were in Isaac's loins, and must therefore cry out with Isaac's mouth, "Do it not! Thou art bringing everything to naught."

Why then did Abraham do it? For God's sake, and (in complete identity with this) for his own sake. He did it for God's sake because God required this proof of his faith; for his own sake he did it in order that he might furnish the proof. The unity of these two points of view is perfectly expressed by the word which has always been used to characterize this situation: it is a trial, a temptation—but what does that mean? What ordinarily tempts a man is that which would keep him from doing his duty, but in this case the temptation is itself the ethical—which would keep him from doing God's will. . . .

Therefore, though Abraham arouses my admiration, he at the same time appalls me. He who denies himself and sacrifices himself for duty gives up the finite in order to grasp the infinite, and that man is secure enough. The tragic hero gives up the certain for the still more certain, and the eye of the beholder rests upon him confidently. But he who gives up the universal in order to grasp something still higher which is not the universal—what is he doing? Is it possible that this can be anything else but a temptation (*Anfechtung*)? And if it be possible, . . . but the individual was mistaken—what can save him? He suffers all the pain of the tragic hero, he brings to naught his joy in the world, he renounces everything—and perhaps at the same instant debars himself from the sublime joy which to him was so precious that he would purchase it at any price. Him the beholder cannot understand nor let his eye rest confidently upon him. . . .

The story of Abraham contains therefore a teleological suspension of the ethical. As the individual he became higher than the universal: this is the paradox which does not permit of mediation. It is just as inexplicable how he got into it as it is inexplicable how he remained in it. If such is not the position of Abraham, then he is not even a tragic hero but a murderer. To want to continue to call him the father of faith, to talk of this to people who do not concern themselves with anything but words, is thoughtless. A man can become a tragic hero by his own powers—but not a *knight of faith*.[8] When a man enters upon the way, in a certain sense the hard way of the tragic hero, many will be able to give him counsel; to him who follows the narrow way of faith no one can give counsel, him no one can understand. Faith is a miracle, and yet no man is excluded from it; for that in which all human life is unified is passion, and faith is a passion.

QUESTIONS

1. *Why could Brutus's act, in condemning his son to death, be considered ethical?*

2. *What is the difference between Brutus and Abraham from the point of view of morality?*

3. *How does de Silentius (Kierkegaard's "author" of this passage) feel about Abraham's decision to sacrifice his son? Why does he feel this way?*

Jean-Paul Sartre

Kierkegaard was a great original thinker in the history of philosophy. His way of approaching philosophical problems was radical and his answers, such as they were, were not very comforting. After Kierkegaard's death, the next philosopher to work in this radically subjective way was Friedrich Nietzsche (1844–1900). Nietzsche, like Kierkegaard, used his personal experience as the takeoff point for his philosophical speculations and he, too, condemned systematic attempts to discover the truth. But he substituted for Kierkegaard's fierce, personal Christianity his own passionate atheism, declaring that "God is dead" and loudly condemning what he saw as theoretical absurdities in Christian thought.

And so Kierkegaard and Nietzsche developed the two main trends in existential thought. The followers of Kierkegaard have tied in existentialism with personal religious experience, and the followers of Nietzsche have looked at the human dilemma in the absence of God.

In the twentieth century, there have been both religious and atheistic existentialists in abundance, but the most famous of all existentialists was a short, ugly French atheist, Jean-Paul Sartre (1905–80), who became the best-known intellectual of his time. A man of enormous moral courage with a flair for publicity, he was so famous that 50,000 people attended his funeral, the largest turnout for a funeral of any public figure in recent French history. His stature was such that Charles de Gaulle, the first President of the French Fifth Republic and a bitter political enemy of Sartre, once said, "Sartre is France."

It is true that in France intellectuals are venerated as they are nowhere else. But what was the appeal of this intellectual? His philosophy invoked words like "negation," "despair," and "forlornness." He was an atheist in a Catholic country; he worked for a variety of communist causes and considered himself a communist "fellow traveller." Contradictions abound in his life as well. Although a fellow traveller, he was extremely critical of a number of policies and actions of the communists. He considered that his goal was to oppose the bourgeoisie, and yet he spent many years working on a study of the life and writings of Gustave Flaubert, a quintessentially bourgeois writer of the nineteenth century.

His popularity seems to stem, in part, from the popularity of existentialism in postwar France, which made everyone aware of Sartre's existence, if not his thought. It is partly due to the popularity of his plays and novels, for Sartre was a writer as much as a philosopher. It was also helped by his genius for self-publicity, and it was certainly helped by his reputation as a man of profound moral courage, who was willing to stand up for his beliefs and take the consequences. His unorthodox lifestyle also made good newspaper copy. For over fifty years he was intimately involved with the writer Simone de Beauvoir, although they never married nor even lived together. Both, also, had outside affairs, the details of which they did not spare each other. Sartre once said that all his other relationships were "contingent," but that his relationship with de Beauvoir was "necessary." This is particularly interesting because of his philosophy wherein he denies that anything can be necessary.

In both his personal life and his philosophy, Sartre vigorously undermined the idea that there can be a separation of professional and personal behavior. You are what you do; you cannot legitimately claim that you have separate standards for your job and for the rest of your life. If you try to identify yourself as, for example, a lawyer, you are not identifying yourself as a person but as a thing—in this case, a lawyer. When you do that, you are trying to limit your freedom. Sartre argues, however, that although people always try to limit their freedom, there is no way that they can legitimately do so. By saying "I can only do certain things because I am a lawyer and my job requires it," an attempt is made to limit your freedom by your job, and to define yourself according to your job. Sartre says that it is very human to exist, and so you choose, at each moment, to act in accordance with the usual standards of behavior in your job. Your job does not make you do it; you make yourself do it.

There is a problem in dealing with Sartre from an ethical perspective. Sartre promised, at the end of *Being and Nothingness*, to write a book on ethics. He never did, although he worked on the project, on and off, for some twenty years. In 1972, he said that his ideas had changed so much that the project no longer had any meaning for him. Nevertheless, there is an ethical substratum to a great deal of his writing, and it would be impossible to ignore the ethical implications of his ideas.

The closest Sartre came to writing the book on ethics was in a talk he gave that was later published as a small book. In English, the title of this book was given as either *Existentialism* or *Existentialism Is a Humanism*. It became enormously popular, probably because the writing style is simple and engaging and the ethical ideas are provocative, even if Sartre thought they greatly oversimplified his views.

The opinion that he expressed that has the greatest impact is the idea that "man is nothing else but what he makes of himself." In other words, human beings are defined by what they do and have done. Your worth is determined not by your potential and talents, but by what you have done. If you have talent as a painter, but have never painted a great picture, you are then defined not by your talent but by your failure. You are not a talented painter, but simply a painter who has never painted a great picture.

Sartre was very concerned that people understood his belief that each of us should take total responsibility for our actions. He felt that because our actions involved choice, each action we choose should reflect and influence not only ourselves, but the whole world as well. To Sartre, each action has a responsibility that is greater than we usually imagine.

Sartre uses three terms to describe the nature of this responsibility and, in typical existential fashion, these words are laden with negative connotations. The words are *anguish, forlornness,* and *despair*. Sartre says that a state of anguish, forlornness, and despair is essential to the human condition. By "anguish," he means the feeling that persons have when they realize that when they choose an action, they are making a choice not only for themselves but one that affects all people. By "forlornness," he means the feeling that comes from realizing that we cannot rely on God, or any law-giving or supernatural force, to guide us in our ethical choices. Therefore, we must find it in ourselves to be good, for there is no external force compelling us to be good. As for "despair," it is the feeling that comes from the realization that we cannot bend the world to our will, and we ought to confine our thoughts and desires to what we can actually do and control.

From this we can gather that Sartre's existentialist ethics has a tough-minded realism to it. You are responsible, but you cannot depend on God for principles to follow, and you cannot even control much of what happens. Nevertheless, Sartre argued that one is compelled to do things and to do good, because it is the nature of being a responsible member of the human race that we should try to do good in the world to the best of our ability.

Although he has not presented anything like a systematic

approach to the problems of ethics, the ideas he throws out are so provocative that, ironically, they are among the most widely understood and debated ideas in the corpus of Sartrean thought.

QUESTIONS

1. *Why do you think Sartre believes that there is something disturbing about the tendency of people to define themselves according to their jobs?*

2. *What does Sartre mean by each of the terms:* anguish, forlornness, *and* despair? *Why do you think he uses such negatively tinged words?*

ACTIVITIES

❶ Sartre talked about the tendency of people to define themselves, according to their jobs or to the roles that they play. Can you think of examples, in your own life, where you behaved in a way that was phony because you thought you had to, for one reason or another? Describe such an experience.

❷ Think of at least three morally admirable things you could be doing with your time, right now, rather than doing this assignment. Write these three things down. How can you justify not doing these things? Do you intend to do them some day? If you do not, how do you justify your lack of personal and social responsibility?

❸ Write a thoughtful answer of at least 500 words. Then do something useful that will help other people. Before you hand in your essay, briefly explain in a footnote what useful act you performed.

The Zen Perspective

Religion and Ethics

Before considering the rather original Zen Buddhist ethical perspective, we should look at the place of ethics in religion as a whole. First, we must distinguish between the type of religious ethics that Kierkegaard advocated and the ethical perspectives offered by religions. Kierkegaard's religious person does not follow rules, but the direct orders of God. (He felt that the religious perspective was only possible in religions that had a personal God; it does not exist in polytheistic and pantheistic religions.) On the other hand, religions generally offer ethical prescriptions or prohibitions. Those who follow these rules are at the ethical stage in Kierkegaard's scheme.

In other words, religious ethics are often rule-based, or *deontological*, in character. The rules serve many functions, not the least of which is that they bind the members of the faith together in their sense of right and wrong. Problems arise from differing interpretations of these rules. This can lead to some strange consequences. While the Ten Commandments explicitly prohibit killing, many people who consider themselves good Christians and Jews have no compunction about fighting in wars. This contradiction requires elaborate rationalization, and it has long been the job of scholars to find these justifications. The whole idea of a "holy war" may seem ludicrous to one who wants to take the Bible literally; but the holy war has been very much a part of Christian history, and it has been the job of many people to find a way to make sense of such an apparent contradiction.

So it is clear that, although religious ethics may often appear to be naively prescriptive, in reality, the ethics of any religion that has gained significance is an exceedingly complex affair. The naive formulations in holy books are often alluded to when convenient, and they are frequently a rallying cry of any fundamentalist movement in the religion. Just as Martin Luther wanted to return to the original word of the Bible, Christian and Muslim fundamentalists today claim they are returning to the true articles of their faith through what they call a literal reading of the sacred texts. In certain Muslim countries, this is written into law; in Saudi Arabia, the *Qur'an* is the law of the land. But even here, there is the problem of interpretation. The *Qur'an* says that the penalty for stealing is that the right hand should be chopped off; but in reality, not every case of stealing is punished in this way. Sometimes the culprit is merely imprisoned.

The ethical perspective of religion, in fact, is considerably more complex than it would seem in the holy books. A simple phrase can be subjected to the most elaborate analysis. The holy prescriptions also can be inconvenient at times, and may then need to be changed to suit certain political purposes. There is also the problem that the ethics of any religion, when it grafts itself onto a new culture, may have to compromise with the prevailing ethical standards of the people who have been converted if the religion wants to make any serious inroads into that society. We must also not forget that religious institutions are used as agents of the upper orders in society to help maintain their status, and the ethics of the religion will frequently be modified to express the interests of the ruling class.

For example, we can look at the differing interpretations of the biblical perspective on wealth as evidence of the ways the ruling classes have used the Bible to control people. The New Testament phrase "a rich man can no more enter the kingdom of Heaven than a camel could pass through the eye of a needle" was used in the Middle Ages, and in Catholic and Orthodox countries until the present day, to assure the poor that, although they might be doing badly in this life, they will get their reward in the next life. They therefore had no need to try to grab their share of wealth, for they would be rewarded for their poverty in eternity. A cynic might note that the rich were not exactly rushing to give up all their wealth in return for a seat in heaven. But they had a ready supply of servants and peasants who could feel at least a little better knowing that their misery would end once they were dead.

Among some Protestant churches, the story changed some-what, but the interpretation remained consistent with the interests of the ruling classes. Some of these groups have chosen to ignore the camel passage and, instead, use a few passages selected from the Epistles to try to justify their belief that people's wealth shows that they are favored in the eyes of God. One must, according to this doctrine, strive for wealth. When you succeed, God is pleased; if you fail, it's your own fault. This doctrine suits the ruling classes in a capitalist society very well. Capitalists value continued entre-preneurship, consumerism, and circulating wealth. Keeping every-one in search of the big bucks creates even bigger bucks for the already rich. The rich, in this scheme, have the added advantage of having people look up to them as models to be emulated.

This is not to imply that these interpretations were deliber-ately developed by the rich to serve their ends. These things develop in the course of time, helped along by rationalizations, necessity, and self-interest. The ruling class does not need to use religion cynically and deliberately, although they clearly do that sometimes. Purely in the course of trying to protect themselves, they will use their power to alter religious ethics to suit their needs.

So far, we have looked only at the rules a religion imposes and the people who impose those rules. There is another way to look at the ethics of a religion, however, one that looks not at its actual, prescriptive, and ethical content, contained in the writings or oral traditions of the religion, but that instead considers the world-view that the religion offers, and then examines how this world-view affects the ethical thinking of the adherents of the faith. For example, a religion that has the concept of "sin" is going to operate very differently from a religion that lacks this idea. The concept of "karma" implies that there will be consequences for all of a person's actions. This has far-reaching ethical implications that might not be immediately apparent. How can the idea of "forgiveness" account for the difference between Catholic and Protestant ethics? How about visions of the Apocalypse? It seems evident that someone who believed in the inevitability of the Apocalypse would see the world differently and might behave differently than someone without this belief. How about the agnosticism in some forms of Buddhism? The absence of God in these views is bound to influence behavior in some ways.

It is in this spirit that we are going to look at a religion. When we look at Zen Buddhism, and consider the perspective that it comes from, we will try to see how this way of looking at the world would influence the ethical choices made by followers of this faith.

QUESTIONS

1. *How do religions differ from the religious person in Kierkegaard's schemes?*

2. *Why is it difficult to figure out exactly what the ethical perspective of a given religion is?*

3. *How and why do the ruling classes modify religious ethics to suit their ends?*

The Development of Zen Buddhism

The Buddhist religion begins with the work of a single individual, Siddhartha Gautama, who lived in the fifth century B.C., and whose teaching became the basis of the doctrines of Buddhism. He was called "the Buddha," meaning "the enlightened one." His teachings became subject to dispute over time, and just as Christianity divided into Roman Catholicism, Eastern Orthodoxy, and Protestantism and Islam split in Sunni and Shi'ite sects, Buddhism divided into Mahayana and Theravada Buddhism.

The Theravada school follows the earliest surviving written sources of the teachings of the Buddha more closely. The Mahayana school emphasizes the meaning of the life of the Buddha. It claims that the teachings of the earliest texts do not give a broad enough appreciation of the scope of his thoughts, for he revealed his most important ideas to only a small group of intimates. We must look to the example of his life if we are to discover his true ideas.

On the whole, the Mahayana path represents a viewpoint that is closer to other religions than the Theravada path. The Theravada, for example, tends to eschew metaphysical speculation as a useless waste of time, closely following what the Buddha himself said. Theravada Buddhism tends to emphasize the importance of individual effort to reach Nirvana. The Buddha is considered a saintly man, but there is no attempt to turn him into a god. Rituals are kept to a minimum, and the primary practice of the monk is meditation. Because the emphasis is so clearly on individual salvation, emphasis is on the monk rather than on the lay practitioner of the faith. Theravada Buddhism has no gods. Mahayana, on the other hand, has an elaborate metaphysics; although the Mahayana do not necessarily deify the Buddha, there is a definite tendency in this direction. They are much more concerned with the role of the layman in their religion, and the emphasis is on the role of religion in the world. The Mahayana ideal is not the Arhat, or saint, of the Theravadins, but the Bodhisattva, a person who, although at the brink of Nirvana, chooses to renounce transcending this world in order to make his enlightenment available to others.

Today, the Mahayana school holds sway in the Buddhism practiced in China, Japan, Tibet, Mongolia, and Korea, while the Theravada school is dominant in Sri Lanka, Burma, and Thailand. Within the Mahayana, there are various branches, representing everything from the complexities of Zen to the simplistic formulas of the Nichiren sect, with its very atypical (for Buddhism) emphasis on achieving material wealth through prayer. The origin of the word "Zen" itself shows a good deal about the transfer of ideas from one place to another. The Japanese word Zen means meditation, and it is derived from the Chinese word *Ch'an*, which is derived from the Sanskrit word *dhyana*. Meditation and meditative discipline are central to Zen practices, as they are to many forms of Buddhism. But the aim of meditation is altered from its Indian goal of control of the mind, and one's responses to the environment to the more typically Chinese emphasis on sudden illumination. The moment of illumination, called *satori* in Japanese, is a highly valued step on the way to enlightenment. Also, in line with Chinese thinking, is the emphasis on the harmony between human beings and nature, a concept that we see in the earlier writings of the Taoist philosophers. However, it does not figure prominently in any of the pre-Chinese Buddhist texts.

Ch'an Buddhism was first clearly recognized as a movement in China under the guidance of Hui-neng in the seventh century. It was a recognized part of Chinese society for many centuries before it travelled to Japan in the twelfth and thirteenth centuries. In the centuries that followed, Zen became influenced by Japanese culture, particularly in its aesthetic aspects. Zen adepts may display their understanding of the illumination received through Zen practice in various arts. The Japanese tea ceremony, where the simple act of serving and drinking tea is imbued with an elaborate ritual, designed to draw one's attention to the details of a usual daily occurrence, has its origins in Zen as well. Zen also became closely associated with the Samurai class in Japanese society. The practice of Zen meditation had the highly practical purpose of increasing an adept's concentration, which would lead that person to become a more skilled warrior.

Despite the emphasis on intuition, immediate illumination, spontaneity, and the harmony of human beings and nature, all of which will be clear from reading the selections that follow, there are certain elements of the Zen tradition that link Zen not only with its Mahayana roots, but with traditions of scriptural authority. Zen adepts take reincarnation and karma seriously. They emphasize the need for the individual to be released from the world of suffering, and the misery of attachment to things in this world, all typically Buddhist concerns. Their recognition of the value of the Bodhisattva is Mahayana, and their devotion to the person of the Buddha is a fact which was occasionally obscured in some of the Zen stories. These stories approvingly report incidents such as the Chinese monk who chopped up a wooden image of the Buddha for firewood. Zen is also imbued with elaborate rituals, and the life of a Zen monk is extremely structured, with every minute of the day accounted for rigidly.

Zen also makes a great deal about trying to see the truth directly, without words. Illumination may come from the simplest action, and it may not be possible to reduce the truth of the illumination to words. Nevertheless, the volume of Zen literature is enormous, and there is even a scriptural basis for the Zen teachings in, among other sources, the Lankavatra Sutra which reached China in the fifth century. This sutra (holy book) emphasizes that pure consciousness can be identified with the Buddha nature. Ultimate truth and Buddhahood are achievable through immediate mystical experience, rather than through rational thought. Since the appearance of this sutra, much has been written about the inadequacy of words.

Within Zen itself, there are two major schools, the Rinzai and the Soto. The somewhat more violent methods of the Rinzai have made good newspaper copy in the West. The basic technique to achieve enlightenment in both sects is to engage in meditation or za-zen. This meditation may be extremely long and rigorous. A sesshin, or sitting meditation, may go on for sixteen hours a day for a solid week. While meditating, there may be someone who walks around, hitting people on the back with a stick in order to remind meditators to stay awake, or simply to rouse devotees to a higher level of consciousness. It should be emphasized that, particularly in the Rinzai sect, the emphasis is on passing illumination from teacher to student, so it is not possible to achieve satori simply through one's own efforts. The Roshi (teacher) gives the student a koan, or a problem for meditation. Through meditation on this koan the devotee may, with the help of the teacher, achieve enlightenment. Typically, the first koan that is given to a new aspirant is "mu," which means "nothing" in Japanese. One may then spend the next several years meditating on nothing. This attempt is to break down the normal way of thinking and looking at the world. When these conceptual barriers are broken down, enlightenment may occur.

There is one other aspect of Zen that should be mentioned. Zen, like other forms of Mahayana Buddhism, emphasizes the ability of lay people to partake in that religion. Zen has thus become associated with various secular arts. One can achieve enlightenment without becoming a monk. Zen methods and thinking have been applied to swordsmanship, painting, and martial arts. When people speak of a "Zen attitude" towards things, they are referring to an approach that intensely concentrates on the task at hand, and intuitively and spontaneously reacts to the needs of the moment. If you are washing dishes, for example, in the Zen mold, you would be completely focused on that task and not grumble about how much you hate washing dishes, and not talk to someone or listen to the radio. You would be so focused on the task that you would not even be analyzing your dishwashing technique; you would just do it. The dishes would be washed perfectly, and your achievement would seem both artless and effortless.

The connection that can be made between Zen and existentialism should be quite clear. Both are concerned with the individual's response to the world. Both aim at enlightening the individual. Both approaches eschew formulaic ethical prescriptions. Both emphasize experience as a means to the truth and embrace, rather than deny, the absurdity of the world. The differences should be clear as well. Zen is a discipline, tied to particular practices. Existentialism is a philosophical movement whose participants are linked by a very tenuous list of theoretical and methodological similarities. Existentialism is a label imposed on some writers. Zen Buddhism is a spiritual path and way of life chosen by Zen adherents.

The fact that Zen and existentialism became popular at the same time has led some people to see more of a connection than is actually there. Both became associated with a "do-your-own-thing" type of beatnikism. In very different ways, Zen and existentialism are far from the undisciplined hedonism that some people have seen in them. Both do, however, try to force your mind out of traditional grooves of thought, and this may have led to confusion.

Since the waning of the fad, however, quite a few westerners have taken up a serious study of Zen practice. Some have even been honored with the title of Roshi. In many ways, Zen is more vital in the West than it is in Japan, and Zen theory and practice have been changing in response to western influence.

QUESTIONS

1. *How do the Theravada and Mahayana branches of Buddhism differ?*

2. *How does the origin and practice of Zen show how Buddhism changed as it was adapted by different cultures?*

3. *How is Zen linked to its Mahayana roots?*

4. *What is a "Zen attitude" towards things? Give an example that shows you understand what this means.*

5. *How is Zen like existentialism? How is it different?*

ACTIVITIES

❶   Do some task that you normally dislike doing, but do it with a Zen attitude. It could be cleaning your room, washing the dishes, doing your homework. Were you successful in maintaining your Zen attitude? How did it feel? Get into a Zen attitude and write a 300-word report on the experience.

Characteristics of Zen Buddhism

The short essay from the writings of D.T. Suzuki that follows is from his *Essays in Zen Buddhism.*[9] Suzuki's books popularized Zen in the West. "Beat Zen" got its start from passages like the one presented. It should be kept in mind that Suzuki was not a scholar, nor a Zen master himself. His knowledge of Zen was rather journalistic. If you take care not to take his more abstract and philosophical concepts too seriously, you can get some feeling for the spirit and feeling of Zen. The Zen stories reveal varieties of the Zen approach to life, state of nothingness when a person's spirit, if freed from the cycle of reincarnations, disappears completely.

1. Neglect of form is generally characteristic of mysticism, Christian, or Buddhist, or Islamic. When the importance of the spirit is emphasized, all the outward expressions of it naturally become things of secondary significance. Form is not necessarily despised, but attention to it is reduced to a minimum, or we may say that conventionalism is set aside and individual originality is asserted in its full strength. But because of this there is a forceful tone of inwardness perceivable in all things connected with Zen. As far as form is concerned, nothing beautiful or appealing to the senses may be observable here, but one feel something inward or spiritual asserting itself in spite of the imperfection of the form, perhaps because of this very imperfection. The reason is this: when the form is perfect, our senses are satisfied too strongly with it and the mind may at least temporarily neglect to exercise its more inner function. The efforts concentrated too greatly in the outwardness of things fail to draw out what inner meaning there is in them. So Tanka (Tan-hsia) burned a wooden image of Buddha to make a fire, and idolatry was done away with. Kensu (Hsien-tzu) turned into a fisherman against the conventionality of monastery life. Daito Kokushi (1282–1360) became a beggar and Kanzan Kokishi (1277–1360) was a cowherd.

2. The inwardness of Zen implies the directness of its appeal to the human spirit. When the intermediary of form is dispensed with, one spirit speaks directly to another. Raise a finger and the whole universe is there. Nothing could be more direct than this in this world of relativity. The medium of communication or the symbol of self-expression is curtailed to the shortest possible term. When a syllable or a wink is enough, why spend one's entire life in writing huge books or building a grandiose cathedral?

3. Directness is another word for simplicity. When all the paraphernalia to express ideas are discarded, a single blade of

grass suffices to stand for Buddha Vairochana sixteen feet high. Or a circle is the fullest possible symbol for the immeasurability of the truth as realised in the mind of a Zen adept. This simplicity also expresses itself in life. A humble straw-thatched mountain retreat, a half of which is shared by white clouds, is enough for the sage. The potatoes roasted in the ashes of a cow-dung fire appease his hunger, as he casts a contemptuous look upon an envoy from the Imperial court.

4. Poverty and simplicity go hand in hand, but to be merely poor and humble is not Zen. It does not espouse poverty just for the sake of poverty. As it is sufficient with itself, it does not want much—which is poverty to others, but sufficiency to oneself. Rich and poor—this is a worldly standard; for the inwardness of Zen poverty has nothing to do with being short of possessions, or being rich with the owning of material wealth.

5. Facts of experience are valued in Zen more than representations, symbols, and concepts, that is to say, substance is everything in Zen and form nothing. Therefore, Zen is radical empiricism. This being so, space is not something objectively extending, time is not to be considered a line stretched out as past, present, and future. Zen knows no such space, no such time, and, therefore, such ideas as eternity, infinitude, boundlessness, etc., are mere dreams to Zen. For Zen lives in facts. Facts may be considered momentary but momentariness is an idea subjectively constructed. When Zen is compared to a flash of lightning which disappears even before you have uttered the cry "Oh!", it is not to be supposed that mere quickness is the life of Zen. But we can say that Zen eschews deliberation, elaboration. When a roof leaked, a Zen master called out to his attendants to bring in something to keep the tatami dry. Without a moment's hesitation, one of them brought in a bamboo basket, while another went around and searching for a tub took it to the master. The master was immensely pleased, it is said, with the first monk with the basket. It was he who understood the spirit of Zen better than the one who was deliberate though his wisdom proved far more practical and useful. This phase of Zen is technically known as "non-discrimination."

6. What might be designated "eternal loneliness" is found at the heart of Zen. This is a kind of sense of the absolute. In the *Lankavatara Sutra* we have what is known there as the "truth of solitude" (*viviktadharma* in Sanskrit). The experience of this seems to wake the feeling of eternal loneliness. This does not mean that

we all feel solitary and long forever for something larger and stronger than ourselves. This feeling is cherished more or less by all religious souls; but what I mean here is not this kind of solitariness, but the solitariness of an absolute being, which comes upon one when a world of particulars moving under the conditions of space, time, and causation is left behind, when the spirit soars high up in the sky and moves about as it lists like a floating cloud.

7. When all these aspects of Zen are confirmed, we find a certain definite attitude of Zen towards life generally. When it expresses itself in art, it constitutes what may be called the spirit of Zen estheticism. In this we shall then find simplicity, directness, abandonment, boldness, aloofness, unworldliness, innerliness, the disregarding of form, free movements of spirit, the mystic breathing of a creative genius all over the world—whether it be painting, calligraphy, gardening, tea-ceremony, fencing, dancing, or poetry.

QUESTIONS

1. *What are the seven characteristics of Zen that Suzuki lists in the selection from* Essays in Zen Buddhism?

2. *What does Suzuki mean when he describes Zen as "radical empiricism"?*

3. *What ethical consequences can you see developing from the Zen world view? How would you imagine that Zen masters would make ethical decisions, if true to the spirit of their beliefs?*

Zen Stories[10]

IS THAT SO?

The Zen master Hakuin was praised by his neighbors as one living a pure life.

A beautiful Japanese girl whose parents owned a food store lived near him. Suddenly, without any warning, her parents discovered she was with child.

This made her parents angry. She would not confess who the man was, but after much harassment at last named Hakuin.

In great anger the parents went to the master. "Is that so?" was all he would say.

After the child was born it was brought to Hakuin. By this time he had lost his reputation, which did not trouble him, but he took very good care of the child. He obtained milk from his neighbors and everything else the little one needed.

A year later the girl-mother could stand it no longer. She told her parents the truth—that the real father of the child was a young man who worked in the fishmarket.

The mother and father of the girl at once went to Hakuin to ask his forgiveness, to apologize at length, and to get the child back again.

Hakuin was willing. In yielding the child, all he said was: "Is that so?"

OBEDIENCE

The master Bankei's talk were attended not only by Zen students but by persons of all ranks and sects. He never quoted sutras nor indulged in scholastic dissertations. Instead, his words were spoke directly from his heart to the hearts of his listeners.

His large audiences angered a priest of the Nichiren sect because the adherents had left to hear about Zen. The self-centered Nichiren priest came to the temple, determined to debate with Bankei.

"Hey, Zen teacher!" he called out. "Wait a minute. Whoever respects you will obey what you say, but a man like myself does not respect you. Can you make me obey you?"

"Come up beside me and I will show you," said Bankei.

Proudly the priest pushed his way through the crowd to the teacher.

Bankei smiled. "Come over to my left side."

The priest obeyed.

"No," said Bankei, "We may talk better if you are on the right side. Step over here."

The priest proudly stepped over to the right.

"You see," observed Bankei, "you are obeying me and I think you are a very gentle person. Now sit down and listen."

THE MOON CANNOT BE STOLEN

Ryokan, a Zen master, lived the simplest kind of life in a little hut at the foot of a mountain. One evening a thief visited the hut only to discover there was nothing in it to steal.

Ryokan returned and caught him. "You may have come a long way to visit me," he told the prowler, "and you should not return empty-handed. Please take my clothes as a gift."

The thief was bewildered. He took the clothes and slunk away.

Ryokan sat naked, watching the moon. "Poor fellow," he mused, "I wish I could give him this beautiful moon."

QUESTIONS

1. *What does the story "Is That So?" reveal about Hakuin's attitude towards life? What does it reveal about his ethics and what lesson can we learn from him?*

2. *What is striking about Bankei's method of dealing with the Nichiren monk? What lesson is being taught in this story?*

3. *What Buddhist virtue does Ryokan exemplify? What impact would his attitude have on a person's ethical perspective?*

4. *What is the significance of Ryokan's musing about the moon?*

ACTIVITIES

❶ Look back to the selection from Kierkegaard's Either/Or. At one point, the author notes how he was able to derive great pleasure from watching beads of sweat form on a man's brow. Both Kierkegaard and the Zen adept delight in saying or doing things that are deliberately surprising. What is the difference between the arbitrariness of Kierkegaard's aesthetic character and the surprises of the Zen practitioner?

Different Perspectives

The selections from existential and Zen writings in this unit were designed to force us to look at our world in different ways. The activities have also been designed to get you to think a little differently, to see both the complexity of life and to see how possible it is to look at things differently or to behave differently. Immanuel Kant once said that reading of works of David Hume "awakened him from his dogmatic slumber." Many people have felt the same way when reading Kierkegaard or Sartre, and the precise purpose of the Zen experience is to enlighten you. Of course, the Zen aim is not to see the complexity of the world, but to see through the apparent complexity to the simplicity and harmony of the universe. But, first, one must go through the trials of complexity. Like the existentialists, the Zen adepts know that only by seeing the world through varying lenses can we truly make our own choices. The spontaneity and apparent simplicity of Zen is only achieved through a long and arduous struggle; that which looks easiest is actually the most difficult to attain.

Endnotes for Chapter 4

1. "Rotation of Crops". Reprinted by permission of Princeton University Press from *Either/Or Volume I* by Sören Kierkegaard, translated by Howard V. Hong and Edna Hong. Copyright 1987, Princeton University Press, pp. 295–300.

2. Reprinted by permission of Princeton University Press from *Fear and Trembling* by Sören Kierkegaard, translated by Walter Lowrie. Copyright 1941, renewed 1982, Princeton University Press, pp. 68–71 and 77.

3. Brutus's son took part in a conspiracy to restore the outlawed monarchy. Brutus condemned his son to death, as was required by law.

4. *telos*: justification.

5. *dialectic*: a technical term, referring to a process by which one passes thoughts over into their opposites, and then merges them into a higher unity.

6. *teleological suspension of the ethical*: a justifiable suspension of ethical rules.

7. *universal*: Kierkegaard means universal rules of morality.

8. Abraham is a knight of faith because he carries the will of God with him and acts on God's command.

9. Reprinted with the permission of Random Century Ltd. from *Essays in Zen Buddhism*, 3rd series, by D. T. Suzuki. Copyright 1953, Rider and Co.

10. Reprinted with permission of Charles E. Tuttle Co., Inc., from *Zen Flesh, Zen Bones*, compiled by Paul Reps, translated and transcribed by Nyogen Senzaki and Paul Reps. Copyright 1957, Charles E. Tuttle Co., Inc.

CHAPTER 5

ETHICS AND PSYCHOLOGY:
The Problem of Evil

We consider the problem of evil from two perspectives within psychology. We first look at the psychoanalytical approach, with particular emphasis on the writings of Wilhelm Reich. We then look at the experiments of Stanley Milgram, including selections from his book, Obedience to Authority, *where the problem of the ability of otherwise "good" people to commit horrible acts received its classic experimental consideration. The ethics of Milgram's experiments themselves are also discussed.*

Why is there evil in this world? The question is a cliché, but is no less disturbing for being one. Is there evil because people are basically bad? Is there evil because people are basically good but are capable of being corrupted? Is evil due to human weakness or original sin? Or is evil due to people being caught in the web of desire, as the Buddhists would say?

The human capacity for evil is profound. Everyday, from the drunken husband who beats his wife, to the mother who inflicts subtle psychological torture on her children, to the Indonesian police and the Chinese army, we are surrounded by evidence of the capacity we have for hurting one another. Why does this happen?

There have been many theories from philosophers and holy men who try to explain evil, but some of the most interesting theories have come from psychologists. In this chapter, we will examine the works of two psychologists who have delved into this issue. They come from radically different perspectives, but both have some profound insights into the subject. Knowledge may not be enough to end evil in this world; but insight into evil can certainly change the lives of those exposed to these ideas.

The Origins of Psychoanalysis

On a dark evening in the autumn of 1880, "Anna O." was up all night, caring for her sick father. She was consumed with worry and fatigue. As she drifted off to sleep, she hallucinated about a black snake coming out of the wall. She tried to drive the creature off, but she could not move her arm. As she looked at her hand, she saw her fingers change into little snakes with death heads where her nails should have been. When the hallucination vanished, she tried to speak but could not. When she finally was able to talk, she remembered the words of an English prayer. For the next year and a half, she could neither move her arm nor speak German, her native language. (She spoke only English.)

Anna O. consulted a psychiatrist, Dr. Josef Breuer, about her condition. Breuer hypnotized her, and she recalled the snake incident under hypnosis. When she came out of the hypnotic state, Breuer told her what she had recalled. She then clearly remembered the incident and, amazingly, her symptoms disappeared.

Breuer told the story of Anna O. to his colleague and friend, Sigmund Freud. Freud was fascinated by the fact that a repressed memory could cause such symptoms, and that recalling the memory could lead to an alleviation of the symptoms. He persuaded Breuer to collaborate on a book about this case and other cases of hysteria that had been cured in this manner. With their little opus, *Studies in Hysteria*, the psychoanalytic era of psychiatry began.

Breuer and Freud soon parted company, and it was left to Freud to develop the theory of psychoanalysis. This was the first attempt to develop a systematic understanding of the unconscious and irrational forces that govern most of our behavior. Although orthodox Freudian therapy has been modified through the years, and the unconscious forces that determine our behavior are probably somewhat different from what Freud's own theories would indicate, the approach and some of the ideas of Freud continue to influence the way we think today.

The significant parts of Freud's theories for our study deal with his understanding of the irrational forces that control human behavior. Freud noted that we are not led by reason, but often by forces beyond our conscious control. Frequently, some physical or emotional trauma that occurred in the first five years of life becomes the basis for neurotic behavior as an adult.

In the early years of the century, Freud had many students and disciples who carried Freudian ideas throughout the world, although each of his important disciples differed from the master on many important points of interpretation.

We will consider the life and career of one of his most colorful and eccentric followers, who carried Freud's insights in areas of social and political concern in a way that made a fascinating contribution to our understanding of the irrational forces in human nature. The man we will discuss is Wilhelm Reich (pronounced "Reish").

ACTIVITIES

❶ Freud's discovery of the unconscious origin of much irrational human behavior has greatly influenced thought in the twentieth century. But the influence of Freud in the areas of philosophy, sociology, and anthropology has been equaled by his influence on people in the creative arts. Writers, painters, and filmmakers have used psychoanalytic ideas as the takeoff point for many of their flights of imagination. In this activity, you will be a writer who composes a story that describes some irrational act on the part of your main character. The irrational act will make sense only when you uncover some relevant childhood trauma. The story could be based on your own experience, on a true event you have heard about, or it could be something you make up. It should be 1,000–1,500 words long.

Wilhelm Reich

One of the most original thinkers to emerge from the psychoanalytical school of thought was Wilhelm Reich (1897–1957). He carried the insights of Freud on sexuality and the workings of the unconscious into much broader fields of social concern. His restless mind probed the darker side of human nature, even while he continued to hold to the idea that people are basically good; and it was he alone, among psychologists, who was able to see both the ascendancy and the horrors of Nazism.

Reich's difficult life seemed to confirm the horrible possibilities of the human soul. He began to study psychoanalysis in 1920, and very quickly became a favorite of Freud. He was young and dynamic, and it was clear that Freud hoped that he would remain loyal to an orthodox Freudian approach to psychoanalysis. But by 1925, Reich had a falling out with the master over the question of a death instinct in human nature. Freud thought that there was a death instinct in people, but Reich denied it. The strain of the feud led to a breakdown of Reich's health, and, soon after, he developed tuberculosis. After recovering, he began to work with working-class adolescents in Vienna and later in Berlin and, as a result of these experiences, became aware of forces that influence people in ways that Freud never saw. He became conscious of the role of class in the development of a person's character problems. The working-class adolescents whom he saw had very different problems from the middle-class, middle-aged Viennese women who formed the bulk of Freud's patients. He also began to look into the relationship between psychological problems and the psychological manifestations of these problems. All of this moved him away from the procedures of orthodox psychoanalysis, during which the patients merely talked about their experiences. Reich increasingly looked at social problems and issues, and was interested in the way that political movements could use the neuroses of people to their own advantage.

With the advent of Nazism, Reich found himself unwelcome in Germany. He moved to Denmark, Sweden, and Norway over the next few years, in each country embroiling himself in controversies that made it necessary for him to leave the country. He arrived in the United States in 1940 and, except for a few brief incidents, led a peaceful existence for the next eight years. In 1948, an article by a woman named Mildred Edie Brady, appeared in *Harper's* magazine, accusing Reich of running a sex clinic. Despite gross inaccuracies in her account, the Food and Drug Administration used the article as a reason to hound Reich, to interfere with his work, and finally, to bring him to court. In 1956, on very dubious charges, he was jailed and his books were burned, including writings that had nothing to do with the case at hand. Reich died in jail in 1957, and the associate who was jailed with him, his life work ruined, immediately committed suicide after his release in 1958. Ironically, Reich, who had done so much to uncover the forces in human beings that make fascism possible, died at the hands of these extreme right-wing forces in a country that he himself had continually exalted for its advocacy of freedom.

Reich's theories covered vast ground in many fields. He was a restless, eclectic thinker who suggested new ideas and then left the details for others to work out. Unfortunately, his writing assumes that the reader shares and understands his extraordinary, idiosyncratic vocabulary. In order to understand the language in any of his books, it is necessary to have read his earlier writings; and his very first article is only intelligible to those who have read extensively in the earlier psychoanalytical literature. However, interspersed in the jargon, repetitious passages, and peculiar digressions, there are passages of powerful insight and even eloquence.

Reich dealt at length with the fundamental question of evil. Why is there war? Why are people so vicious and cruel? In dealing with these questions, he came up with fascinating theories that postulate a historical basis for the existence of evil in the world today.

According to Reich, mental illness only began to develop in human beings when we began to settle down into permanent farming communities. Once society became organized in this way, we became removed from nature; we sought to control nature rather than to work with it. As early agricultural societies developed, it became necessary to control and suppress natural human instincts, such as sex. Women became commodities, and marriage developed as an economic institution. In the process of suppressing natural urges, in the course of thinking of future gain (important in agriculture), people became rigid and lost touch with their instincts. Reich based a good deal of this theory on a study of life in the Trobriand Islands, off the coast of New Guinea, by the great anthropologist Bronislaw Malinowski. Malinowski found people at the very crossroads of the development of early agricultural societies. Some members of society had complex and rigid social roles, complete with marriages and dowries, while others maintained the more fluid, interpersonal relations that are more typical of preagricultural societies.

According to Reich, over a period of several thousand years, as agricultural society developed, human beings changed from relatively healthy animals, in touch with their environment, into complex, neurotic, alienated people. No longer were we animals, participants in nature; we became people, masters of nature, who were at the same time detached from it. In the process, we became detached from our own feelings as well. Reich saw the story of the Garden of Eden as a parable of this change.

Physically, these changes in human behavior and perception manifested themselves in what Reich called "armor." Many animals turn physically rigid when faced with danger. But only modern humans have bodies that are chronically rigid.

Reich found that people typically were armored in seven bands across the body. These bands fall across the eyes, jaw, throat, chest, diaphragm, stomach, and pelvis. The effects of armoring can be illustrated by a simple exercise. Sit up very straight, stick out your chest and stare rigidly ahead; note how difficult it is to think or feel clearly while you maintain such a posture. When armoring becomes chronic, a person feels nothing, or has feelings that are distorted and confused. Armoring makes it easier to repress feelings, particularly sexual feelings. But the feelings, repressed or not, are still there. What do we do with them?

Reich looked at many ways in which these distorted or hidden feelings either came out or were used for some secondary purpose. But he was especially fascinated with the way repressed feelings could be used by cynical politicians for political purposes.

The Nazis, according to Reich, had a profound instinctive understanding of the relationship between repressed sexuality and anger. In their program, in their advertising and policies, they advocated the repression of sexual desire and the focus of hate on certain specific sources—either the Jews, the Slavs, or the architects of the Treaty of Versailles, which had so humiliated Germany. In an extraordinary analysis of Nazi propaganda, *The Mass Psychology of Fascism*, Reich shows how deliberately and consistently the Nazis were able to link hatred, the value of sexual repression, and the love of the fatherland, and how Hitler was able to tap on people's sexual repression as a tool to further the Nazi cause. What is truly extraordinary is that this analysis was made in 1933, before the Nazis came to power, and that he predicted that the Nazis' ability to mobilize the irrational potential in human beings linked to people's chronically armored pelvises would lead the Nazis to their initial victory.

A person who has a high energy level and an insuperable pelvic block will become what Reich called an "emotional plague character." Emotional plague shows itself in many ways: in vicious gossip, political intolerance, race hatred, and a desire to control others. According to Reich, anyone can suffer from a temporary attack of the plague, but a person afflicted with a true emotional plague is constantly doing these things. Reich saw both fascism and communism as endemic outbreaks of emotional plague behavior. The characteristic that linked these movements with the emotional plague was their intolerance. Neither fascist nor communist countries can tolerate any opposition to their views. People who think differently are regarded as threats to be tortured or eliminated. This irrational behavior stems from the need of the emotional plague character to control his or her environment which, in turn, stems from the inability to tolerate sensation, or change. Terrified of feeling anything, afraid of losing control, and giving in to murderous impulses, such people feel the need to impose their own standards on others and to make the world conform to their needs. Unfortunately, because of the ability of politicians to influence laws, Reich noted how many plague characters enter politics and then try to impose their own agendas on everyone else. Because the need to achieve their goals is so intense, they are always willing to subscribe to the idea that the end justifies the means.

In an emotional plague character, the reason given for an action is always a lie. For example, a politician who suffers from an "attack" of the plague may start a vicious rumor about an opponent. He or she will swear, up and down, that the rumor is true; or that it is being spread because "people have the right to know the true nature of my opponent's character"; or that the rumor "did not originate with my office." The need to lie about one's actions and motives are merely examples of the plague-ridden nature of such a personality.

Reich felt that modern humans had become increasingly mechanical in their thinking and functioning, which made them unable to feel or think clearly, and therefore more prone to accept the distortions of the emotional plague characters. Mechanical thinking for Reich was manifest in such things as the tendency to try to quantify everything—the concern with test scores, averages, calories in the diet. It was also evident in the concern for order and regularity in life, the desire to follow procedures and orders.

He felt that the attempts to organize life in a mechanical way were doomed to failure; despite all attempts to turn humans into machines, at bottom we are living, breathing, unpredictable animals. What happens to people, however, is quite interesting. Because we are unwilling to accept our true nature, we are inclined to interpret our inner feelings—our passions, our desires and longings—in a mystical way. Rather than accept their passions as evidence of our true nature (or according to Reich, our nature as human *animals*), we mystify them, turn our passions into religious ecstasy or, more sinisterly, into the hatred that infests those who desire racial or ethnic purity.

Reich blamed the wars and destruction of the twentieth century on the mechanistic and mystical habits and tendencies of modern human society. The combination of a mechanical way of looking at the world and the mystical belief in such entities as the fatherland, the state, the workers, the saints, or the holy war have made hideous destruction possible and acceptable to the people who hold to these mechanical/mystical ideas. Reich places the blame for these problems on both science and religion, for science has mechanized experience while religion has mystified it.

In contrast to these ideas, Reich believes that there is a healthier way of looking at problems. He calls this approach "functionalism." The functional approach is flexible; it studies living things as vital, changing entities, tries to explain their behavior in ways that take into account the fact that living things are always changing. It takes the quantification of experience through tests, statistics, and measurements with some skepticism, realizing, for example, that a test which shows that a person has high blood pressure is not really taking into account the person or the situation, but merely comparing the numbers of that minute with some statistical norm. The functionalist neither mystifies experience as religion does nor mechanizes it, as many people do in science. The functionalist has a much greater tolerance for change and uncertainty, and need not believe that there is one answer to a problem, or that he or she has found the truth about the world.

Reich does not give us a clear picture of how functionalism would actually work. This is partly because functionalism, by nature, is so flexible. The functional physician, for example, would probably have no set ways to treat patients. Such a person could take the same disease in two people and treat them in radically different ways. The functional scientist would not claim that an answer to the problem was found but that a new way of looking at it made sense, given the information at hand. Functionalist educators would not assume that a child who scores poorly on tests is stupid; they would understand that tests measure only part of the experience.

Functional thinking has become more common these days. The arrogant certainty of the world view of many scientists and religious leaders has been tempered by the wars and destruction of this century. Moreover, the constant changes in scientific knowledge and theory have undermined any idea that science has found the truth. But there are many people to whom the functional perspective seems threatening or immoral, and they have become particularly vocal in recent years. The tolerance and flexibility Reich hoped for is far from being generally accepted today.

QUESTIONS

1. What factors in history have led man to develop mental illness, according to Reich?

2. What does Reich mean by armoring? What effects can armoring have on a person's behavior? What can releasing the armor do?

3. According to Reich, how did the Nazis use repressed sexual energy to their advantage?

4. What are emotional plague characters and how do such persons act? Why are they so dangerous?

5. How have mechanical and mystical ideas interacted so that it is hard for us to understand living beings?

6. How have mechanical persons interpreted the nonmechanical part of their nature?

❶   Write a summary of Reich's ideas, as presented in these passages.

❷   Look through news magazines and newspapers. Find evidence of behavior in them that illustrates emotional plague reactions and the mechanical way people look at the world.

The Obedience Experiments

Although Reich's ideas are fascinating, they hardly constitute a scientific study of the problem of evil. He was an astute observer of human nature, but his theories are usually generalizations that are not subject to proof. Are there factors that can be scientifically studied that can give us some insight into the problem of evil?

Such a study was made by Stanley Milgram at Yale University in 1961. He conducted a set of experiments designed to test the degree to which people were willing to obey an authority figure who asked them to perform acts which directly conflicted with their ethical beliefs. As Milgram noted, there is no belief more universal than the idea that one should not harm another person who does not deserve punishment. We simply have to look at the rationalizations used by governments who torture their people to weigh its truth. They either lie outright and deny that the tortures are occurring, or they go to elaborate lengths to make the atrocities sound justified.

Milgram's experiments led to spectacular, disturbing results. The number of people willing to torture an innocent man, simply because a man in a lab coat told them to do so, was astonishing. The study was replicated at several universities in the United States and in both European and Asian countries. The results were always the same: most people will obey an authority rather than their conscience. How could this be? Why would people do this? Milgram wrestled with these questions and studied them in the series of experiments we will now examine.

These experiments are so crucial to any understanding of ethics that we have included large segments of Milgram's book *Obedience to Authority*. Milgram's lucid prose speaks for itself; all we must do is wrestle with the deeper implications of the study.

Obedience to Authority[1]

The first selection we have included from Milgram's book shows how the experiment was set up. Read this excerpt carefully. Notice the stages he went through to put the experiment together and the care that went into planning it.

EXCERPT 1

Simplicity is the key to effective scientific inquiry. This is especially true in the case of subject matter with a psychological content. Psychological matter, by its nature, is difficult to get at and likely to have many more sides to it than appear at first glance. Complicated procedures only get in the way of clear scrutiny of the phenomenon itself. To study obedience most simply, we must create a situation in which one person orders another person to perform an observable action, and we must note when obedience to the imperative occurs and when it fails to occur.

If we are to measure the strength of obedience and the conditions by which it varies, we must force it against some powerful factor that works in the direction of disobedience, and whose human import is readily understood.

Of all moral principles, the one that comes closest to being universally accepted is this: one should not inflict suffering on a helpless person who is neither harmful nor threatening to oneself. This principle is the counterforce we shall set in opposition to obedience.

A person coming to our laboratory will be ordered to act against another individual in increasingly severe fashions. Accordingly, the pressures for disobedience will build up. At a point not known beforehand, the subject may refuse to carry out this command, withdrawing from the experiment. Behavior prior to this rupture is termed *obedience*. The point of rupture is the act of *disobedience* and may occur sooner or later in the sequence of commands, providing the needed measure.

The precise mode of acting against the victim is not of central importance. For technical reasons, the delivery of electric shock was chosen for the study. It seemed suitable, first, because it would be easy for the subject to understand the notion that shocks can be of graded intensity; second, its use would be consistent with the general scientific aura of the laboratory; and finally, it would be relatively easy to simulate the administration of shock in the laboratory.

Let us now move to an account of the details of the investigation.

Obtaining Participants for the Study

Yale undergraduates, being close at hand and readily available, would have been the easiest subjects to study. Moreover, in psychology it is traditional for experiments to be carried out on undergraduates. But for this experiment the use of undergraduates from an elite institution did not seem wholly suitable. The possibility that subjects from Yale would have heard of it from fellow students who had already participated in it seemed too great a risk. It appeared better to draw subjects from a much larger source, the entire New Haven community of 300,000 people. There was a second reason for relying on New Haven rather than the university: the students were too homogeneous a group. They were virtually all in their late teens or early twenties, were highly intelligent, and had some familiarity with psychological experimentation. I wanted a wide range of individuals drawn from a broad spectrum of class backgrounds.

To recruit subjects, an advertisement was placed in the local newspaper. It called for people of all occupations to take part in a study of memory and learning, and it offered $4 payment and 50 cents carfare for one hour of participation. A total of 296 responded. As these were not sufficient for the experiment, this mode of recruitment was supplemented by direct mail solicitation. Names were sampled from the New Haven telephone directory, and a letter of invitation was sent to several thousand residents. The return rate for this invitation was approximately 12 percent. The respondents, for whom we had information on sex, age, and occupation, constituted a pool of subjects, and specific appointments were made with participants a few days before they were to appear in the study.

Typical subjects were postal clerks, high school teachers, salesmen, engineers, and laborers. Subjects ranged in educational level from one who had not finished high school to those who had doctoral and other professional degrees. Several experimental conditions (variations of the basic experiment) were contemplated, and from the outset, I thought it important to balance each condition for age and occupational types. The occupational composition for each experiment was: workers, skilled and unskilled: 40 percent; white-collar, sales, businesses: 40 percent; professionals: 20 percent. The occupations were intersected with three age categories (subjects in twenties, thirties, and forties assigned to each experimental condition in the proportions of 20, 40 and 40 percent respectively).

Locale and Personnel

The experiment was conducted in the elegant Interaction Laboratory of Yale University. This detail is relevant to the perceived legitimacy of the experiment. In some subsequent variations, the experiment was dissociated from the university. The role of experimenter was played by a thirty-one-year-old high school teacher of biology. Throughout the experiment, his manner was impassive and his appearance somewhat stern. He was dressed in a gray technician's coat. The victim was played by a forty-seven-year-old accountant, trained for the role; he was of Irish-American descent and most observers found him mild-mannered and likable.

Procedure

One naive subject and one victim performed in each experiment. A pretext had to be devised that would justify the administration of electric shock by the naive subject. (This is true because in every instance of legitimate authority the subordinate must perceive some connection, however tenuous, between the specific type of authority and the commands he issues.) The experimenter oriented the subjects toward the situation in which he wished to assess obedience with the following instructions:

Psychologists have developed several theories to explain how people learn various types of material.

Some of the better-known theories are treated in this book. (The subject was shown a book on the teaching-learning process.)

One theory is that people learn things correctly whenever they get punished for making a mistake.

A common application of this theory would be when parents spank a child if he does something wrong.

The expectation is that spanking, a form of punishment, will teach the child to remember better, will teach him to learn more effectively.

But actually, we know very little about the effect of punishment on learning, because almost no truly scientific studies have been made of it in human beings.

For instance, we don't know how much punishment is best for learning—and we don't know how much difference it makes as to who is giving the punishment, whether an adult learns best from a younger or an older person than himself—or many things of that sort.

So in this study we are bringing together a number of adults of different occupations and ages. And we're asking some of them to be teachers and some of them to be learners.

We want to find out just what effect different people have on each other as teachers and learners, and also what effect *punishment* will have on learning in this situation.

Therefore, I'm going to ask one of you to be the teacher here tonight and the other one to be the learner.

Does either of you have a preference?

[Subject and accomplice are allowed to express preference.]

Well, I guess the fairest way of doing this is for me to write the word *Teacher* on one slip of paper and *Learner* on the other and let you both draw.

[The subject draws first, then the accomplice.]

Well, which of you is which?

All right. Now the first thing we'll have to do is to set the Learner up so that he can get some type of punishment.

If you'll both come with me into this next room.

The drawing described above had been rigged so that the subject was always the teacher and the accomplice always the learner. (Both slips contained the word "Teacher.") Immediately after the drawing, the teacher and learner were taken to an adjacent room and the learner was strapped into an "electric chair" apparatus.

The experimenter explained that the straps were to prevent excessive movement while the learner was being shocked. The effect was to make it appear impossible for him to escape from the situation. An electrode was attached to the learner's wrist, and electrode paste was applied "to avoid blisters and burns." Subjects were told that the electrode was attached to the shock generator in the adjoining room.

To improve credibility the experimenter declared, in response to a question by the learner, "Although the shocks can be extremely painful, they cause no permanent tissue damage."

Learning Task

The lesson conducted by the subject was a paired-associate learning task. The subject read a series of word pairs to the learner, and then read the first word of the pair along with four terms. For example, the subject read such pairs as:

blue box
nice day
wild duck
etc.

Then, in the testing sequence he would read:
blue: sky   ink   box   lamp

The learner was to indicate which of the four terms had originally been paired with the first word. He communicated his answer by pressing one of four switches in front of him, which lit up one of four numbered quadrants in an answer box located on top of the shock generator.

Shock Generator

The instrument panel consisted of 30 lever switches set in a horizontal line. Each switch was clearly labeled with a voltage designation that ranged from 15 to 450 volts. The labels showed a 15-volt increment from one switch to the next, going from left to right. In addition, the following verbal designations were clearly indicated for groups of four switches, going from left to right: Slight Shock, Moderate Shock, Strong Shock, Very Strong Shock, Intense Shock, Extreme Intensity Shock, Danger: Severe Shock. Two switches after this last designation were simply marked XXX.

When a switch was depressed, a pilot light corresponding to each switch was illuminated in bright red; an electric buzzing was heard; an electric blue light, labeled "voltage energizer," flashed; the dial on the voltage meter swung to the right, and various relay clicks were sounded.

The upper left-hand corner of the generator was labeled SHOCK GENERATOR, TYPE ZLB, DYSON INSTRUMENT COMPANY, WALTHAM, MASS. OUTPUT 15 VOLTS-450 VOLTS.

Sample Shock

Each subject was given a sample shock from the shock generator, prior to beginning his run as teacher. This shock was always 45 volts and was applied by pressing the third switch of the generator. The shock was applied to the wrist of the subject, and the jolt strengthened the subject's belief in the authenticity of the generator.

Shock Instructions

The subject was told to administer a shock to the learner each time he gave a wrong response. Moreover—and this is the key command—the subject was instructed to "move one level higher on the shock generator each time the learner gives a wrong answer." He was also instructed to announce the voltage level before administering a shock. This served to continually remind the subjects of the increasing intensity of shocks administered to the learner. If the subject reached the 30th shock level (450 volts), he was instructed to continue the procedure using this maximum voltage. After two further trials, the experimenter called a halt to the experiment.

Experimenter Feedback

At various points in the experiment the subject would turn to the experimenter for advice on whether he should continue to administer shocks. Or he would indicate that he did not wish to go on.

The experimenter responded with a sequence of "prods," using as many as necessary to bring the subject into line.

Prod 1:   Please continue, or, Please go on.

Prod 2:   The experiment requires that you continue.

Prod 3:   It is absolutely essential that you continue.

Prod 4:   You have no other choice, you must go on.

The prods were made in sequence: Only if Prod 1 had been unsuccessful could Prod 2 be used. If the subject refused to obey the experimenter after Prod 4, the experiment was terminated. The experimenter's tone of voice was at all times firm, but not impolite. The sequence was begun anew on each occasion that the subject balked or showed reluctance to follow orders.

Special Prods

If the subject asked if the learner was liable to suffer permanent physical injury, the experimenter said:

Although the shocks may be painful, there is no permanent tissue damage, so please go on. (Followed by Prods 2, 3, and 4, if necessary.)

If the subject said that the *learner* did not want to go on, the experimenter replied:

Whether the learner likes it or not, you must go on until he has learned all the word pairs correctly. So please go on. (Followed by Prods 2, 3, and 4, if necessary.)

Feedback from the Victim

In all conditions the learner gave a predetermined set of responses to the word-pair test, based on a schedule of approximately three wrong answers to one correct answer.

The victim's responses were a key element in the situation and needed to be worked out carefully. In pilot studies, at first no vocal feedback from the victim was used. It was thought that the verbal voltage designations on the control panel would create sufficient pressure to curtail the subject's obedience. However, this proved not to be the case. In the absence of protests from the learner, virtually every subject in the pilot study, once commanded, went blithely to the end of the board, seemingly indifferent to the verbal designations. This deprived us of an adequate basis for measuring obedient tendencies. A force had to be introduced that would strengthen the subject's resistance to the experimenter's commands, and reveal individual differences in terms of a distribution of break off points.

This force took the form of protests from the victim. Initially, mild protests were used, but these proved inadequate. Subsequently, more vehement protests were inserted into the experimental procedure. To our consternation, even the strongest protests from the victim did not prevent many subjects from administering the harshest punishment ordered by the experimenter. But the protests did lower the mean of the maximum shocks somewhat and created some spread in the subject's performance; therefore, the victim's cries were recorded on tape and incorporated into the regular experimental procedure.

The situation did more than highlight the technical difficulties of finding a workable experimental procedure: it indicated that subjects would obey authority to a greater extent than we had supposed. It also pointed to the importance of feedback from the victim in controlling the subject's behavior.

Each vocal response of the victim was coordinated to a particular voltage level on the shock generator. It is difficult to convey on the printed page the full tenor of the victim's responses, for we have no adequate notion for vocal intensity, timing, and general qualities of delivery. In general, however, the victim indicated no discomfort until the 75-volt shock was administered, at which time there was a little grunt. Similar reactions followed the 90- and 105-volt shocks, and at 120 volts the victim shouted to the experimenter that the shocks were becoming painful. Painful groans were heard on administration of the 135-volt shock, and at

150 volts the victim cried out, "Experimenter, get me out of here! I won't be in the experiment any more! I refuse to go on!" Cries of this type continue with generally rising intensity, so that at 180 volts the victim cried out, "I can't stand the pain," and by 270 volts his response to the shock was definitely an agonized scream. Throughout, from 150 volts on, he insisted that he be let out of the experiment. At 300 volts the victim shouted in desperation that he would no longer provide answers to the memory test.

At this juncture, it was found, subjects would usually turn to the experimenter for guidance. The experimenter would instruct the subject to treat the absence of a response as a wrong answer, and to shock the subject according to the usual schedule. He advised the subjects to allow 5 to 10 seconds before considering no response as a wrong answer, and to increase the shock level one step each time the learner failed to respond correctly. At 315 volts, after a violent scream, the victim reaffirmed vehemently that he was no longer a participant. He provided no answers, but shrieked in agony whenever a shock was administered. After 330 volts he was not heard from, nor did his answers reappear on the four-way signal box.

Measures

The main measure for any subject is the maximum shock he administers before he refuses to go any further. In principle this may vary from 0 (for a subject who refuses to administer even the first shock) to 30 (for a subject who administers the highest shock on the generator).

Interview and Debriefing

An important aspect of the procedure occurred at the end of the experimental session. A careful postexperimental treatment was administered to all subjects. The exact content of the session varied from condition to condition and with increasing experience on our part. At the very least every subject was told that the victim had received no dangerous electric shocks. Each subject had a friendly reconciliation with the unharmed victim and an extended discussion with the experimenter. The experiment was explained to defiant subjects in a way that supported their decision to disobey the experimenter. Obedient subjects were assured that their behavior was entirely normal and that their feelings of conflict or tension were shared by other participants. Subjects were told that they would receive a comprehensive report at the conclusion of the experimental series. In some instances, additional detailed and lengthy discussions of the experiment were also carried out with individual subjects.

When the experimental series was complete, subjects received a written report which presented details of the experimental procedure and results. Again, their own part in the experiments was treated in a dignified way and their behavior in the experiment respected. All subjects received a follow-up questionnaire regarding their participation in the research, which again allowed expression of thoughts and feelings about their behavior.

Recapitulation

In this situation the subject must resolve a conflict between two mutually incompatible demands from the social field. He may continue to follow the orders of the experimenter and shock the learner with increasing severity, or he may refuse to follow the orders of the experimenter and heed the learner's pleas. The experimenter's authority operates not in a free field but against ever-mounting countervailing pressures from the person being punished.

This laboratory situation gives us a framework in which to study the subject's reactions to the principal conflict of the experiment. Again, this conflict is between the experimenter's demands that he continue to administer the electric shock and the learner's demands, which become increasingly insistent, that the experiment be stopped. The crux of the study is to vary systematically the factors believed to alter the degree of obedience to the experimental commands and to learn under what conditions submission to authority is most probable and under what conditions defiance is brought to the fore.

What the experimental situation does is to condense the elements present when obedience occurs in the larger world such that the essential ingredients are brought into a relatively narrow arena where they are open to scientific scrutiny. The power of the situation derives from the fact that we are able to see, and the subject can experience, the concurrent operation of antagonistic forces that in the larger world rarely impinge on him at the identical instant.

QUESTIONS

1. Why does Milgram say "simplicity is the key to effective scientific inquiry"?

2. What purpose was served by asking people to act against their moral principles?

3. Why did Milgram consider Yale undergraduates unsuitable subjects?

4. What significance could be attached to the setting of the experiment?

5. What did the naive subjects think that they were doing in this experiment?

6. Why did the experimenter always give the same prods?

7. Why was verbal feedback needed in order to generate any significant disobedience?

8. Why was the debriefing necessary?

9. What could the experimental results tell us about people in the "real world"?

EXCERPT 2

Now let us look at the actual performance of subjects in the experiment. To begin, we shall consider the results of the Remote-Feedback variation (Experiment 1). It differs slightly from the usual situation in that no vocal complaint is heard from the victim. He is placed in another room where he cannot be seen by the subject, nor can his voice be heard; his answers flash silently on the signal box. However, at 300-volts the laboratory walls resound as he pounds in protest. After 315 volts, no further answers appear, and the pounding ceases.

It is instructive to reprint the subjects' remarks at the point of defiance, as transcribed from the tape recordings:

"I think he's trying to communicate, he's knocking. . . . Well it's not fair to shock the guy . . . these are terrific volts. I don't think this is very humane. . . . Oh, I can't go on with this; no, this isn't right. It's a hell of an experiment. The guy is suffering in there. No, I don't want to go on. This is crazy." (Subject refuses to administer more shocks.)

"He's banging in there. I'm gonna chicken out. I'd like to continue, but I can't do that to a man. . . . I'm sorry I can't do that to a man. I'll hurt his heart. You take your check. . . .No really, I couldn't do it."

Of the 40 subjects, 26 obeyed the orders of the experimenter to the end, proceeding to punish the victim until they reached the most potent shock available on the generator. After the 450-volt shock was administered three times, the experimenter called a halt to the session.

Subjects were frequently in an agitated state. Sometimes, verbal protest was at a minimum, and the subject simply got up from his chair in front of the shock generator, indicating that he wished to leave the laboratory. Some obedient subjects expressed reluctance to administer shocks beyond the 300-volt level and displayed tensions similar to those who defied the experimenter.

After the maximum shocks had been delivered, and the experimenter called a halt to the proceedings, many obedient subjects heaved sighs of relief, mopped their brows, rubbed their fingers over their eyes, or nervously fumbled cigarettes. Some shook their heads, apparently in regret. Some subjects had remained calm throughout the experiment and displayed only minimal signs of tension from beginning to end.

Bringing the Victim Closer

An experiment differs from a demonstration in that in an experiment, once an effect has been observed, it becomes possible to alter systematically the conditions under which it is produced, and in this way to learn the relevant causes.

What we have seen thus far applies only to a situation in which the victim is out of sight and unable to communicate with his own voice. The recipient of the punishment is thus remote, nor does he indicate his wishes very clearly. There is pounding on the wall, but this has an inherently ambiguous meaning; possibly, some subjects did not interpret this pounding as evidence of the victim's distress. The resulting obedience may be attributable to this. Perhaps there will be no obedience when the victim's suffering is more clearly communicated; when the victim is given a sense of presence, and he is seen, heard, and felt.

Behavior noted in our pilot studies lent credence to this notion. In those studies the victim could be dimly perceived by the subject through a silvered glass. Subjects frequently averted their eyes from the person they were shocking, often turning their heads in an awkward and conspicuous manner. One subject explained, "I didn't want to see the consequences of what I had done." Observers noted:

> . . . subjects show a reluctance to look at the victim, whom they could see through the glass in front of them. When this fact was brought to their attention, they indicated that it caused them discomfort to see the victim in agony. We note, however, that although the subject refuses to look at the victim, he continues to administer shocks.

This suggested that the salience of the victim may have, in some degree, regulated the subject's performance. If in obeying the experimenter the subject found it necessary to avoid scrutiny of the victim, would the reverse be true? If the victim were rendered increasingly more salient to the subject, would obedience diminish? A set of four experiments was designed to answer this question. We have already described the Remote condition.

Experiment 2 (Voice-Feedback) was identical to the first except that vocal protests were introduced. As in the first condition, the victim was placed in an adjacent room, but his complaints could be heard clearly through the walls of the laboratory.

Experiment 3 (Proximity) was similar to the second, except that the victim was placed in the same room as the subject, a few feet from him. thus he was visible as well as audible, and voice cues were provided.

Experiment 4 (Touch-proximity) was identical to the third, with this exception: the victim received a shock only when his hand rested on a shock plate. At the 150-volt level the victim demanded to be let free and refused to place his hand on the shock plate. The experimenter ordered the subject to force the victim's hand onto the plate. Thus obedience in this condition required that the subject have physical contact with the victim in order to give him punishment at or beyond the 150-volt level.

Forty adult subjects were studied in each condition. The results revealed that obedience was significantly reduced as the victim was rendered more immediate to the subject.

Thirty-five percent of the subjects defied the experimenter in the Remote condition, 37.5 percent in Voice-Feedback, 60 percent in Proximity, and 70 percent in Touch-Proximity.

Shock Level	Verbal Designation and Voltage Level	Experiment 1 Remote (*n* = 40)	Experiment 2 Voice Feedback (*n* = 40)	Experiment 3 Proximity (*n* = 40)	Experiment 4 Touch-Proximity (*n* = 40)
	Slight Shock				
1	15				
2	30				
3	45				
4	60				
	Moderate Shock				
5	75				
6	90				
7	105			1	
8	120				
	Strong Shock				
9	135		1		1
10	150		5	10	16
11	165		1		
12	180		1	2	3
	Very Strong Shock				
13	195				
14	210				1
15	225			1	1
16	240				
	Intense Shock				
17	255				1
18	270			1	
19	285		1		1
20	300	5*	1	5	1

Shock Level	Verbal Designation and Voltage Level	Experiment 1 Remote (*n* = 40)	Experiment 2 Voice Feedback (*n* = 40)	Experiment 3 Proximity (*n* = 40)	Experiment 4 Touch-Proximity (*n* = 40)
	Extreme Intensity Shock				
21	315	4	3	3	2
22	330	2			
23	345	1	1		1
24	360	1	1		
	Danger: Severe Shock				
25	375	1		1	
26	390				
27	405				
28	420				
	XXX				
29	435	26	25	16	12
Mean Maximum Shock Level		27.0	24.53	20.80	17.88
Percentage Obedient Subjects		65.0%	62.5%	40.0%	30.0%

*Indicates that in Experiment 1, five subjects administered a maximum shock of 300 volts.

QUESTIONS

1. *What can we conclude from the fact that the first two experiments had almost identical levels of compliance? Were there any differences* *between the two experiments in terms of the shock levels at which disobedience occurred? What do these results suggest?*

2. *What can be concluded from the fact that after experiments 2 and 3, the compliance levels dropped? What does this suggest about the relative strength of the power of moral belief and of the human inclination towards obedience?*

3. *Looking at the results of the experiments, one notices the time at which disobedience occurs. What can be concluded about the distribution of disobedient moments in the last three experiments?*

EXCERPT 3

Experiment 5: A New Base Line Condition

After the proximity series was completed, the experiment was moved out of the elegant Yale Interaction Laboratory to more modest quarters in the basement of the same building. The new laboratory was functional but somewhat plain, with bare steam pipes running along the ceiling, and a concrete floor, instead of the posh rugs and drapes of the former locale. I wondered whether the less impressive quarters would lead to a lesser level of obedience. In any case it was necessary to establish a new base-line condition. It was modeled on the Voice-Feedback condition, with a slight alteration. The learner would not merely respond with cries of anguish, but would introduce remarks about a heart problem. Perhaps this new element would provide additional justification for disobeying and make such a course of action seem even more compelling and necessary. . . .

The experimenter replies in a confident, somewhat dismissive tone that although the shocks may be painful, they cause no permanent tissue damage, and then proceeds with the experimental routines.

The new series of protests, which was to serve as a standard for all subsequent experiments, paralleled the first set, with the exception that reference is made to the learner's heart condition at 150, 195, and 330 volts. The exact schedule of protests is as follows:

Experiment 5: New Base-Line Condition

The Learner's Schedule of Protests

75 volts	Ugh!
90 volts	Ugh!
105 volts	Ugh! (louder)
120 volts	Ugh! Hey, this really hurts.
135 volts	Ugh!!
150 volts	Ugh!!! Experimenter ! That's all. Get me out of here. I told you I had heart trouble. My heart's starting to bother me now. Get me out of here, please. My heart's starting to bother me. I refuse to go on. Let me out.
165 volts	Ugh! Let me out! (shouting)
180 volts	Ugh! I can't stand the pain. Let me out of here! (shouting)
195 volts	Ugh! Let me out of here. Let me out of here. My heart's bothering me. Let me out of here! You have no right to keep me here! Let me out! Let me out of here! Let me out! Let me out of here! My heart's bothering me. Let me out! Let me out!
210 volts	Ugh!! Experimenter! Get me out of here. I've had enough. I won't be in the experiment any more.
225 volts	Ugh!
240 volts	Ugh!
255 volts	Ugh! Get me out of here.
270 volts	(Agonized scream.) Let me out of here. Let me out of here. Let me out of here. Let me out. Do you hear? Let me out of here.
285 volts	(Agonized scream.)
300 volts	(Agonized scream.) I absolutely refuse to answer any more. Get me out. Get me out of here.
315 volts	(Intensely agonized scream.) I told you I refuse to answer. I'm no longer a part of this experiment.
330 volts	(Intense and prolonged agonized scream.) Let me out of here. Let me out of here. My heart's bothering me. Let me out, I tell you. (Hysterically) Let me out of here. Let me out of here. You have no right to hold me here. Let me out! Let me out! Let me out! Let me out of here! Let me out! Let me out!

Neither the less elegant laboratory nor the mention of a heart condition leads to greater disobedience. Twenty-six of the 40 subjects continued to the end in the present condition, compared with 25 out of 40 in the Voice-Feedback condition, merely a slight variation. The distribution of breakoff points is show in Table 3.

Probably there is nothing the victim can say that will uniformly generate disobedience; for the teacher's actions are not controlled by him.

In the postexperimental interview subjects were asked, "What is the maximum sample shock you would be willing to accept?" Three defiant subjects would accept shocks more powerful than they had administered. Of the 26 obedient subjects, 7 were willing to sample the 450-volt shock they had just administered, while 19 were not. In most cases there is a marked discrepancy between the shock the subject administered and the level he would be willing to accept as a sample. . . . [Some] subjects who administered 450 volts . . . were not willing to sample more than 45 volts. Similar and even more extreme results are found in all experimental conditions when this question was asked.

Experiment 6: Change of Personnel

Is it possible that the subjects respond principally to the personalities of the experimenter and victim? Perhaps the experimenter came across as a more forceful person than the victim, and the subject allied himself with the more impressive personality. The following experimenter comparison came about inadvertently, but it can shed some light on this point. In order to speed up the running of the experiment, we had set up a second team, consisting of a new experimenter and a new victim. In the first team the experimenter was a somewhat dry, hard, technical-looking man. the victim in contrast was soft, avuncular, and innocuous. These personal characteristics were more or less reversed in the second team. The new experimenter was rather soft and unaggressive. The alternate victim in contrast, was played by a man possessing a hard bony face and prognathic jaw, who looked as if he would do well in a scrap. The results, shown in Table 3, indicate that the change in personnel had little effect on the level of obedience. The personal characteristics of the experimenter and victim were not of overriding importance.

Experiment 7: Closeness of Authority

We saw in the proximity experiments that the spatial relationship between subject and victim affected the level of obedience. Would not the relationship of subject to experimenter also play a part?

There are reasons to feel that, on arrival, the subjects were oriented primarily to the experimenter rather than to the victim. They had come to the laboratory to fit into the structure that the experimenter—not the victim—would provide. They had come less to understand the behavior than to reveal that behavior to a competent scientist, and they were willing to display themselves as the scientist's purposes required. Most subjects seemed quite concerned about the appearance they were making before the experimenter, and one could argue that this preoccupation in a relatively new and strange setting made the subjects somewhat insensitive to the triadic nature of the social situation. The subjects were so concerned about the show they were putting on for the experimenter that influences from other parts of the social field did not receive much weight. This powerful orientation to the experimenter would account for the relative insensitivity of the subject to the victim and would also lead us to believe that alterations in the relationship between subject and experimenter would have important consequences for obedience.

In another series of experiments we varied the physical closeness of the experimenter and the degree of surveillance he exercised. In Experiment 5 the experimenter sat just a few feet away from the subject. In Experiment 7, after giving initial instructions, the experimenter left the laboratory and gave his orders by telephone.

Obedience dropped sharply when the experimenter was physically removed from the laboratory. The number of obedient subjects in the first condition (26) was almost three times as great as in the second (9), in which the experimenter gave his orders by telephone. Subjects seemed able to resist the experimenter far better when they did not have to confront him face to face.

Moreover, when the experimenter was absent, subjects displayed an interesting form of behavior that had not occurred under his surveillance. Though continuing with the experiment, several subjects administered lower shocks than were required and never informed the experimenter of their deviation from the correct procedure. Indeed, in telephone conversations some subjects specifically assured the experimenter that they were raising the shock level according to instruction, while, in reality, they repeatedly used the lowest shock on the board. This form of behavior is particularly interesting: although these subjects acted in a way that clearly undermined the avowed purposes of the experiment, they found it easier to handle the conflict in this manner than to precipitate an open break with authority.

Other conditions were completed in which the experimenter was absent during the first segment of the experiment but reappeared shortly after the subject had refused to give higher shocks when commanded by telephone. Although he had exhausted his power via telephone, the experimenter could frequently force further obedience when he reappeared in the laboratory.

This series of experiments showed that the physical presence of an authority was an important force contributing to the subject's obedience or defiance. Obedience to destructive commands was in some degree dependent on the proximal relations between authority and subject, and any theory of obedience must take account of this fact.

Experiment 8: Women as Subjects

In the experiments described thus far the subjects were adult males. Forty women were also studied. They are of particular theoretical interest because of two general sets of findings in social psychology. First, in most tests of compliance, women are more yielding than men (Weiss, 1969; Feinberg, mimeo). And thus in the present study they might have been expected to show more obedience. On the other hand, women are thought to be less aggressive and more empathic than men; thus their resistance to shocking the victim would also be higher. In principle, the two factors ought to work in opposite directions. The results are shown in Table 3. The level of obedience was virtually identical to the performance of men; however, the level of conflict experienced by the women was on the whole higher than that felt by our male subjects.

There were many specifically feminine styles in handling the conflict. In postexperimental interviews women, far more frequently than men, related their experience to problems of rearing children.

The women were studied only in the role of teachers. It would be interesting to move them into other roles. As victims, they would most likely generate more disobedience, for cultural norms militate against hurting women even more strongly than hurting men. (Similarly, if a child were placed in the victim's role, disobedience would be much greater.)

It would be especially interesting to place women in the position of authority. Here it is unclear how male subjects and other women would respond to her. There is less experience with women bosses; on the other hand many men may want to show their toughness before a women experimenter, by carrying out her callous orders without emotion.

[In experiment 9, the learner only agrees to be in the experiment if he has the power to terminate it if the shocks are too painful. Thus when the subject continues to shock the learner over his protests he is violating a prior contract that the subject and experimenter made with the learner. Although more subjects disobeyed, the lower level of compliance may have been a chance variation.]

[In experiment 10, the laboratory was moved out of Yale University into a rather run-down office building in Bridgeport, Connecticut. The experimenters now claimed to be an independent research group, and they made no mention of any connection with Yale University. The lower level of compliance in this experiment may be due to chance.]

[In experiment 11, subjects choose their own shock levels. In other words, the experimenter just instructed the naive subject to give whatever shock he wanted. Milgram ran this experiment to see if the reason people obeyed the experimenter is because they wanted to give painful shocks. Maybe people are inherently sadistic. The results of this variation, however, undermine that idea.]

MAXIMUM SHOCKS ADMINISTERED IN EXPERIMENTS 5, 6, AND 7

Shock Level	Verbal Designation and Voltage Level	Experiment 5 New Base Line ($n = 40$)	Experiment 6 Change of Personnel ($n = 40$)	Experiment 7 Experimenter Absent ($n = 40$)
	Slight Shock			
1	15			
2	30			
3	45			
4	60			

Shock Level	Verbal Designation and Voltage Level	Experiment 5 Remote (n = 40)	Experiment 6 Voice Feedback (n = 40)	Experiment 7 Proximity (n = 40)
	Moderate Shock			
5	75			
6	90	1		1
7	105			1
8	120		2	
	Strong Shock			
9	135			1
10	150	6	4	7
11	165		1	3
12	180	1	3	1
	Very Strong Shock			
13	195		1	5
14	210		2	
15	225			1
16	240			
	Intense Shock			
17	255			
18	270	2	2	3
19	285			
20	300	1	1	3
	Extreme Intensity Shock			
21	315	1	2	
22	330	1	1	1
23	345			
24	360		1	2
	Danger: Severe Shock			
25	375	1		
26	390			
27	405			1
28	420			1

Shock Level	Verbal Designation and Voltage Level		Experiment 5 New Base Line ($n = 40$)	Experiment 6 Change of Personnel ($n = 40$)	Experiment 7 Experimenter Absent ($n = 40$)
	XXX				
29		435			
30		450	26	20	9
Mean Maximum Shock Level			24.55	22.20	18.15
Percentage Obedient Subjects			65.0%	50.0%	20.5%

MAXIMUM SHOCKS ADMINISTERED IN
EXPERIMENTS 8, 9, 10, AND 11

Shock Level	Verbal Designation and Voltage Level	Experiment 8 Women ($n = 40$)	Experiment 9 Enters with Prior Conditions ($n = 40$)	Experiment 10 Experimenter Absent ($n = 40$)	Experiment 11 Subject Chooses Shock Level* ($n = 40$)
	Slight Shock			2†	
1	15				3
2	30				6
3	45				7
4	60				7
	Moderate Shock				
5	75				5
6	90				4
7	105			1	1
8	120			1	1

Shock Level	Verbal Designation and Voltage Level	Experiment 8 Women (n = 40)	Experiment 9 Enters with Prior Conditions (n = 40)	Experiment 10 Experimenter Absent (n = 40)	Experiment 11 Subject Chooses Shock Level* (n = 40)
	Strong Shock				
9	135		1		3
10	150	4	7	7	1
11	165	1	2		
12	180	2	1	1	
	Very Strong Shock				
13	195		1	3	
14	210	1			
15	225				
16	240				
	Intense Shock				
17	255		1		
18	270	2	2	1	
19	285				
20	300	1	1	4	
	Extreme Intensity Shock				
21	315		3	1	
22	330	2		1	
23	345	1	1		
24	360		1		
	Danger: Severe Shock				
25	375		1		
26	390		1		1
27	405				
28	420				

Shock Level	Verbal Designation and Voltage Level	Experiment 8 Women (n = 40)	Experiment 9 Enters with Prior Conditions (n = 40)	Experiment 10 Experimenter Absent (n = 40)	Experiment 11 Subject Chooses Shock Level* (n = 40)
	XXX				
29	435				
30	450	26	16	19	1
Mean Maximum Shock Level		24.573	21.40	20.95	5.50
Percentage Obedient Subjects		65.0%	40.0%	47.5%	2.5%[‡]

*Indicates the maximum shock chosen by the subject, no matter at what point it occurred in his sequence of choices.

[†]Two subjects in Bridgeport refused to administer even the lowest shock.

[‡]Percentage of subjects who used the last shock on the generator. Does not indicate obedience, as subjects chose their own level.

ACTIVITIES

❶ Analyze the effect that the new series of variations had on the obedience levels of the subjects. Discuss not only the number of subjects who obeyed the experimenter to the end, but also speculate on any significance that you can attach to the shock levels at which disobedience tended to occur. (In this context, however, one should keep in mind that what appears significant may not be so statistically. For example, experiment 7 shows that, when different people were used as victim and experimenter, the compliance level dropped from 65% to 50%. Apparently, this could be due to chance. However, it would still be valuable to consider whether this small drop in obedience may be due to some factor in the personalities involved.)

In a series of experiments we have omitted (experiments 12–16), Milgram varies the positions of authority in the experiment. The purpose of these experiments was to make sure that it was obedience to an authority figure that was causing compliance. Evidently, it was, for people refused to shock a victim who demanded to be shocked. They refused to listen to someone who was not an authority figure when he demanded that they shock the victim, and they did nothing when two authority figures contradicted each other.

The final set of experiments, included in this excerpt , treat the issues of conformity and obedience.

EXCERPT 4

The individual is weak in his solitary opposition to authority, but the group is strong. The archetypic event is depicted by Freud (1921), who recounts how oppressed sons band together and rebel against the despotic father. Delacroix portrays the mass in revolt against unjust authority; Gandhi successfully pits the populace against British authority in nonviolent encounter; prisoners in Attica Penitentiary organize and temporarily challenge prison authority. The individual's relationship with his peers can compete with, and on occasion supplant, his ties to authority.

Distinction Between Conformity and Obedience

At this point a distinction must be made between the terms *obedience* and *conformity*. Conformity, in particular, has a very broad meaning, but for the purposes of this discussion, I shall limit it to the action of a subject when he goes along with his peers, people of his own status, who have no special right to direct his behavior. Obedience will be restricted to the action of the subject who complies with authority. Consider a recruit who enters military service. He scrupulously carries out the orders of his superiors. At the same time he adopts the habits, routines, and language of his peers. The former represents obedience and the latter, conformity.

A series of brilliant experiments on conformity has been carried out by S.E. Asch (1951). A group of six apparent subjects was shown a line of a certain length and asked to say which of three other lines matched it. All but one of the subjects in the group had been secretly instructed beforehand to select one of the "wrong" lines on each trial or in a certain percentage of the trials. The naive subject was so placed that he heard the answers of most of the group before he had to announce his own decision. Asch found that under this form of social pressure a large fraction of subjects went along with the group rather than accept the unmistakable evidence of their own eyes.

Asch's subjects *conform* to the group. The subjects in the present experiment *obey* the experimenter. Obedience and conformity both refer to the abdication of initiative to an external source. But they differ in the following important ways:

1. Hierarchy. Obedience to authority occurs within a hierarchical structure in which the actor feels that the person above has the right to prescribe behavior. Conformity regulates the behavior among those of equal status; obedience links one status to another.

2. Imitation. Conformity is imitation but obedience is not. Conformity leads to homogenization of behavior, as the influenced person comes to adopt the behavior of peers. In obedience, there is compliance without imitation of the influencing source. A soldier does not simply repeat an order given to him but carries it out.

3. Explicitness. In obedience, the prescription for action is explicit, taking the form of an order or command. In conformity, the requirement of going along with the group often remains implicit. Thus, in Asch's experiment on group pressure, there is no overt requirement made by group members that the subject go along with them. The action is spontaneously adopted by the subject. Indeed, many subjects would resist an explicit demand by group members to conform, for the situation is defined as one consisting of equals who have no right to order each other about.

4. Voluntarism. The clearest distinction between obedience and conformity, however, occurs after the fact—that is, in the manner in which subjects explain their behavior. Subjects *deny* conformity and *embrace* obedience as the explanation of their actions. Let me clarify this. In Asch's experiments on group pressure, subjects typically understate the degree to which their actions were influenced by members of the group. They belittle the group effect and try to play up their own autonomy, even when they have yielded to the group on every trial. They often insist that if they made errors in judgment, these were nonetheless their own errors, attributable to their faulty vision or bad judgment. They minimize the degree to which they have conformed to the group.

In the obedience experiment, the reaction is diametrically opposite. Here the subject explains his action of shocking the victim in denying any personal involvement and attributing his behavior exclusively to an external requirement imposed by authority. Thus, while the conforming subject insists that his autonomy was not impaired by the group, the obedient subject asserts that he had no autonomy in the matter of shocking the victim and that his actions were completely out of his own hands.

Why is this so? Because conformity is a response to pressures that are implicit, the subject interprets his own behavior as voluntary. He cannot pinpoint a legitimate reason for yielding to his peers, or he denies that he has done so, not only to the experimenter but to himself as well. In obedience the opposite is true. The situation is publicly defined as one devoid of voluntarism, for there is an explicit command that he is expected to obey. The subject falls back on his public definition of the situation as the full explanation of his action.

So the psychological effects of obedience and conformity are different. Both are powerful forms of social influence, and we may now investigate their role in this experiment.

Experiment 17: Two Peers Rebel

We have said that the revolt against malevolent authority is most effectively brought about by collective rather than individual action. This is a lesson that every revolutionary group learns, and it can be demonstrated in the laboratory with a simple experiment. We have previously seen that there is a marked discrepancy between the subjects' moral principles and their actual performance in the laboratory. Despite their protests and obvious conflict in shocking the victim, a substantial number of subjects are unable to defy the experimenter's authority, and they proceed to administer the highest shock levels commanded by him.

We may now examine in what degree group influence can release the subject from authoritarian control and allow him to act in a direction congruent with his values and personal standards. The strategy is to replicate the basic experiment, but with this difference: the subject is placed in the midst of two peers who defy the experimenter and refuse to punish the victim against his will. In what degree will the pressure created by their actions affect the naive subject's behavior?

Technique

Four apparent subjects appear at the laboratory to take part in an experiment on the "effects of collective teaching and punishment on memory and learning." Three of them are confederates of the experimenter and one is a naive subject. The experimenter explains that three teachers and one learner are to be used in the study, and by means of a rigged drawing, the naive subject is assigned the position of teacher 3. The roles of teacher 1, teacher 2, and learner are filled by the confederates. The learner is strapped into the electric chair and the three teachers are seated before the shock generator. Teacher 1 is told to read the list of word pairs, teacher 2 tells the subject whether his answer is correct or incorrect, and teacher 3 (the naive subject) administers punishment. As in the basic experiment, the subjects are instructed to raise the shock level one step each time the learner makes an error.

Behavior of Confederates

The confederates comply with the experimenter's orders through the 150-volt shock, which provokes the victim's first vehement protest. At this point teacher 1 informs the experimenter that he does not wish to participate further because of the learner's complaints. The experimenter insists that teacher 1 continue. However, teacher 1 is not swayed by the experimenter's commands, gets up from his chair in front of the shock generator, and takes a seat in another part of the room. Since the experimenter's effort to get the subject to return to the generator are futile, the experimenter instructs the remaining two subjects to continue with the experiment. Teacher 3 (the naive subject) is to handle the reading of word pairs, in addition to his regular job of administering electric shock to the learner.

After shock level 14 (210 volts) is administered, teacher 2, expressing concern for the learner, refuses to participate further. The experimenter orders him to continue, but he too leaves his chair in front of the generator and seats himself at an opposite corner of the room, saying, "I'm willing to answer any of your questions, but I'm not willing to shock that man against his will. I'll have no part of it."

At this point the naive subject is seated alone in front of the shock generator. He has witnessed the defiant actions of two peers. The experimenter orders him to continue, stating that it is essential that the experiment be completed.

The results of the experiment are shown in Table 5. In this group setting, 36 of the 40 subjects defy the experimenter (while the corresponding number in the absence of group pressure is 14). The effects of peer rebellion are impressive in undercutting the experimenter's authority. Indeed, of the score of experimental variations completed in this study, none was so effective in undercutting the experimenter's authority as the manipulation reported here.

Reactions to the Defiant Peers

The reactions of naive subjects to the defiant confederates varied considerably and were in part dependent on the exact point where the subject himself defied the experimenter. A subject who quit simultaneously with the first confederate stated, "Well, I was already thinking about quitting when the guy broke off." Most defiant subjects praised the confederates with such statements as, "I thought they were men of good character, yes I do. When the victim said 'Stop,' they stopped" (broke off at shock level 11). "I think they were very sympathetic people . . . and they were totally unaware of what was in store for them" (broke off at shock level 14).

A subject who defied the experimenter at level 21 qualified his approval: "Well, I think they should continue a little further, but I don't blame them for backing out when they did."

Four defiant subjects definitely acknowledged the importance of the confederates' actions to their own defiance: "The thought of stopping didn't enter my mind until it was put there by the other two" (broke off at shock level 14). "The reason I quit was that I did not wish to seem callous and cruel in the eyes of the other two men who had already refused to go on with the experiment" (broke off at shock level 14). A majority of defiant subjects, however, denied that the confederates' action was the critical factor in their own defiance.

A closer analysis of the experimental situation points to several factors that contribute to the group's effectiveness:

1. The peers instill in the subject the *idea* of defying the experimenter. It may not have occurred to some subjects as a possibility.

2. The lone subject in previous experiments had no way of knowing whether, if he defies the experimenter, he is performing in a bizarre manner or whether this action is a common occurrence in the laboratory. The two examples of disobedience he sees suggest that defiance is a natural reaction to the situation.

3. The reactions of the defiant confederates define the act of shocking the victim as improper. They provide social confirmation for the subject's suspicion that it is wrong to punish a man against his will, even in the context of a psychological experiment.

4. The defiant confederates remain in the laboratory even after withdrawing from the experiment (they have agreed to answer postexperimental questions). Each additional shock administered by the naive subject then carries with it a measure of social disapproval from the two confederates.

5. As long as the two confederates participate in the experimental procedure, there is a dispersion of responsibility among the group members for shocking the victim. As the confederates withdraw, responsibility becomes focused on the naive subject.

6. The naive subject is a witness to two instances of disobedience and observes the *consequences* of defying the experimenter to be minimal.

7. The experimenter's power may be diminished by the very fact of failing to keep the two confederates in line, in accordance with the general rule that every failure of authority to exact compliance to its commands weakens the perceived power of the authority (Homans, 1961).

The fact that groups so effectively undermine the experimenter's power reminds us that individuals act as they do for three principal reasons: they carry certain internalized standards of behavior; they are acutely responsive to the sanctions that may be applied to them by authority; and finally, they are responsive to the sanctions potentially applicable to them by the group. When an individual wishes to stand in opposition to authority, he does best to find support for his position from others in his group. The mutual support provided by men for each other is the strongest bulwark we have against the excesses of authority. (Not that the group is always on the right side of the issue. Lynch mobs and groups of predatory hoodlums remind us that groups may be vicious in the influence they exert.)

Experiment 18: A Peer Administers Shocks

Authority is not blind to the uses of groups and will ordinarily seek to employ them in a manner that facilitates submission. A simple variation of the experiment demonstrates this possibility. Any force or event that is placed between the subject and the consequences of shocking the victim, any factor that will create distance between the subject and the victim, will lead to a reduction of strain on the participant and thus lessen disobedience. In modern society others often stand between us and the final destructive act to which we contribute.

Indeed, it is typical of modern bureaucracy, even when it is designed for destructive purposes, that most people involved in its organization do not directly carry out any destructive actions. They shuffle papers or load ammunition or perform some other act which, though it contributes to the final destructive effect, is remote from it in the eyes and mind of the functionary.

To examine this phenomenon within the laboratory, a variation was carried out in which the act of shocking the victim was removed from the naive subject and placed in the hands of another participant (a confederate). The naive subject performs subsidiary acts which, though contributing to the over-all progress of the experiment, remove him from the actual act of depressing the lever on the shock generator.

And the subject's new role is easy to bear. Table 5 shows the distribution of breakoff points for 40 subjects. Only 3 of the 40 refuse to participate in the experiment to the end. They are accessories to the act of shocking the victim, but they are not psychologically implicated in it to the point where strain arises and disobedience results.

Any competent manager of a destructive bureaucratic system can arrange his personnel so that only the most callous and obtuse are directly involved in violence. The greater part of the personnel can consist of men and women who, by virtue of their distance from the actual acts of brutality, will feel little strain in their performance of supportive functions. They will feel doubly absolved from responsibility. First, legitimate authority has given full warrant for their actions. Second, they have not themselves committed brutal physical acts.

MAXIMUM SHOCKS ADMINISTERED IN GROUP EXPERIMENTS

Shock Level	Verbal Designation and Voltage Level	Experiment 17 Two Peers Rebel (n = 40)	Experiment 18 Peer Administers Shocks (n = 40)
	Slight Shock		
1	15		
2	30		
3	45		
4	60		
	Moderate Shock		
5	75		
6	90		
7	105	1	
8	120		
	Strong Shock		
9	135		
10	150	3	1
11	165	4	
12	180	1	1
	Very Strong Shock		
13	195	4	
14	210	12	
15	225		
16	240		
	Intense Shock		
17	255		
18	270	4	
19	285		
20	300	2	1
	Extreme Intensity Shock		
21	315	3	
22	330	1	
23	345		
24	360		

Shock Level	Verbal Designation and Voltage Level	Experiment 17 Two Peers Rebel (*n* = 40)	Experiment 18 Peer Administers Shocks (*n* = 40)
	Danger: Severe Shock		
25	375	1	
26	390		
27	405		
28	420		
	XXX		
29	435		
30	450	4	37
Mean Maximum Shock Level		16.45	28.65
Percentage Obedient Subjects		10.0%	92.5%

QUESTIONS

1. What is the distinction that Milgram wants to make between obedience and conformity? Why is this distinction important?

2. What were the results when two peers rebelled? To what can we attribute this change?

3. What were the results of experiment 18? To what can we attribute these results? Many people consider the results of this experiment to be more important than any other in the entire series. Why would this be so?

EXCERPT 5

To broaden our understanding of why some people obey and others defy the experimenter, a number of individual tests were given in the subjects. To see whether obedient and disobedient subjects differ in their concept of responsibility, subjects in the first four experimental conditions were exposed to a "responsibility clock." This consisted of a disk which the subject could center. The subject, after performing in the experiment, was asked to "cut slices of pie" proportional to the responsibility of the three participants in the experiment (experimenter, subject, and victim). We asked, "How much is each of us responsible for the fact that this person was given electric shocks against his will?" The experimenter read off the results directly on the back of the disk, which is graduated in the manner of a 360-degree protractor.

On the whole, the subjects did not have very much difficulty performing the task.

The major finding is that the defiant subjects see themselves as principally responsible for the suffering of the learner, assigning 48 percent of the total responsibility to themselves and 39 percent to the experimenter. The balance tips slightly for the obedient subjects, who do not see *themselves* as any more responsible than the experimenter, and indeed, are willing to accept slightly less of the responsibility. A larger difference occurs in assigning responsibility to the learner. The obedient subjects assign him about twice as large a share of the responsibility for his own suffering as do the defiant subjects. When questioned on this matter, they point to the fact that he volunteered for the experiment and did not learn very efficiently.

Thus, the defiant subjects, more often than obedient subjects, attribute primary responsibility to themselves. And they attribute less responsibility to the learner. Of course, these measures were obtained after the subject's performance, and we do not know if they constitute enduring predispositions of the obedient and defiant subjects, or whether they were post facto adjustments of thought. . . .

I had also collected background information on subjects immediately after participation in the experiment. The findings, although generally weak, pointed in the following directions. Republicans and Democrats were not significantly different in obedience levels; Catholics were more obedient than Jews or Protestants. The better educated were more defiant than the less well educated. Those in the moral professions of law, medicine, and teaching showed greater defiance than those in the more technical professions, such as engineering and physical science. The longer one's military service, the more obedience—except that former officers were less obedient than those who served only as enlisted men, regardless of length of service. These were the findings when subjects in the first four experimental conditions (the proximity series) were studied. Many of these findings "wash out" when further experimental conditions were added in, for reasons that were somewhat mysterious to me. (It is true, of course, that the meaning of obedience and disobedience changes from one condition to the next.) My over-all reaction was to wonder at how few correlates there were of obedience and disobedience and how weakly they are related to the observed behavior. I am certain that there is a complex personality basis to obedience and disobedience. But I know we have not found it.

In any event it would be a mistake to believe that any single temperamental quality is associated with disobedience or to make the simpleminded statement that kindly and good persons disobey while those who are cruel do not. There are simply too many points in the processes at hand at which various components of the personality can play complicated roles to allow any oversimplified generalizations. Moreover, the disposition a person brings to the experiment is probably less important a cause of his behavior than most readers assume. For the social psychology of this century reveals a major lesson: often, it is not so much the kind of person a man is as the kind of situation in which he finds himself that determines how he will act.

QUESTIONS

1. *What differences could be noted between obedient and defiant subjects in terms of how they assigned responsibility for shocking the victim?*

2. *Was there any correlation between a person's background, education, religion, and job, and his or her tendency to obey authority?*

3. *What general conclusion did Milgram come to about the correlates of obedience and disobedience?*

ACTIVITIES

❶ Some people have complained that the obedience study was unethical. There are two ways in which the experiment has been said to be ethically compromised. The first problem stems from the fact that the naive subject is lied to about the nature and purpose of the experiment. The second problem is that the obedient subjects suffered enormous stress and conflict over the pain they were causing. Was it right for Milgram and his associates to lie to people this way? Was it right for them to allow the subjects to suffer real pain for the sake of the experiment?

❷ Milgram argued that fewer than 1 percent of all subjects, who answered a questionnaire on their participation in the experiment, indicated that they regretted taking part in it. They said this, even though they knew they had been lied to, and many admitted suffering enormous stress and anxiety during the experiment. If we are judging the ethics of the experiment, does it matter that everyone felt fine about it? Give reasons for your answer.

Obedience and Conformity

The obedience experiments clearly show the harrowing possibilities for destruction that people have within them. All that we need is a sufficiently persuasive authority figure and many, if not most, people will follow along, unless compelling social factors counteract the power of the authority. Perhaps the results should not have been so surprising. People have followed leaders into battle, have committed mass suicide, and have engaged in massive national outbreaks of atrocities when mobilized by those in power. When moral behavior has occurred, it may be, as Milgram suggests, that it is the result not of principle but of the powerful effect of conformity.

We can see the effects of authority and conformity in the behavior of Americans during the Vietnam War. In the early stages, most people supported the war effort, and many people blindly went off to get killed without having more than the vaguest idea of what they were fighting for. The formulaic response—"we are here to fight communism"—was repeated, and it seemed to suffice. However, when opposition to the war began not only to grow but to gain press coverage, it became the thing to do. Soon the power of the military and the government was undermined. It is revealing to note the phrase that was used to describe the early opponents of the war. They were called "prematurely moral," as though showing moral courage before it was socially appropriate was a sin.

What this suggests is that morality—acting on principle rather than obedience or conformity—remains conspicuously unrewarded. Given that this is true, then perhaps we can actually view the results of the Milgram experiments in a more positive light. Remember that at least one-third of all people in the basic conditions (experiments 1, 2, 5, 6, 8) disobeyed. These people had the strength to follow conviction over authority. Given how powerful authority is and given that so much of our training in life is geared towards obedience, it shows that moral courage still exists. What people with strength and conviction need to do is to make their views known. If others see the example of moral courage that they provide, then, through the effects of conformity, moral behavior can be encouraged.

We can see the powerful way in which conformity interacts with authority to create both good and evil. The extraordinary conformity with Nazism can be seen as a case where a malevolent authority interacted with the effects of conformity to allow a mass orgy of evil. On the other hand, the extraordinary moral courage displayed by the Indians in combating British rule in the 1930s and '40s can also be seen as a conformity effect. They saw Gandhi and his followers fighting back in a distinctive way, and people were given the courage to display bravery themselves, just as seeing two peers rebel in the laboratory gave many people the courage to stand up to the experimenter in the obedience experiments.

In this context, we must also consider the relative places of conformity, obedience, and morality in the lives of people. One of the ironies of life is that before one can make autonomous moral decisions, one must be able to conform and obey. Small children, once they become aware of the fact that they are separate beings, are quite egocentric. In the process of growing up, they learn to conform to the behavior, speech patterns, and rules of their peers. We notice, for example, that children of parents who speak heavily accented English speak with the accent of their peers, not of their parents. Learning to conform to peers is an essential phase of social and emotional development. Obedience develops along with conformity, but it is clear that obedience is more difficult to learn and that it requires a more sophisticated consciousness.

With a young child, authority can be maintained by the sheer fact that the adult is bigger than the child, and it does not take long for the child to sense both his or her own weakness in the face of adults and a dependence on them. But, over time, if the child does not internalize the need of obedience, it can be very difficult for the child to accept authority. And yet the acceptance of authority of some sort or other is essential for social systems to run smoothly.

A person who cannot conform or accept authority is likely to be a social menace. Criminals are notorious for their inability to accept the legitimate demands for conformity and obedience that are necessary to maintain any semblance of order in a society. In the process, they show a blatant disregard for the rights and interests of others and a lack of moral concern. The people studied in the obedience experiments, whether disobedient or obedient, did not, as a rule, display this egotistical lack of concern. They were often highly concerned about the victim that they were shocking, and even those obedient subjects, who showed little concern for the victim generally, saw their obedience not as a self-serving act but as a virtuous decision, because by obeying, they were helping to maintain the natural order of society. They were paid to do a job; the experimenter knew better than they did what was going on; the demands of science required that the experiment be completed. These were the types of excuses that people used to justify their obedience.

In most cases, it is clear that such obedience to the requests of authority figures is not only justifiable but necessary. For a person to disobey, it requires that, first of all, the subject recognize that this is an extraordinary situation where the usual rules do not apply. There is rarely a conflict between the demands of authority and the demands of morality. The obedient subjects just acted as though the situation were normal, and they were acting as any good law-abiding person would. On the other hand, the disobedient subjects were not criminals, not moral egoists who were acting out of self-interest, but people who, under most circumstances, would obey or conform to the rules of society. These people, however, had reached a higher stage of development in which they were able to see that, in some circumstances, obedience is wrong.

We can then see that there are three stages in the hierarchy of human moral development, with each stage requiring that one may be able to function at the lower stage. One must first be able to conform; then one can learn to obey; finally, one can learn to be moral. Moral claims made by those who cannot conform or obey (like the rantings of political terrorists) are usually nothing more than articulate justifications of the most grotesque manifestations of egotism. Moralistic slogans are not the same as moral actions, and the use of political slogans with a moralistic slant has been a great boon to some of the more articulate criminal elements in our society. It is not this type of civil disobedience that is required in situations like the Milgram experiments, but disobedience born of human compassion, a willingness to take responsibility for one's actions, and recognition that the means do not always justify the end.

QUESTIONS

1. *What are the three levels of moral development listed in this article? Why are the two lower levels considered preconditions for the third stage?*

2. *Have you ever been in a situation in which someone was not sure whether they were acting from genuine moral principles or from egocentric motives? What kind of conflict did this involve? What did you do?*

3. *How did you justify your behavior?*

Ethics and Alienation

One of the most vivid images in the work of Karl Marx is his picture of "alienated labor." He described the nineteenth-century factory worker as profoundly out of touch with the product he or she produces. The worker may spend years sewing buttons on shirts, but never completes the work on a single shirt, nor does he or she own the shirts or the buttons. Therefore, there is little pride in the work accomplished. It is not his or her shirt, or factory, or sewing machine. To a machine, the operator is a replaceable part, not a person. This feeling of being disassociated from what you are producing or doing is called *alienation*. It is even more prevalent today than when Marx described it one hundred years ago.

The simple act of eating chicken can show us the extent of modern alienation. A modern city dweller can go into a supermarket and buy a box of chicken thighs, pull them out of the plastic wrapper, wash them, and stick them on the grill. One wonders if this rectangular slab ever lived and breathed. When a farmer in Thailand grabs a chicken that he or she has fed, slits its throat, bleeds it, plucks its feathers, disembowels it, and breaks its bones, there is an intimate sense of what is actually involved in eating chicken. No wonder it seems necessary to appease the gods before consumption. The modern city dweller hardly needs to dirty his or her hands. To such a person, appeasing the gods is an anthropological curiosity, and even its Christian equivalent, saying grace, may seem like a stupid ritual. One is alienated from what is involved in eating chicken because one has had so little to do with the process.

But alienation, in the modern world, strikes much deeper than plastic supermarket chickens. It permeates our society. We do not know the people who build our houses, grow our food, or make our clothes. Some companies are involved in everything from animal feed to weapons. You could be contributing to a war effort when you buy Rover doggie treats. And in the area where alienation meets weapons, we find the place where ethics is most difficult and most essential.

Modern technology has made killing easy and impersonal. It has also managed to spread the responsibility around, so that no one feels that they are really to blame. Missiles can kill countless people from a distance; even dropping a bomb from an airplane removes the killer from the victim. And who is responsible for the carnage caused by these acts? The bomb dropper? The person who assigned the task? The military leader who decided to bomb that town? The strategist who developed the policy that certain types of bombs should be used on certain types of targets? The overseers of military policy? The politicians who started the war? Everyone, except the politicians, could say that they were taking orders. And the politicians rarely decide that any particular target should be hit, so they, too, can pass the blame for specific wartime atrocities.

There are others, outside of the chain of command, who do their own part to make these modern weapons possible. There is the vast cooperative effort of scientists, engineers, workers and business people who develop weapons in the first place. They, too, are in some way responsible for the destruction that occurs, but they are even more alienated from the act than those in the military chain. No one screams in pain when the blueprints are approved; no limbs are severed when the parts are stuck together. But without the cooperation of those who design and build the weapons, wars would not be possible.

In the last of the obedience experiments, the naive subject did not have to administer shocks, but had to help the experiment along. Almost everyone complied completely; only three out of forty subjects refused to be an adjunct to shocking another person. Everyone, except the person who drops the bomb, is an adjunct to the act in modern war; and the person who drops the bomb would be severely punished if he or she refused. It is precisely this type of situation that most requires everyone involved to be ethically conscious, and yet this is also a situation where alienation makes ethical thinking most difficult.

Historically, the evolution of this vast, interdependent culture is very recent. We are not mentally or emotionally equipped to respond ethically to remote acts and distant responsibilities. It is precisely these difficult cases, though, that demand our conscious, ethical attention. The alienation of modern war shows more clearly than any other situation the need for ethics in today's world.

QUESTIONS

1. *What other examples of alienation are there in the modern world? What are the ethical implications of these cases?*

2. *What is the relationship between Reich's idea of the mechanical nature of modern people and the concept of alienation?*

3. *How could alienation contribute to the levels of compliance in the obedience experiments? Could there be a relation between Reich's concept of mechanism and the willingness of people to comply with malevolent authority? Can you justify your answer?*

Endnotes for Chapter 5

1. Reprinted with the permission of Harper Collins Publishers Inc. from *Obedience to Authority* by Stanley Milgram. Copyright 1974, Harper and Row.

CHAPTER 6

ETHICS AND THE ENVIRONMENT:
Pollution and the Pocketbook

In this chapter we look at the interaction of personal and political factors in attitudes towards the environment. A description of the problem of acid rain is used as an example of an environmental problem; we then consider the political factors involved in legislating about acid rain, with a selection from Richard Cohen's Washington at Work. *The overall attitude towards environmental issues (and the political problems involved) is further considered through the selections taken from the ancient classic* Dao de Jing.

I t was not so long ago that the consensus of most people—or at least most people who wrote about such issues—was that the morally correct thing to do was to alter the environment to suit the needs of people. The nineteenth-century notions of progress imposed on the leaders of that time a moral obligation to carve up nature to suit our needs. If this meant destroying forests, or driving out forest-dwelling people, or destroying certain species of birds, then so be it. There were those who condemned these practices, but their objections stemmed from romantic or sentimental notions; it was generally believed that such practices were not intrinsically harmful. Environmental pollutants were recognized as health hazards, but no one had any idea what to do about them or how dangerous they were, and the issue was not widely studied.

It was only in the years after World War II that widespread concern about environmental pollutants developed. The explosion of atomic bombs in the late 1940s and '50s led to extraordinary health problems among those exposed to the blasts, and made people aware of a connection between harmful things in the environment and diseases. In 1952, London experienced a hideous, pollution-related smog that caused many deaths and diseases among susceptible people, forcing scientists and the government to look at the effects of pollution on human lives. Since then, concern about the environment has gone from a rather esoteric issue to a safely mainstream political position. Although associated in the public imagination with the political left in the United States, even the most conservative politicians now feel constrained to temper their prodevelopment, anticonservation positions by trying to show that what they propose will not really damage the environment.

Acid Rain

Silent Spring

Perhaps the most important event in the development of an environmental consciousness was the publication in 1962 of *Silent Spring* by Rachel Carson. Her book was concerned with the effect of pesticide use on the environment; but perhaps its greatest impact came from the philosophical position it suggested. Carson believed that it was essential to test the environmental effects of pesticides *before* allowing them onto the market. She was concerned that indiscriminate use of chemical pesticides would upset the natural ecology in a way that would create more problems than they would solve. In general, her position was that we must work with nature rather than attempting to conquer it. This idea is so commonplace today that it is hard to imagine how radical it was in 1962. The negative reaction to *Silent Spring* was so vociferous (and unfair) that many people believe it was responsible for Carson's premature death in 1964.

But, in the long run, the basic tenets proposed in her book have become standard, accepted beliefs. No one seriously proposes the indiscriminate use of dangerous chemicals, and no one suggests that we can totally manipulate the natural environment to suit our needs. But given this consensus, it is interesting to see how society goes about trying to regulate and control pollution, and how the ethical issues become altered by practical concerns. The example we will look at concerns acid rain, an issue on which there is little, if any, dispute about facts, and one in which there is no genuine moral problem involved. The weight given to these facts and the solutions proposed to the problem indicate that ethical flexibility (that is, rationalization) comes easily in the face of economic necessity.

The Acid-Rain Problem

The following description from Roy Gould's *Going Sour* gives us the standard information on the nature of the acid-rain problem.[1]

The Problem in Brief

Acid rain is caused by sulfur dioxide (SO_2) and nitrogen oxides (NO_x) released to the air during the burning of coal, oil and other fossil fuels.[2] Within hours to days, these pollutants are oxidized in the air to form acid sulfate and acid nitrate—commonly known as sulfuric acid and nitric acid. The acids are brought to earth in rain, snow and other forms of precipitation such as dew, mist and frost. Even when the sun shines, microscopic particles of acid sulfate and acid nitrate continually trickle to earth as "dry deposition," a kind of acid fallout which adds as much acidity to the environment as acid rain itself. The various pathways by which acid returns to earth are collectively termed "acid deposition," but this book will use the popular term "acid rain" except where confusion would arise.

The continual shower of acid extends over most of eastern North America from the Gulf of Mexico to northern Canada and out over the Atlantic Ocean. About two thirds of the acidity is acid sulfate, while one-third is acid nitrate. The most seriously affected regions are the northeastern U.S. and Ontario, Canada, which not only receive the most acidic rain but are also the most sensitive to acid rain, because their underlying rocks and soils cannot neutralize the incoming acidity. Other sensitive regions include parts of the Appalachian Mountains, the Great Smoky Mountains, the Boundary Waters Canoe Area in northern Minnesota, and parts of the Rocky Mountains. However, there are pockets of susceptibility throughout the eastern U.S. Furthermore, the direct effects of airborne acid may be felt in a very broad region.

We all contribute to acid rain every time we light a match, drive the family car, or burn any fuel. However, most of the pollution that causes acid rain comes from just a few large sources. Nearly three quarters of the SO_2 emitted east of the Mississippi River comes from power plants, and nearly half of that from just the forty largest coal-fired power plants. A single one of the largest coal-fired plants, such as the Muskingum plant in Ohio, annually emits about as much SO_2 as the Mt. St. Helens volcano—some 200,000 tons a year.

The largest plants use very tall smokestacks, some of which rival the Empire State Building in height. SO_2 from these "superstacks" can be carried hundreds or even thousands of miles downwind, remaining aloft long enough for a considerable fraction of the SO_2 to be converted to acid before returning to earth. Thus the largest plants contribute preferentially both to the formation of acid rain and to the transport of air pollution across state and national boundaries. The 50 largest coal-fired power plants are mostly clustered in the Midwest and the Ohio and Tennessee Valleys, and are currently the focus of Congressional efforts to reduce acid rain. SO_2 is emitted from many of these plants without any pollution controls.

The sources of NO_x emissions are more widely distributed. About 44% comes from transportation (motor vehicles and, to a lesser extent, trains and planes). The remaining 56% of NO_x emissions comes chiefly from the smokestacks of power plants and other industrial sources. A small percentage comes from homes and businesses. Although Congressional attention has focused on SO_2 emissions—the major cause of acid rain—NO_x contributes a significant and growing share of the acidity in rain.

Every state contributes to its own acid rain. However, large amounts of air pollution are carried between states. For example, New York's Adirondack Mountains, an area hard-hit by acid rain, is downwind of the major sulfur emitters in both the Midwest and Canada. According to a variety of studies, including computer calculations and actual field measurements, more than 50% of the acid sulfate in the Adirondacks comes from Midwestern SO_2 emissions, about 20% comes from the large metal smelters in Ontario, Canada, while less than 10% comes from the Northeast itself. Thus even if the Northeast completely eliminated all of its SO_2 emissions, there would be little impact on the amount of acid rain in the region.

But the inequity between regions goes even deeper. Northeastern power plants burn relatively clean oil, in contrast to the cheap, high-sulfur coal burned by midwestern plants. As a result, northeasterners pay up to 4 times more for their electricity. Midwesterners pay an artificially low price for electricity, because part of the real cost of producing electricity—dealing with the consequences of pollution—has been shifted to northeasterners and other parties downwind. Under even the most costly plans for reducing SO_2 emissions, midwesterners would still pay less for electricity than do northeasterners.

The technological solutions to acid rain are at hand, but the political obstacles have been formidable. The midwestern electric utilities and the coal industry have formed a powerful coalition to block legislation aimed at cleaning up acid rain. It is not hard to see why: Reducing SO_2 emissions from power plants would increase the cost of generating electric power. It would also reduce the demand for high-sulfur coal, leading to a decline in production and the loss of thousands of jobs in the industry. The battle lines have been clearly etched between the Midwest and the Northeast.

Another storm has been brewing to the north. The United States sends Canada more than 5 million tons of airborne acid sulfate annually—about 20% of the sulfur emitted in the eastern U.S., and two to three times more sulfur than the U.S. receives from Canada. Considering that Canada has more resources at risk to acid rain than any other nation in the world, it is not surprising that Canada's Minister of the Environment, John Roberts, described acid rain as "the single most important issue" between the two nations.

QUESTIONS

1. *What are some of the sources of acid rain?*

2. *What political problems are created by the fact that acid rain travels?*

ACTIVITIES

❶   This selection does not discuss the actual impact of acid rain on the environment. It should be noted that acid rain can cause the death of a wide variety of fish and other creatures that live in the water, and that it has been connected with the death and stunted growth of many trees. Acidic drinking water is more likely to contain lead and other toxic chemicals. Look up more information on acid rain; try to find specific examples of destruction caused by it.

More on Acid Rain

It is clear from Gould's description of the acid-rain problem that, perhaps, the most interesting ethical dilemma it presents is that pollution, created in one place, is carried to another. Therefore, those who are causing the problem are not suffering the consequences of their action. This has created interregional and international tensions, as became evident in the Gould article. The problem becomes how to convince those who have something to lose by cleaning up their factories that their efforts would be worthwhile. Philosophers may argue that one should think of the greater good, or consider the long-term consequences of actions; but it is difficult to achieve that end when people stand to lose jobs, or when they will be unable to afford to heat their houses.

On the problem of acid rain, the American government waffled and avoided the issues, but finally addressed the problem in the 1990 Clean Air Act Amendments. We all agree that acid rain is bad, and the following selection shows a fascinating aspect of a complex web of competing interests.

Legislating Against Acid Rain[3]

In the final hectic days, as senior lawmakers were dashing from one meeting to another, some clean-air sessions moved to a large room in the Capitol that was a half-minute walk from Majority Leader Mitchell's office. There, the negotiators engaged in the final major round of high-stakes poker on acid rain, the issue that had been the most divisive during Senate and House deliberations.

They largely retained the Senate's acid-rain agreement, which was based on Bush's innovative plan for allowance-trading and a 10-million ton annual cut from the 1980 level of sulfur dioxide emissions. In addition to the Bush–Mitchell link on acid rain and the fact that the House had prevailed on most other issues in the conference committee, the decision to take most of the Senate plan reflected more practical considerations. It was the final major issue facing the conferees and the congressional session was running out of time for full-fledged bargaining. "It was distressing that much of our work in the House got lost," said Rep. Sharp of Indiana.

Sharp and other Midwest lawmakers worked during the final days of the congressional session to salvage a form of pork-barrel aid: additional allowances to ease the pain for their local coal-fired utilities that would be hardest hit by the new rules reducing their acid-rain emissions. Their continuing effort, led by Sharp, to achieve a more direct form of national cost sharing to finance the clean-up never had much chance of success. But Sharp kept the faith for his region. He rejected on principle, he said, a Senate proposal that was designed to placate him with aid narrowly targeted to his local Indiana utility in lieu of the broader Midwest.

The Midwesterners among the House conferees settled on a last-gasp proposal to give 200,000 additional credits to Illinois, Indiana, and Ohio utilities each year until 1999. Because each credit permitted the emission of another ton of sulfur dioxide, the change would allow some of the dirty utilities to meet the new requirements without spending $50 million or more to scrub their emissions. The plan had been developed when EPA staff recalculated the nationwide acid-rain total, including emissions from Energy Department plants. But when the proposal was presented on Oct. 20 at a private, late Saturday-night meeting of the key conferees, the initial reaction was not positive. "It resulted in a Midwest-bashing speech by Max Baucus, who told us that we didn't know what was good for us," said Representative Eckart of Ohio. "He and I had an exchange that was not friendly."

Eckart then walked the Midwest's proposal to Mitchell's office, telling him that the talks were at an impasse and that the region badly needed help. "George Mitchell suggested that if I put together an acid-rain offer that was a balance, he would go along with the 200,000 credits," Eckart said. After some additional shuttle diplomacy that produced relatively minor concessions by the Midwesterners, Mitchell agreed after midnight to override Baucus' opposition and Eckart took the plan back to the House conferees for their okay.

QUESTIONS

1. *Why do you think Representative Sharp rejected a plan that would have helped his own constituents financially, but would not have benefited the region?*

2. *In view of the fact that these concessions would create more acid rain for a period of ten years, what do you think of the efforts of the midwestern representatives to force concessions on the bill?*

Ethical Issues in the Clean-Air Agreement

There are several fascinating ethical questions left by this congressional discussion. We note, for example, that Rep. Sharp takes a moral stand on the issue of aid to his region. The aid that he was proposing was that utilities in his region be allowed to continue to pollute more vigorously than utilities in other parts of the country. Rep. Sharp would simply not consider an offer to allow only his local utility to continue polluting; he insisted that all midwestern utilities be allowed to pollute at higher than national levels until 1999. This was, for him, a *moral* issue! We are clearly dealing with competing moral principles here, and for Rep. Sharp, the more important moral issue was loyalty to his region.

Nevertheless, it is probably true that all the players in this little drama, whatever their competing desires, agreed that, in the long run, there must be a significant and serious reduction in the emissions that cause acid rain. It was that fundamental agreement that made it possible for everyone to settle on a final proposal.

Lao Zi and the *Dao de Jing*

Although clarity is usually considered a virtue in writing, it is interesting to note that the most famous and debated works are notably ambiguous and subject to many interpretations; the Bible, Kant's *Critique of Pure Reason*, and the *Dao de Jing* come to mind immediately. It is funny that, especially with the first two of these, there are people who are convinced that they know exactly and precisely what is being said. The obvious and deliberate ambiguities of classical Chinese are such that it would be hard to believe that one had discovered the "true" *Dao de Jing*. But the massive differences between the translations of this text make one wonder if there is any way to get a grip on it. As a philosophical adjunct to our chapter on environmental ethics, it makes for an interesting study, for it has been seen both as a work of philosophical speculation that emphasized the need for humans to harmonize with nature and as a sort of ancient version of Machiavelli's *The Prince* —advice to a ruler on how to maintain control of a state. There are so many English translations of the work—well over fifty—that it is easy for even a person who knows no Chinese to get a sense of the immense possibilities for interpretation of this little set of writings.

Everything about the work is obscure. We are not even certain if Lao Zi was a real person. The collection of sayings, gathered under his name, may be nothing more than a group of poems and aphorisms, collected over a period of several centuries, that represented a certain school of thought, not unlike the so-called "writings" of Hippocrates. Be that as it may, most commentators and translators impose a sort of unity on the writings by interpreting them in a way that brings out a certain consistency of thought. Whether we are speaking of a king, or a sage, or an ordinary person, one is still advised to follow a path that does not encourage resistance, whether the resistance comes from invading armies, bad ideas, or poor advisors. And few would disagree that the *Dao de Jing* way cannot be described or spoken of adequately. This leaves us fumbling about to figure out what "the way" is, but we can certainly sense that whatever it is, it refers to a path of living that is centered in harmony with the universe.

This sort of vague talk is precisely what antienvironmentalists have always accused "tree huggers" of preaching. There can be no doubt that many fuzzy-brained types, who support environmental issues, do so based on knee-jerk responses that reflect their own emotional needs. Many of these people have also been attracted to the incoherent side of Daoism. But just as there is a scientifically sound basis to a good deal of environmentalist thought, going right back to Rachel Carson, who was a meticulous researcher, there is within the Daoist perspective a good deal of simple, practical advice for living.

ACTIVITIES

❶ Let us look at some selections from *Dao de Jing* and see how they reflect both a general philosophical position and some simple, practical ideas. In doing so, bear in mind that, in many editions, this work, is referred to as the *Tao Te Ching* and the author is called Lao Tzu. These spellings were based on the Wade-Giles transliterations of Chinese sounds. Today, it is standard to use the Pinying transliterations. If one comes across a complete copy of the translation we have used in this text, note that D. C. Lau used the Wade-Giles system, as did virtually everyone else at the time.

Selections from the *Dao de Jing*[4]

EXCERPT 1

LIII

120   Were I possessed of the least knowledge, I would, when walking on the great way, fear only paths that lead astray. The great way is easy, yet people prefer by-paths.

121   The court is corrupt,
The fields are overgrown with weeds,
The granaries are empty;
Yet there are those dressed in fineries,
With swords at their sides,
Filled with food and drink,
And possessed of too much wealth.
This is known as taking the lead in robbery.

121a   Far indeed is this from the way.

QUESTIONS

1. *What could be meant by "the great way"? What clues do we get about the nature of the great way by reading the rest of the selection?*

2. *Could this selection be interpreted as a plea for moderation on all things? Explain your answer.*

EXCERPT 2

LIX

137 In ruling the people and in serving heaven it is best
 for a ruler to be sparing.
It is because he is sparing
That he may be said to follow the way from the
 start;
Following the way from the start he may be said to
 accumulate an abundance of virtue;
Accumulating an abundance of virtue there is
 nothing he cannot overcome;
When there is nothing he cannot overcome, no one
 knows his limit;
When no one knows his limit
He can possess a state;
When he possesses the mother of a state
He can then endure.
This is called the way of deep roots and firm stems
 by which one lives to see many days.

QUESTIONS

1. *What could be meant by saying that a ruler should be "sparing"?*

2. *What relationship could you imagine between "being sparing" and "accumulating an abundance of virtue"?*

3. *Why would it be an advantage for a ruler to make sure that no one knows his limits?*

EXCERPT 3

LXIV

152 It is easy to maintain a situation while it is still secure;
 It is easy to deal with a situation before symptoms develop;

It is easy to break a thing when it is yet brittle;
It is easy to dissolve a thing when it is yet minute.

152a Deal with a thing while it is still nothing;
Keep a thing in order before disorder sets in.

153 A tree that can fill the span of a man's arms
Grows from a downy tip;
A terrace nine storeys high
Rises from hodfuls of earth;
A journey of a thousand miles
Starts from beneath one's feet.

154 Whoever does anything to it will ruin it; whoever lays hold
of it will lose it.

154a Therefore the sage, because he does nothing, never ruins
anything; and, because he does not lay hold of
anything, loses nothing.

155 In their enterprises the people
Always ruin them when on the verge of success.
Be as careful at the end as at the beginning
And there will be no ruined enterprises.

156 Therefore the sage desires not to desire
And does not value goods which are hard to come by;
Learns to be without learning
And makes good the mistakes of the multitude
In order to help the myriad creatures to be natural and to
refrain from daring to act.

QUESTIONS

1. *How could the first six lines of this selection be relevant to a nation's environmental policy?*

2. *What is implied in the line "Whoever does anything to it will ruin it"?*

3. *What is meant by saying that the sage does nothing?*

4. *What advantage does the sage have by desiring "not to desire"?*

5. *Is number 156 contradictory?*

Further Remarks on Lao Zi

The philosophy of Lao Zi reflects an attitude of noninterference in the natural order of the world. The prevailing analogy for the sage is that the sage is like water: soft, apparently weak, but relentlessly strong and durable over time. The respect that sage has for the natural order of the world is part of his strength. This concept of leadership has seemed to many to be appropriate in a world of limited resources, and it may explain the increased awareness of the views of Lao Zi during a period of increased environmental sensitivity.

Endnotes for Chapter 6

1. Reprinted with permission of Roy Gould, from *Going Sour*, by Roy Gould. Copyright 1985, Birkhauser.

2. Nitrogen oxides are a mixture of nitric oxide, NO, and nitrogen dioxide, NO_2, collectively abbreviated NO_x, where $x = 1$ or 2.

3. Reprinted with permission of Macmillan Publishing Company, from *Washington at Work: Back Rooms and Clean Air*, by Richard Cohen. Copyright 1992, Macmillan Publishing Company.

4. Reprinted with the permission of Penguin Books Ltd., from *Tao Te Ching*, by Lao Tzu, translated by D. C. Lau (Penguin Classics, 1963). Copyright 1963, D. C. Lau.

CHAPTER 7

ETHICS AND JOURNALISM:
The News or the Truth

The objectivity of news reporting in a free society is the subject of the first part of this chapter. To what extent can news reporters be objective? To what extent are they, consciously or unconsciously, biased in their presentation? These issues are explored in an essay by the author, in an essay by Noam Chomsky, "Propaganda, American Style," and in a case study that considers the news media's approach to a questionable story that linked Dan Quayle to a man who claimed he sold the ex-vice president marijuana. The possibility of manipulation is further considered in the selections from The Prince, *by Machiavelli, who explicitly considers how the rulers of a nation can manipulate public opinion to their advantage.*

In general, most reporters working for newspapers or for radio or television stations today would agree that they are obligated to tell the truth. They would further agree that they are obligated to omit certain facts in presenting the story. They would probably also admit that these omissions create a certain bias to the story.

The morality of a reporter is a strange one. The reporter is obligated to get information about events from grieving relatives, to record events but not interfere with them during natural or human disasters, and to create interesting, supposedly factual stories on a minimum amount of information in a minimum amount of time. In accordance with the ethical standards of the profession, the reporter is required to be cruel and detached, to drag reluctant information from the unfortunate, and to turn that information into reports that give the appearance of verisimilitude. As an employee of a company (these days, usually a media conglomerate with interests in many things besides the newspaper or television station where the reporter works), it is hard to believe that a reporter is able to be sufficiently critical about issues that directly concern his or her employers.

The classic case of this lack of objectivity occurred when Time-Life merged with Warner Brothers, creating an instant corporate giant that controlled huge areas of news and entertainment. The event was big news in all the news magazines, which provided analyses of the meaning of the merger, its impact on American news and entertainment, how it reflected the corporate mood of the 1980s, and so on. However, in *Time* magazine the story merited only the briefest mention. In this instance, the omission in *Time* was so striking that, shortly afterwards, the magazine issued a rather convoluted justification for this behavior.

Nevertheless, both the style and the manner of most American news simulates objectivity, in contrast to the style and manner of totalitarian news agencies who do little to hide their frankly propagandistic intent. As a result, most people in totalitarian countries have little faith in the information they receive. In democratic countries, by contrast, people are quite willing to believe that the news they receive in their paper, or on television, is fundamentally true. This faith imposes a greater moral burden on the reporter in a democracy, for the reporter's words are likely to be believed.

For this reason, it becomes important to understand and to work through the bias that does exist in reporting material in a democratic society. Perhaps the most forceful exposition of these biases is in the writing of Noam Chomsky, famous for his work in psycholinguistics, but also a tireless chronicler of media bias. Even his turgid writing style can hide neither the passion behind his conviction nor the sheer wealth of information he presents.

Propaganda, American Style[1]

Pointing to the massive amounts of propaganda spewed by governments and institutions around the world, observers have called our era the age of Orwell. But the fact is that Orwell was a latecomer on the scene. As early as World War I, American historians offered themselves to President Woodrow Wilson to carry out a task they called "historical engineering," by which they meant designing the facts of history so that they would serve state policy. In this instance, the U.S. government wanted to silence opposition to the war. This represents a version of Orwell's *1984*, even before Orwell was writing.

In 1921 the famous American journalist Walter Lippmann said that the art of democracy requires what he called the "manufacture of consent." This phrase is an Orwellian euphemism for thought control. The idea is that in a state such as the U.S., where the government can't control the people by force, it had better control what they think.

The Soviet Union is at the opposite end of the spectrum from us in its domestic freedoms. It's essentially a country run by the bludgeon. It's very easy to determine what propaganda is in the USSR: what the state produces is propaganda.

That's the kind of thing that Orwell described in *1984* (not a very good book in my opinion). *1984* is so popular because it's trivial and because it attacks our enemies. If Orwell had dealt with a different problem—ourselves—his book wouldn't have been popular. In fact, it probably wouldn't have been published.

In totalitarian societies where there's a Ministry of Truth, propaganda doesn't really try to control your thoughts. It just gives you the party line. It says, "Here's the official doctrine; don't disobey and you won't get in trouble. What you think is not of great importance to anyone. If you get out of line we'll do something to you because we have force."

Democratic societies can't work like that, because the state is much more limited in its capacity to control behavior by force. Since the voice of the people is allowed to speak out, those in power better control what that voice says—in other words, control what people think.

One of the ways to do this is to create political debate that appears to embrace many opinions, but actually stays within very narrow margins. You have to make sure that both sides in the debate accept certain assumptions—and that those assumptions are the basis of the propaganda system. As long as every one accepts the propaganda system, then debate is permissible.

The Vietnam War is a classic example of America's propaganda system. In the mainstream media—the *New York Times*, CBS, and so on—there was a lively debate about the war. It was between people called "doves" and people called "hawks." The hawks said, "If we keep at it we can win." The doves said "Even if we keep at it we probably can't win, and besides, it would probably be too costly for us, and besides, maybe we're killing too many people."

Both sides agreed on one thing: We had a right to carry out aggression against South Vietnam. Doves and hawks alike refused to admit that aggression was taking place. They both called our military presence in Southeast Asia the defense of South Vietnam, substituting "defense" for "aggression" in the standard

Orwellian manner. In reality, we were attacking South Vietnam just as surely as the Soviets later attacked Afghanistan.

Consider the following facts. In 1962 the U.S. Air Force began direct attacks against the rural population of South Vietnam with heavy bombing and defoliation. It was part of a program intended to drive millions of people into detention camps where, surrounded by barbed wire and armed guards, they would be "protected" from the guerrillas they were supporting—the "Viet Cong," the southern branch of the former anti-French resistance (the Vietminh). This is what our government calls aggression or invasion when conducted by some official enemy. The Saigon government had no legitimacy and little popular support, and its leadership was regularly overthrown in U.S.-backed coups when it was feared that they might arrange a settlement with the Viet Cong. Some 70,000 "Viet Cong" had already been killed in a U.S.-directed terror campaign before the outright U.S. invasion took place in 1962.

Like the Soviets in Afghanistan, we tried to establish a government in Saigon to invite us in. We had to overthrow regime after regime in that effort. Finally, we simply invaded outright. That is plain, simple aggression. But anyone in the U.S. who thought that our policies in Vietnam were wrong in principle was not admitted to the discussion about the war. The debate was essentially over tactics.

Even at the peak of opposition to the U.S. war, only a minuscule portion of the intellectuals opposed the war out of principle—on the grounds that aggression is wrong. Most intellectuals came to oppose it—well after leading business circles did—on the "pragmatic" grounds that the costs were too high.

Strikingly omitted from the debate was the view that the U.S. could have won, but that it would have been wrong to allow such military aggression to succeed. This was the position of the authentic peace movement but it was seldom heard in the mainstream media.

If you pick up a book on American history and look at the Vietnam War, there is no such event as the American attack on South Vietnam. For the past 22 years, I have searched in vain for even a single reference in mainstream journalism or scholarship to an "American invasion of South Vietnam" or American "aggression" in South Vietnam. In the American doctrinal system, there is no such event. It's out of history, down Orwell's memory hole.

If the U.S. were a totalitarian state, the Ministry of Truth would simply have said, "It's right for us to go into Vietnam.

Don't argue with it." People would have recognized that as the propaganda system, and they would have gone on thinking whatever they wanted. They could have plainly seen that we were attacking Vietnam, just as we can see that the Soviets are attacking Afghanistan.

People are much freer in the U.S.; they are allowed to express themselves. That's why it's necessary for those in power to control everyone's thought, to try to make it appear as if the only issues in matters such as U.S. intervention in Vietnam are tactical: Can we get away with it? There is no discussion of right or wrong.

During the Vietnam War, the U.S. propaganda system did its job partially but not entirely. Among educated people it worked very well. Studies show that among the more educated parts of the population, the government's propaganda about the war is now accepted unquestioningly.

One reason that propaganda often works better on the educated than on the uneducated is that educated people read more, so they receive more propaganda. Another is that they have jobs in management, media, and academia and therefore work in some capacity as agents of the propaganda system—and they believe what the system expects them to believe. By and large, they're part of the privileged elite, and share the interests and perceptions of those in power.

On the other hand, the government had problems in controlling the opinions of the general population. According to some of the latest polls, over 70 percent of Americans still thought the war was, to quote the Gallup Poll, "fundamentally wrong and immoral, not a mistake."

Due to the widespread opposition to the Vietnam War, the propaganda system lost its grip on the beliefs of many Americans. They grew skeptical about what they were told. In this case there's even a name for the erosion of belief. It's called the "Vietnam Syndrome," a grave disease in the eyes of America's elites because people understand too much.

Let me give one more example of the powerful propaganda system at work in the U.S.—the congressional vote on contra aid in March 1986. For the three months prior to the vote, the administration was heating up the political atmosphere, trying to reverse the congressional restrictions on aid to the terrorist army that's attacking Nicaragua.

I was interested in how the media was going to respond to the administration campaign for the contras. So I studied two national newspapers, the *Washington Post* and the *New York Times*. In January, February, and March, I went through every one of their editorials, opinion pieces, and the columns written by their own columnists. There were 85 pieces. Of these, all were anti-Sandinista. On that issue, no discussion was tolerable.

There are two striking facts about the Sandinista government, as compared with our allies in Central America—Honduras, Guatemala, and El Salvador. One is that the Sandinista government doesn't slaughter its population. That's a well-recognized fact. Second, Nicaragua is the only one of those countries in which the government has tried to direct social services to the poor. This too is not a matter of debate; it is conceded on all sides to be true.

On the other hand, our allies Guatemala and El Salvador are among the world's worst terrorist states. So far in the 1980s they have slaughtered over 150,000 of their own citizens with U.S. support. These nations do little for their populations except torture, terrorize, and kill them.

Honduras is a little different. In Honduras there's a government of the rich that robs the poor. It doesn't kill on the scale of El Salvador or Guatemala, but a large part of the population is starving to death.

So in examining the 85 editorials, I also looked for those two facts about Nicaragua. The fact that the Sandinistas are radically different from our Central American allies in that they don't slaughter their population was not mentioned once. That they have carried out social reforms for the poor was referred to in two phrases, both buried. Two phrases in 85 columns on one crucial issue, zero phrases in 85 columns on another.

That's really remarkable control over thought on highly debated issue. After that I went through all the editorials on El Salvador and Nicaragua in the *New York Times* from 1980 to the present; it's essentially the same story.

Nicaragua, a country under attack by the regional superpower, did on October 15, 1985, what we did in Hawaii during World War II: instituted a state of siege. There was a huge uproar in the mainstream American press—editorials, denunciations, claims that the Sandinistas are totalitarian Stalinist monsters and so on.

Two days after that, on October 17, El Salvador renewed its state of siege. Instituted in March 1980 and renewed monthly afterwards. El Salvador's state of siege was far more harsh than Nicaragua's. It blocked freedom of expression, freedom of movement, and virtually all civil rights. It was the framework within which the U.S.-trained and -organized army has carried out torture and slaughter.

The *New York Times* considered the Nicaraguan state of siege a great atrocity. The Salvadoran state of siege, far harsher in its measures and its application, was never mentioned in 160 *New York Times* editorials on Nicaragua and El Salvador, up until now [mid-1986, the time of this interview].

We are often told the country is a budding democracy, so it can't possibly be having a state of siege. According to news reports on El Salvador, Duarte is heading a moderate centrist government under attack by terrorists of the left and of the right. This is complete nonsense. Every human rights investigation, even the U.S. government in private, concedes that terrorism is being carried out by the Salvadoran government itself. The death squads are the security forces. Duarte is simply a front for terrorists. But that is seldom said publicly.

All of this falls under Walter Lippmann's notion of "the manufacture of consent." Democracy permits the voice of the people to be heard, and it is the task of the intellectual to ensure that this voice endorses what leaders perceive to be the right course. Propaganda is to democracy what violence is to totalitarianism. The techniques have been honed to a high art in the U.S. and elsewhere, far beyond anything that Orwell dreamed of. The device of feigned dissent (as practiced by the Vietnam-era "doves," who criticized the war on the grounds of effectiveness and not principle) is one of the more subtle means, though simple lying and suppressing fact and other crude techniques are also highly effective.

For those who stubbornly seek freedom around the world, there can be no more urgent task than to come to understand the mechanisms and practices of indoctrination. These are easy to perceive in the totalitarian societies, much less so in the propaganda system to which we are subjected and in which all too often we serve as willing or unwitting instruments.

QUESTIONS

1. *If you have read* 1984 *or are familiar with Orwell's work, do you consider Chomsky's statement true that "*1984 *is so popular because it's trivial and because it attacks our enemies."?*

2. *How do the leaders of a democratic society control the way people think and how was the Vietnam war an example of this procedure?*

3. *What was striking about the debate on American policy in Nicaragua and in newspapers during 1985 and 1986? How was the policy in Nicaragua different from that in El Salvador?*

Postscript to Chomsky

Chomsky's most interesting point is that propaganda is both more necessary and more subtle in a democratic society than in a totalitarian one, and that the purposes of media censorship are quite different in the two types of societies. In a totalitarian state, the propaganda machine churns out material that lets people know what they are supposed to say and how they are supposed to act. The consequences of saying or doing anything else are immediately apparent, but there is no serious attempt to affect the way people think. In a "free" society, it is important to establish the boundaries of the debate, because people can, in fact, say what they think. So ideas that are dangerous to the security of the state must be either marginalized or eliminated entirely. It becomes necessary to affect not merely what people do, but what they think.

This level of thought control seems virtually impossible to mandate. And yet anyone familiar with the writings in the mainstream press in even a western European country, such as France or England, must be impressed by the astonishing uniformity and agreement of opinions and attitudes expressed in the American media. The fundamental beliefs of Americans in their own rightness and goodness have been so thoroughly inculcated that dissension is contained within a rather narrow range of opinions. At the extreme left, we have the *Nation*; at the right, Rush Limbaugh, with anything more extreme effectively marginalized. There is no socialist mainstream opinion expressed, and the far right opinions, expressed in a magazine such as *American Opinion*, have greater readership but no more respect. The opinions expressed on television fall into an even narrower range of positions, as becomes clear from the allegedly confrontational "Crossfire" program; there opinions vary from center to center/right and are put forth by people who then "debate" minutae, or rather, pompously assert positions and interrupt each other without listening.

In a sense, this is not a true ethical problem, for we cannot say that people who present these positions are deliberately trying to narrow the range of acceptable opinion. But it does let us see how narrow the range of ethically acceptable positions are in this country. Where ethical issues truly become important is when we start to consider the way in which specific issues are deliberately distorted by newspapers and television, and the rationalizations that are offered for these distortions. The next selection describes a fascinating case of media self-censorship, one that could certainly inspire those inclined to conspiracy theories, to concoct elaborate fantasies of extraordinary cooperation.

Dan Quayle, Pothead, and "The Information Police"[2]

EXCERPT 1

Within days after George Bush chose Dan Quayle as his running-mate, controversies swirled around reports that Quayle's family wealth and connections enabled him to enter the National Guard to avoid military service in Vietnam, and that similar favoritism got him into law school. Most of the hullabaloo was short-lived: Republican strategists popularized the idea that journalists were unfairly picking on him.

Yet a hidden story of the 1988 campaign was the manipulation of the federal prison system for partisan political purposes, a story involving the Justice Department's collaboration with top Bush-Quayle campaign managers to suppress allegations that Dan Quayle repeatedly purchased marijuana while in law school. Mass media refused to report what was going on, imposing a virtual blackout before the election and declining to publicize dramatic new evidence that emerged afterwards.

"In a free society," *USA Today* editorialized on Election Day, November 8, 1988, "the news media are obligated to feed all the information they can to the public. People can then use that information as they wish—or they can ignore it. They don't need information police standing in the way." The editorial's clarion call for uncowed media (part of an argument favoring exit polls of voters) was terribly ironic, since it came from one of the "information police" giants standing in the way of news involving a Quayle accuser, who remained sequestered in a solitary cell even as the editorial rolled off *USA Today*'s presses.

Four days before the election that delivered George Bush to the Oval Office and put Dan Quayle a heartbeat away, the newspaper near a federal prison in Oklahoma—the *El Reno Daily Tribune*—published a startling front-page article. Written by the paper's news editor, the story disclosed that an inmate, "Brett Kimberlin of Indianapolis, Ind., claims he sold marijuana to Quayle '15 to 20' times between 1971 and 1973. Kimberlin said the sales occurred while Quayle was a law student at Indiana University." An NBC television news crew had filmed Kimberlin at the prison that morning. (The public never saw the footage.)

Journalists immediately deluged the El Reno Correctional Institution with requests to interview Kimberlin. In response, prison authorities scheduled a press conference for that evening at the penitentiary. But when reporters arrived, they were told that the press conference was canceled. Instead of going before news reporters, Kimberlin was put in solitary confinement.

Ordinarily a local newspaper's prominent article with wide interest would have been put on news wires. But this time it didn't get beyond the *El Reno Daily Tribune*. "We checked into this story, we found no substantiation in this matter and we did not run a story," said Robert Shaw, Associated Press bureau chief in Oklahoma City, who sought to justify the news blockade when we reached him by phone. Yet Shaw was not claiming that any inaccuracies existed in the newspaper story—just that AP could not verify the truth of Kimberlin's charges and therefore refused to report on them at all.

Associated Press officials in New York were directly involved in the decision to kill the story, according to AP's national assistant managing editor, Charles Hanley, who confirmed his role in deciding to keep it off the wire. And so it was with every other major news organization in the United States. In the case of

Kimberlin's allegations, and again when federal officials stopped his press conference before it started, top-level national news editors uniformly opted *not* to provide any information to the public. A media logjam continued to block Kimberlin's story.

The mass media remained silent after Kimberlin was again locked in solitary Monday morning—the day before the election—within two hours after noncommercial WBAI Radio in New York City broadcast a taped interview with Kimberlin. That morning, he was scheduled to hold a telephone news conference by way of speakerphone at the Mayflower Hotel in Washington, but his banishment back to solitary made that impossible.

Kimberlin, who'd offered to take polygraph tests, had signed two affidavits swearing that he repeatedly sold marijuana to Quayle. The inmate's assertion could have posed serious problems for the Republican ticket for several reasons. Quayle was adamant that he'd never smoked marijuana, as he reiterated on August 17 just after being named as Bush's running-mate, in answer to a question from ABC's Peter Jennings. Both Bush and Quayle had proclaimed that, as Vice President, Quayle would be in charge of the government's "war on drugs," a plan later dropped. And in his first debate with Michael Dukakis, Bush went out of his way to denounce marijuana use. "For a while, as I recall, it even seems to me that there was talk of legalizing or decriminalizing marijuana and other drugs, and I think that's all wrong," Bush declared. He added: "And we have to be tougher on those who commit crimes. We've got to get after the users more."

Mass media editors—who in the preceding months printed and broadcast totally unsubstantiated rumors that Michael Dukakis had seen a psychiatrist and that his wife Kitty had participated in the burning of an American flag—responded to our inquiries before the election by insisting that the Kimberlin allegations should remain unpublicized out of fairness to the Bush-Quayle team.

QUESTION

1. *What are the specific objections, voiced by the writers, to the way the media handled the situation described?*

EXCERPT 2

Prison Politics

Six weeks after the election, more facts emerged about the inside story behind the Quayle/Kimberlin non-story. On December 19, 1988, the Washington-based weekly journal *Legal Times* front-paged an investigative report which concluded that "Kimberlin's handling by federal prison officials, and the intensive interest in his activities among top GOP campaign aides, suggests that a supposedly apolitical system was being guided by political considerations." Exhaustively researched and written by staff reporter Aaron Friewald, the *Legal Times* article stated: "The Bush-Quayle campaign certainly closely monitored the Kimberlin matter. Mark Goodin, deputy press secretary to the campaign, says he briefed campaign chairman James Baker on Kimberlin's status five times during the final days of the campaign. Goodin, who says he was in regular contact with the Justice Department about Kimberlin, also says that throughout the Nov. 4 weekend, he briefed Lee Atwater, Bush's campaign manager, and Stuart Spencer, Quayle's campaign manager."

In the midst of this intensive briefing process, Kimberlin's scheduled press conference on November 4 was abruptly canceled by J. Michael Quinlan, director of the Federal Bureau of Prisons, an agency administered by the U.S. Department of Justice. Quinlan also gave the order that Kimberlin be isolated, away from any telephone. Those were highly unusual actions. And *Legal Times* observed that "several factors, in addition to Quinlan's personal involvement, lead to the conclusion that the decisions to silence Kimberlin were not simply the product of routine prison administration."

The Justice Department's director of public affairs, Loye Miller, conceded to *Legal Times* the purpose of the disciplinary action: "The Bureau of Prisons caught on that he was going to hold another press conference. So they put him back in." Some officials contended that inmates were simply not allowed to hold press conferences, and that by scheduling one, prison authorities in Oklahoma had violated the federal bureau's procedures. But actually, as *Legal Times* found, "inmate press conferences have been allowed in the past and are not barred by law or policy." What was more, "John Pendleton, congressional liaison for the bureau, says he cannot think of another instance in which the director of the bureau made the decision to place an inmate in administrative detention." Such matters were routinely left to the warden's office at each prison.

"Quinlan's unusual personal involvement in Kimberlin's treatment came amid a flurry of contacts throughout the pre-election weekend among the bureau, high-ranking political appointees at the Justice Department, and senior advisers at Bush-Quayle headquarters," *Legal Times* revealed. Kimberlin's sudden solitary confinement, preventing potentially dramatic press appearances, "served to contain what could nevertheless have been an explosive situation on the eve of the Nov. 8 election," said *Legal Times*. Officials at the Justice Department were acutely aware of just how concerned the campaign managers were as they closely monitored the Kimberlin matter. "Bush-Quayle spokesman Goodin says he kept in close touch with Loye Miller, director of public affairs at the Justice Department, reporting to Campaign Chairman Baker and other senior campaign officials."

While increasingly drawn into fielding pre-election media calls on the matter, Loye Miller apparently served as a savvy switchboard between Bush-Quayle strategists and the ostensibly non-political Bureau of Prisons operating under the wing of the Justice Department. After a long reportorial career that included several years of covering the Reagan White House for Newhouse News Service, Miller was not always forthright while in the employ of the Justice Department, as *Legal Times* discovered: "Miller, after first denying that he discussed the Kimberlin matter with any higher-ups at Justice, now acknowledges that he called Robin Ross, executive assistant to the attorney general. 'I think I thought that if this guy was going to have a press conference, and we were going to get a story out of it, Ross ought to know,' explains Miller."

Kimberlin's legal troubles stretched back to his teens, when he was convicted as a perjurer for testimony he gave about drug dealing. At age 34, he was in his tenth year of serving a 50-year prison sentence as a result of guilty verdicts on charges of smuggling marijuana and involvement in bombings near the Indianapolis Speedway. In summer 1988, a letter to the Parole Commission from former U.S. Solicitor General Erwin Griswold noted that "Kimberlin's prison record has been good" and that "he has received a number of commendations from the prison authorities."

But after he made public his allegations about having been Dan Quayle's pot dealer, Kimberlin's problems kept mounting. In late December 1988, three days after publication of the *Legal Times* exposé, Kimberlin was back in solitary, with the explanation that he had abused telephone privileges in speaking with his attorneys. Kimberlin told us that his unwavering claim about Quayle and pot "can't help me. It can only hurt me. Like this getting thrown in solitary and getting harassed."

Whether Dan Quayle purchased marijuana is in some ways far less important than whether Bush-Quayle campaign officials—including James Baker, on his way to becoming Secretary of State—improperly used the Justice Department to put Kimberlin in solitary confinement, away from the media, for partisan political purposes.

In its detailed reporting, *Legal Times* had broken a significant story. Once *Legal Times* let the cat out of the bag, inquisitive media should have followed up with their own investigations. But that didn't happen. The information police kept standing in the way.

An editor at the Washington bureau of the Associated Press received the advance text of the *Legal Times* exposé the night of December 16, more than 48 hours before publication. But the AP wire never carried a word about it. Nor did the commercial TV and radio networks, PBS, NPR, the news weeklies, the *Washington Post* or the *Los Angeles Times*.

It was the *New York Times*, however, that may have done more than any other media to smother the *Legal Times* exposé. The nation's "newspaper of record" turned the story into old news without ever really reporting at all.

The brief article, appearing on page B9, was a masterpiece of omissions and distortions. According to the *New York Times*, Kimberlin claimed he once sold marijuana to Dan Quayle." The actual claim was "15 to 20 times." The *Times* featured Bureau of Prisons chief Quinlan's assertion that inmate news conferences were not permitted; *Legal Times* had documented that press conferences *were* permitted. The *New York Times* omitted the story's key points: The unprecedented nature of Quinlan's personal intervention resulting in the solitary confinement of a prisoner; the flurry of contacts between Bush-Quayle campaign leaders and Justice Department officials. The only individual quoted in the *Times* story was Loye Miller, the Justice Department official whose veracity about the incident had already been strongly questioned by the *Legal Times* exposé.

We later spoke with the *New York Times* reporter who wrote the article, Michael Wines. "The story had a surface appeal at the beginning because, I mean, it's almost a rule of thumb that if somebody tries to suppress a story it raises the possibility that whatever they're trying to suppress is true," he said. But the story quickly petered out, according to Wines: "I did manage to confirm the fact that they [Bush-Quayle campaign officials] were kept abreast of what this guy was doing. At which point I asked myself—'Okay, what's wrong with that?' " Wines checked with some official sources. "After making telephone calls, I wound up concluding that this was basically a case of one prison inmate who was a publicity hound."

Wines said he might have pursued the story further if he had more time. "But," he hastened to add, "it was after the election and the point in any case was moot. There was a new regime coming in at the Justice Department, in more ways than one, and there was a load of other things on my plate."

QUESTIONS

1. *What was peculiar about the behavior of the prison officials in this case?*

2. *What was the relationship between the prison department and the Bush–Quayle team?*

3. *What do the writers think was the most suspicious aspect of the way this issue was handled?*

4. *How did the* New York Times *article distort the case? What was the writer's excuse for the way he handled the issue?*

Machiavelli

In this chapter, we have been discussing the issue of manipulation. It is therefore appropriate that our choice of philosophical writing be from the work of the man whose name has become synonymous with the cynical control of masses of people. Although this characterization is unfair, there is no doubt that

Machiavelli did offer suggestions for the crass manipulation of the population, and that he was supremely acute in understanding the human frailties that would make such manipulation possible.

Niccolò Machiavelli himself led a life of only modest success. He managed to be on the wrong side, politically, in a number of situations, and seems hardly to have mastered the art of manipulating others in his own lifetime. His most famous work, *The Prince*, was written for Lorenzo de Medici, the ruler of Florence, 1478–92. It was a treatise designed to show how a prince could gain or maintain power in a state, and as such was a practical work. Although Machiavelli has been accused of suggesting the gratuitous use of cruelty and random barbarity, a careful reading of his text will make it clear that, in fact, Machiavelli circumscribed the range of cruelty and made it obvious that one should avoid it unless necessary. He argued, quite realistically, that an act of supposed kindness that weakens the state may lead to greater hardship and more wanton viciousness than a well thought-out cruel act that ends further problems. Few political leaders would disagree with Machiavelli on this point, and history has shown, time and again, how inappropriate acts of pacification, kindness, or acquiescence can lead to immeasurable suffering. Chamberlain's famous appeasement of Hitler, the restoration of ethnic "rights" in the former Yugoslavia, Gorbachev's feebly planned *glasnost* that ultimately weakened and destroyed the Soviet Union are all examples of this problem. It would certainly be more appropriate to call Machiavelli a realist than a sadist, and the following selections will show both his acute understanding of human nature and the realistic streak that made him extraordinarily aware of the dangers of sentimentalizing human behavior.

The Prince[3]

EXCERPT 1

Those Who Come to Power by Crime

. . . Agathocles, the Sicilian, not only from the status of a private citizen but from the lowest, most abject condition of life, rose to become king of Syracuse. At every stage of his career this man, the son of a potter behaved like a criminal; nonetheless he accompanied his crimes with so much audacity and physical courage that when he joined the militia he rose through the ranks to become *praetor*[4] of Syracuse. After he had been appointed to this position, he determined to make himself prince and to possess by force and without obligation to others what had been voluntarily conceded to him. He reached an understanding about this ambition of his with Hamilcar the Carthaginian, who was campaigning with his armies in Sicily. Then one morning he assembled the people and Senate of Syracuse, as if he meant to raise matters which affected the republic; and at a prearranged signal he had all the senators, along with the richest citizens, killed by his soldiers; and when they were dead he seized and held the government of that city, without encountering any other internal opposition. Although he was twice routed and finally besieged by the Carthaginians, not only did he successfully defend the city, but, leaving some of his troops to defend it, he invaded Africa with the rest, and in a short time lifted the siege and reduced the Carthaginians to severe straits. They were compelled to make a pact with him, contenting themselves with the possession of Africa and leaving Sicily to Agathocles. So whoever studies that man's actions will discover little or nothing that can be attributed to fortune, inasmuch as he rose through the ranks of the militia, as I said, and his progress was attended by countless difficulties and dangers; that was how he won his principality, and he maintained his position with many audacious and dangerous enterprises. Yet it cannot be called prowess to kill fellow citizens, to betray friends, to be treacherous, pitiless, irreligious. These ways can win a prince power but not glory. One can draw attention to the prowess of Agathocles in confronting and surviving danger, and his courageous spirit in enduring and overcoming adversity, and it appears that he should not be judged inferior to any eminent commander; nonetheless, his brutal cruelty and inhumanity, his countless crimes, forbid his being honoured among eminent men. One cannot attribute to fortune or prowess what was accomplished by him without the help of either.

One might well wonder how it was that Agathocles, and others like him, after countless treacheries and cruelties, could live securely in his own country and hold foreign enemies at bay, with never a conspiracy against him by his countrymen, inasmuch as many others, because of their cruel behaviour, have not been able to maintain their rule even in peaceful times, let alone in the uncertain times of war. I believe that here it is a question of cruelty used well or badly. We can say that cruelty is used well (if it is permissible to talk in this way of what is evil) when it is employed once for all, and one's safety depends on it, and then it is not persisted in but as far as possible turned to the good of one's subjects. Cruelty badly used is that which, although infrequent to start with, as time goes on, rather than disappearing, grows in intensity. Those who use the first method can, with divine and human assistance, find some means of consolidating their position, as did Agathocles; the others cannot possibly stay in power.

So it should be noted that when he seizes a state the new ruler ought to determine all the injuries that he will need to inflict. He should inflict them once for all, and not have to renew them every day, and in that way he will be able to set men's minds at rest and win them over to him when he confers benefits. Whoever acts otherwise, either through timidity or bad advice, is always forced to have the knife ready in his hand and he can never depend on his subjects because they, suffering fresh and continuous violence, can never feel secure with regard to him. Violence should be inflicted once for all; people will then forget what it tastes like and so be less resentful. Benefits should be conferred gradually; and in that way they will taste better. Above all, a prince should live with his subjects in such a way that no development, either favourable or adverse, makes him vary his conduct. For, when adversity brings the need for it, there is not time to inflict harm; and the favours he may confer are profitless, because they are seen as being forced, and so they earn no thanks.

QUESTIONS

1. *How did Agathocles illustrate the policy of using cruelty wisely?*

2. *How should one inflict injuries on others to assure the security of the state?*

EXCERPT 2

Cruelty and Compassion; and Whether It Is Better to Be Loved than Feared, or the Reverse

Taking others of the qualities I enumerated above, I say that a prince should want to have a reputation for compassion rather than for cruelty: nonetheless, he should be careful that he does not make bad use of compassion. Cesare Borgia was accounted cruel: nevertheless, this cruelty of his reformed the Romagna, brought it unity, and restored order and obedience. On reflection, it will be seen that there was more compassion in Cesare than in the Florentine people, who, to escape being called cruel, allowed Pistoia to be devastated.[5] So a prince should not worry if he incurs reproach for his cruelty so long as he keeps his subjects united and loyal. By making an example or two he will prove more compassionate than those who, being too compassionate, allow disorders which lead to murder and *rapine*.[6] These nearly always harm the whole community, whereas executions ordered by a prince only affect individuals. A new prince, of all rulers, finds it impossible to avoid a reputation for cruelty, because of the abundant dangers inherent in a newly won state. Vergil, through the mouth of Dido, says:

> *Res dura, et regni novitas me talia cogunt*
> *Moliri, et late fines custode tueri.*[7]

Nonetheless, a prince should be slow to take action, and should watch that he does not come to be afraid of his own shadow; his behaviour should be tempered by humanity and prudence so that over-confidence does not make him rash or excessive distrust make him unbearable.

From this arises the following question: whether it is better to be loved than feared, or the reverse. The answer is that one would like to be both the one and the other; but because it is difficult to combine them, it is far better to be feared than loved if you cannot be both. One can make this generalization about men: they are ungrateful, fickle, liars, and deceivers, they shun danger and are greedy for profit; while you treat them well, they are yours. They would shed their blood for you, risk their property, their lives, their children, so long, as I said above, as danger is remote; but when you are in danger they turn against you. Any prince who has come to depend entirely on promises and has taken no other precautions ensures his own ruin; friendship which is bought with money and not with greatness and nobility of mind is paid for, but it does not last and it yields nothing. Men worry less about doing an injury to one who makes himself loved than to one who makes himself feared. The bond of love is one which men, wretched creatures that they are, break when it is to their advantage to do so; but fear is strengthened by a dread of punishment which is always effective.

The prince should nonetheless make himself feared in such a way that, if he is not loved, at least he escapes being hated. For fear is quite compatible with an absence of hatred; and the prince can always avoid hatred if he abstains from the property of his subjects and citizens and from their women. If, even so, it proves necessary to execute someone, this should be done only when there is proper justification and manifest reason for it. But above all a prince should abstain from the property of others; because men sooner forget the death of their father than the loss of their patrimony. It is always possible to find pretexts for confiscating someone's property; and a prince who starts to live by rapine always finds pretexts for seizing what belongs to others. On the other hand, pretexts for executing someone are harder to find and they are less easily sustained.

However, when a prince is campaigning with his soldiers and is in command of a large army then he need not worry about having a reputation for cruelty; because, without such a reputation, he can never keep his army united and disciplined. Among the admirable achievements of Hannibal is included this: that although he led a huge army, made up of countless different races, on foreign campaigns, there was never any dissension, either among the troops themselves or against their leader, whether things were going well or badly. For this, his inhuman cruelty was wholly responsible. It was this, along with his countless other qualities, which made him feared and respected by his soldiers. If it had not been for his cruelty, his other qualities would not have been enough. The historians, having given little thought to this, on the one hand admire what Hannibal achieved, and on the other condemn what made his achievements possible.

That his other qualities would not have been enough by themselves can be proved by looking at Scipio, a man unique in his own time and through all recorded history. His armies mutinied against him in Spain, and the only reason for this was his excessive leniency, which allowed his soldiers more licence than was good for military discipline. Fabius Maximus reproached him for this in the Senate and called him a corrupter of the Roman legions. Again, when the Locri were plundered by one of Scipio's officers, he neither gave them satisfaction nor punished his officer's insubordination; and this was all because of his having too lenient a nature. By way of excuse for him some senators argued that many men were better at not making mistakes themselves than at correcting them in others. But in time Scipio's lenient nature would have spoilt his fame and glory had he continued to indulge it during his command; when he lived under orders from the Senate, however, this fatal characteristic of his was not only concealed but even brought him glory.

So, on this question of being loved or feared, I conclude that since some men love as they please but fear when the prince pleases, a wise prince should rely on what he controls, not on what he cannot control. He should only endeavour, as I said, to escape being hated.

QUESTIONS

1. *Why is it better to be feared than loved? How can one be feared but not hated?*

2. *Why is a reputation for cruelty useful for military discipline? How did Hannibal and Scipio illustrate that point?*

EXCERPT 3

How Princes Should Honour Their Word

Everyone realizes how praiseworthy it is for a prince to honour his word and to be straightforward rather than crafty in his dealings; nonetheless contemporary experience shows that princes who have achieved great things have been those who have given their word lightly, who have known how to trick men with their cunning, and who, in the end, have overcome those abiding by honest principles.

You should understand, therefore, that there are two ways of fighting: by law or by force. The first way is natural to men, and the second to beasts. But as the first way often proves inadequate one must needs have recourse to the second. So a prince must understand how to make a nice use of the beast and the man. The ancient writers taught princes about this by an allegory, when they described how Achilles and many other princes of the ancient world were sent to be brought up by Chiron, the centaur, so that he might train them his way. All the allegory means, in making the teacher half beast and half man, is that a prince must know how to act according to the nature of both, and that he cannot survive otherwise.

So, as a prince is forced to know how to act like a beast, he should learn from the fox and the lion; because the lion is defenceless against traps and a fox is defenceless against wolves. Therefore one must be a fox in order to recognize traps, and a lion to frighten off wolves. Those who simply act like lions are stupid. So it follows that a prudent ruler cannot, and should not, honour his word when it places him at a disadvantage and when the reasons for which he made his promise no longer exist. If all men were good, this precept would not be good; but because men are wretched creatures who would not keep their word to you, you need not keep your word to them. And a prince will never lack good excuses to colour his bad faith. One could give innumerable modern instances of this, showing how many pacts and promises have been made null and void by the bad faith of princes: those who have known best how to imitate the fox have come off best. But one must know how to colour one's actions and to be a great liar and deceiver. Men are so simple, and so much creatures of circumstances, that the deceiver will always find someone ready to be deceived.

There is one fresh example I do not want to omit. Alexander VI was always, and he thought only of, deceiving people; and he always found victims for his deceptions. There never was a man capable of such convincing *asseverations*,[8] or so ready to swear to the truth of something, who would honour his word less. Nonetheless his deceptions always had the result he intended, because he was a past master in the art.

A prince, therefore, need not necessarily have all the good qualities I mentioned above, but he should certainly appear to have them. I would even go so far as to say that if he has these qualities and always behaves accordingly he will find them ruinous; if he only appears to have them they will render him service. He should appear to be compassionate, faithful to his word, guileless, and devout. And indeed he should be so. But his disposition should be such that, if he needs to be the opposite, he knows how. You must realize this: that a prince, and *especially a new prince, cannot observe all those things which give men a reputation for virtue*, because in order to maintain his state he is often forced to act in defiance of good faith, of charity, of kindness, of religion. And so he should have a flexible disposition, varying as fortune and circumstances dictate. As I said above, he should not deviate from what is good, if that is possible, but he should know how to do evil, if that is necessary.

A prince, then, should be *very careful not to say a word which does not seem inspired by the five qualities I mentioned earlier.* To those seeing and hearing him, he should appear a man of *compassion*, a man *of good faith*, a man *of integrity*, a *kind* and a *religious* man. And there is nothing so important as to seem to have this last quality. *Men in general judge by their eyes rather than by their hands;* because everyone is in a position to watch, few are in a position to come in close touch with you. Everyone sees what you appear to be, few experience what you really are. And those few dare not gainsay the many who are backed by the majesty of the state.

In the actions of all men, and especially of princes, where there is no court of appeal, one judges by the result. So let a prince set about the task of conquering and maintaining his state; his methods will always be judged honourable and will be universally praised. The common people are always impressed by appearances and results. In this context, there are only common people, and there is no room for the few when the many are supported by the state. A certain contemporary ruler, whom it is better not to name, never preaches anything except peace and good faith;[9] and he is an enemy of both one and the other, and if he had ever honoured either of them he would have lost either his standing or his state many times over.

Q U E S T I O N S

1. *Why does Machiavelli believe that it is necessary for a prince to be, at times, a great deceiver?*

2. *What does Machiavelli mean when he says that people judge by their eyes, rather than by their hands? How should a prince take advantage of this situation?*

3. *What do you think of Machiavelli's view of human nature? Is he being realistic or cynical?*

Truth and the Media

Machiavelli posits an important distinction between appearance and actual behavior, and maintains that the job of the Prince —or any ruler of a society—is to maintain an appearance of virtue while doing whatever is necessary to maintain the security of the state. The attempts to control the press on the part of politicians through subtle manipulation of facts, careful presentation of ideas, and careful timing of press releases and leaks, are merely twentieth-century variations on this theme. The compliance of the media, in this charade, may seem strange in a so-called free society; but, to a great extent, media people share both the values and the desire for order and peace in their society that political spin doctors are trying to insure. In America, a vigorous, free press was accused of undermining morale and popular support for the Vietnam war. This implies that the job of the press was not to tell the truth, but to be a cheerleader for government policies, even when those policies were incoherent and involved sending many to pointless deaths. During the 1991 slaughter in Iraq and Kuwait, spin doctors and media worked together to create a war picture remarkable for its antiseptic clarity and disregard of the truth. Pictures of death and destruction were nowhere to be seen; instead we saw briefing rooms, interviews with returned heroes and computer simulations of smart bombs hitting targets. It was suggested that these bombs were deadly accurate; only a year after the war was over did we discover that they were certainly deadly, but not all that accurate. Is the job of a journalist in a free society to present only what the censors consider appropriate? Is this ethical? Probably not, in the opinion of many. But Machiavelli would certainly be impressed by the ability of the prince and his minions to create this consensus.

When all is said and done, a journalist does work for a company, and it might well be considered bad form to bite the hand that feeds one. We must also keep in mind that the number of independent news sources that reaches large numbers of people in major cities is fairly limited. If you alienate your boss at, say, Gannett, and you try to find a job at a newspaper in another city, you run a fairly high risk that the newspaper in that city is also run by Gannett. Do you take a chance? And if you say something contrary to your newspaper's position, will your editor run the story?

Endnotes for Chapter 7

1. Reprinted by permission of Noam Chomsky, *Propaganda, American Style*, Utne Review Sept./Oct. 1988, pp. 78–83. Copyright 1988, Noam Chomsky.

2. Reprinted with the permission of the Carol Publishing Group from *Unreliable Sources: A Guide to Detecting Bias in News Media*, by Martin A. Lee and Norman Solomon. Copyright 1990 Martin A. Lee and Norman Solomon.

3. Reprinted with permission of Penguin Books, Ltd., from *The Prince*, by Niccolò Machiavelli, translated by George Bull. Copyright 1961, 1975, 1981, George Bull.

4. *praetor*: an elected official in Ancient Rome who administered civil justice.

5. Pistoia was a subject-city of Florence, which forcibly restored order there when conflict broke out between two rival factions in 1501–2. Machiavelli was concerned with this business at first hand.

6. *rapine*: the violent seizure and carrying off of another person's property.

7. "Harsh necessity, and the newness of my kingdom, force me to do such things and to guard my frontiers everywhere." Aeneid i, 563.

8. *asservations*: emphatic declarations.

9. Ferdinand of Aragon.

CHAPTER 8

ETHICS AND ABORTION:
A Controversy
Dividing a Nation

This chapter begins with a historical consideration of attitudes towards abortion and the development of the present abortion laws. The laws themselves are then examined through a consideration of the relevant Supreme Court decisions. Selections from the various justices' positions—including dissents—are presented. The chapter ends with a consideration of the place of language in framing and encouraging the debate.

In the past few years, the United States has been gripped by a hysterical debate over the issue of abortion. Someone looking from afar at the situation would wonder how this issue became so inflammatory, and what has led to a situation in which, at the height of the conflict—about 1990—there were many people who voted for elected officials purely on the basis of their stand on this single issue.

The purely ethical issues in this situation are fairly easy to outline and have been done so repeatedly. Those who believe that abortion is wrong argue that abortion is the murder of an innocent child. Those who argue in favor of abortion argue that a woman has the right to do what she wants with her own body, and that a fetus carried in her body is still part of her; hence, she has the right to abort it if she wishes. This bald statement of the issue does not give any idea of the legal or linguistic complexity of the problem. For it appears that most people in America believe that abortion is acceptable in some circumstances but not in others. In the minds of most people, aborting a fetus is not an absolute wrong; yet a woman does not have an absolute right to do what she wants with her body. But the issue becomes polarized by the fact that historical and legal aspects of the issue are not properly addressed, and by the extraordinary linguistic gymnastics performed by the defenders of the various positions.

In trying to formulate an intelligent perspective on the issue, it is essential to be aware of some historical background as well as the present legal status of abortion. Perhaps more important, one should consider the reasoning behind these positions and be sufficiently aware of the power of words to distort and inflame opinion. In this way, one can avoid the hysteria surrounding the issue, and make a measured judgment based on facts and genuine moral principles.

Abortion and "Quickening": Law and Custom in the 19th Century

It is interesting that when Justice Harry Blackmun wrote the original majority opinion in *Roe v. Wade,* which established the right of a woman to have an abortion, he felt compelled to enter into a long discussion of the history of abortion law. We have included sections of Blackmun's written opinion in this chapter, but we have largely omitted his discussion of the history of abortion in America. Therefore, we will now briefly summarize the development of American abortion law.

Until about 1850, American law was guided by old English common law, under which abortion was not considered a crime until a woman could feel her child move. In the absence of modern techniques, it was only at this point that a woman could be absolutely sure she was pregnant, and attempts to abort a fetus, at an earlier time, always involved a bit of guesswork. The time when a woman first became aware of her child's movement was called "quickening," which usually occurs in the fourth or fifth month of pregnancy.

It is important to keep in mind that there was no statute law on abortion at all. It was not a major issue in early American history, and when statute law governing abortion came into effect, it was largely due to the efforts of the medical profession to exercise control over what it thought was an area of its domain. We must also keep in mind that the mid- through late nineteenth century was an age when moral legislation became popular. Many laws against adultery, homosexuality, and various specific sexual practices were passed. There may have been a tendency to moralize about abortion as well, although some authorities doubt that the moral issue mattered much. But with the increasing commercialization of abortion in the 1840s, when companies, promising relief of "menstrual blockage," offered their wares on the open market, and when the death rate from abortions was estimated as high as 30 percent, it seemed that the medical profession had an incentive to find some control over the procedure.

It is interesting that in this debate the Catholic Church, now a primary crusader for the restriction of abortions, was pretty much silent. Objections to abortion go way back in Christian history, but the systematic, unified policy of the present-day church did not exist at that time. It also seems that the present-day church position that life begins at conception had not been formulated. Thus abortion before the time of quickening may have been wrong, but it was not murder. Only in the late nineteenth century did the Catholic church position develop in its modern form.

The incidence of abortion by the mid- to late nineteenth century in America was remarkably high. Some estimates put the number of abortions as high as 25 percent of live births. The frequency and openness of abortions undoubtedly contributed to the discomfort of some people, and may have been a factor in the tendency towards restricting the activity. It should also be mentioned that in rural and remote areas during the nineteenth century infanticide was not that uncommon, although the extent of this practice will always be subject to conjecture. We must remember that abortion was then a very risky procedure; infanticide, hideous as it was, may have seemed a safer alternative to the woman.

Throughout this period, abortion was considered horrible by women who engaged in it, but in view of nineteenth-century attitudes towards female sexuality, it is perhaps not surprising that women often did not feel that they were responsible for obtaining an abortion. A theme continually emerges in the letters of the period; a woman, a victim of the insatiable lust of a man, becomes unfortunately pregnant and has to have an abortion. In polite society—and all women who wrote letters were members of polite society—a woman simply did not admit that she wanted or encouraged sex. Therefore, all nonprocreative sex could only stem from the wanton desires of men. Nonprocreative sex with a woman was viewed as a virtual act of rape. It is important to keep this in mind when considering the nineteenth-century attitude towards abortion, because many of today's so-called "pro-life" advocates feel that abortion should be permitted in cases of rape. (This, of course, seriously compromises the traditional pro-life argument that abortion should not be allowed because it is murder. But it just shows how far real people's opinions are from the extreme positions presented as the "two sides" of the debate.)

As a consequence of the changes in the medical profession,

an increasing understanding of the nature of fertility and conception, changing public morality and legalistic political climate, by the late nineteenth-century American law had pretty much developed into the form it took for the first two-thirds of the twentieth century. Abortion was illegal everywhere, and the abortionist became an object of scorn and shame. Rich women could take advantage of the latest medical technology. They could have the procedure performed illegally but relatively safely, while poor women continued to have abortions performed under frightening and unsanitary conditions. In the early 1970s, several states, including New York and Hawaii, made abortions legal. But this trickle of change was to turn into a violent flood when the 1973 *Roe v. Wade* decision suddenly made abortion legal throughout the country.

QUESTIONS

1. *In what ways has modern technology altered our view of acceptable abortion? Explain your answer.*

2. *Why were laws against abortion developed in the nineteenth century?*

3. *Why did women in the nineteenth century feel that they bore no responsibility for abortion? What do you think of their position?*

Legal Decisions Affecting Present-Day Abortion Law

T he two most crucial decisions in present-day abortion law in the United States are *Roe v. Wade*, 1973, and *Planned Parenthood of Southeastern Pennsylvania v. Casey*, 1992. The first decision granted women the fundamental right to have an abortion; the second basically reaffirms Roe, although it is highly critical of some aspects of that decision.

In the following section we have included passages from both Supreme Court decisions. From these we can discern the principles used in determining what is permitted and what is forbidden, according to the Constitution. The eloquent dissension of Justice Scalia on *Casey* presents some interesting points for discussion, both about the nature of abortion law and the nature of the Constitution.

The Supreme Court Opinions on
Roe v. Wade (1973)

MR. JUSTICE BLACKMUN DELIVERED THE OPINION OF THE COURT

This Texas federal appeal and its Georgia companion, *Doe v. Bolton*, present constitutional challenges to state criminal abortion legislation. The Texas statutes under attack here are typical of those that have been in effect in many States for approximately a century. The Georgia statutes, in contrast, have a modern cast and are a legislative product that, to an extent at least, obviously reflects the influences of recent attitudinal change, of advancing medical knowledge and techniques, and of new thinking about an old issue. . . .

The Constitution does not explicitly mention any right of privacy. . . . [But] the Court has recognized that a right of personal privacy, or a guarantee of certain areas or zones of privacy, does exist under the Constitution. In varying contexts, the Court or individual Justices have, indeed, found at least the roots of that right in the First Amendment: in the Fourth and Fifth Amendments: in the penumbras of the Bill of Rights. *Griswold v. Connecticut*: in the Ninth Amendment: or in the concept of liberty guaranteed by the first section of the Fourteenth Amendment. These decisions make it clear that only personal rights that can be deemed "fundamental" or "implicit in the concept of ordered liberty" are included in this guarantee of personal privacy. They also make it clear that the right has some extension to activities relating to marriage: procreation, contraception, family relationships, and child rearing and education.

This right of privacy, whether it be founded in the Fourteenth Amendment's concept of personal liberty and restrictions upon state action, as we feel it is, or . . . in the Ninth Amendment's reservation of rights to the people, is broad enough to encompass a woman's decision whether or not to terminate her pregnancy. The detriment that the State would impose upon the pregnant woman by denying this choice altogether is apparent. Specific and direct harm medically diagnosable even in early pregnancy may be involved. Maternity, or additional offspring, may force upon the woman a distressful life and future. Psychological harm may be imminent. Mental and physical health may be taxed by child care. There is also the distress, for all concerned, associated with the unwanted child, and there is the problem of bringing a child into a family already unable, psychologically and otherwise, to care for it. In other cases, as in this one, the . . . stigma of unwed motherhood may be involved. All these are factors the woman and her responsible physician necessarily will consider in consultation.

On the basis of elements such as these, *appellant*[1] and some *amici*[2] argue that the woman's right is absolute and that she is entitled to terminate her pregnancy at whatever time, in whatever way, and for whatever reason she alone chooses. With this we do not agree. . . . The Court's decisions recognizing a right of privacy also acknowledge that some state regulation in areas protected by that right is appropriate. . . . [A] state may properly assert important interests in safeguarding health, in maintaining medical standards, and in protecting potential life. At some point in pregnancy, these respective interests become sufficiently compelling to sustain regulation of the factors that govern the abortion decision. . . .

Where certain "fundamental rights" are involved, the Court has held that regulation limiting these rights may be justified only by a "compelling state interest," and that legislative enactments must be narrowly drawn to express only the legitimate state interests at stake. . . .

. . . *Appellee*[3] argues that the State's determination to recognize and protect prenatal life from and after conception constitutes a compelling state interest. . . .

The appellee and certain *amici* argue that the fetus is a "person" within the language and meaning of the Fourteenth Amendment. . . . If this suggestion of personhood is established, the appellant's case, of course, collapses, for the fetus' right to life would then be guaranteed specifically by the Amendment. . . .

The Constitution does not define "person" in so many words. [But none of its uses of the word] indicates, with any assurance, that it has any possible prenatal application.

All this, together with our observation that throughout the major portion of the 19th century prevailing legal abortion practices were far freer than they are today, persuades us that the word "person," as used in the Fourteenth Amendment, does not include the unborn. . . .

The pregnant woman cannot be isolated in her privacy. She carries an embryo and, later, a fetus . . . [I]t is reasonable and appropriate for a State to decide that at some point in time another interest, that of health of the mother or that of potential human life, becomes significantly involved. . . .

Texas urges that, apart from the Fourteenth Amendment, life begins at conception and is present throughout pregnancy, and that, therefore, the State has a compelling interest in protecting that life from and after conception. We need not resolve the difficult question of when life begins. When those trained in the respective disciplines of medicine, philosophy, and theology are unable to arrive at any consensus, the judiciary . . . is not in a position to speculate as to the answer. . . .

. . . [W]e do not agree that, by adopting one theory of life, Texas may override the rights of the pregnant woman that are at stake. We repeat, however, that the State does have an important and legitimate interest in preserving and protecting the health of the pregnant woman . . . and that it has still *another* important and legitimate interest in protecting the potentiality of human life. These interests are separate and distinct. Each grows in substantiality as the woman approaches term and, at a point during pregnancy, each becomes "compelling."

With respect to the . . . interest in the health of the mother, the "compelling" point, in the light of present medical knowledge, is at approximately the end of the first trimester. This is so because of the now-established medical fact that until the end of the first trimester mortality in abortion may be less than mortality in normal childbirth. It follows that, from and after this point, a State may regulate the abortion procedure to the extent that the regulation reasonably relates to the preservation and protection of maternal health. . . .

This means, on the other hand, that, for the period of pregnancy prior to this "compelling" point, the attending physician, in consultation with his patient, is free to determine, without regulation by the State, that, in his medical judgment, the patient's pregnancy should be terminated. If that decision is reached, the judgment may be effectuated by an abortion free of interference by the State.

With respect to the . . . interest in potential life, the "compelling" point is at viability. This is so because the fetus then presumably has the capability of meaningful life outside the mother's womb. . . . If the State is interested in protecting fetal life after viability, it may go so far as to proscribe abortion during that period, except when it is necessary to preserve the life or health of the mother.

Measured against these standards, [the Texas state] . . . sweeps too broadly . . . [and] therefore, cannot survive the constitutional attack made upon it here. . . .

QUESTIONS

1. *In what way does the Constitution, according to Justice Blackmun, recognize a right to privacy?*

2. *How does Justice Blackmun connect the privacy right to the right to abortion? When does he believe that abortion is only a limited right?*

3. *Why did the state of Texas believe that a woman does not have the right to abortion? Why does Justice Blackmun believe that the Texas law "sweeps too broadly"?*

MR. JUSTICE REHNQUIST, DISSENTING

. . . I have difficulty in concluding, as the Court does, that the right of "privacy" is involved in this case. Texas . . . bars the performance of a medical abortion by a licensed physician on a plaintiff such as Roe. A transaction resulting in an operation such as this is not "private" in the ordinary usage of that word. Nor is the "privacy" that the Court finds here even a distant relative of the freedom from searches and seizures protected by the Fourth Amendment. . . .

If the Court means by the term "privacy" no more than that the claim of a person to be free from unwanted state regulation of consensual transactions may be a form of "liberty" protected by the Fourteenth Amendment, there is no doubt that similar claims have been upheld in our earlier decisions on the basis of that liberty. I agree with the statement of Mr. Justice Stewart in his concurring opinion that the "liberty," against deprivation of which without due process the Fourteenth Amendment protects, embraces more than the rights found in the Bill of Rights. But that liberty is not guaranteed absolutely against deprivation, only against deprivation without due process of law. The test traditionally applied in the area of social and economic legislation is whether or not a law . . . has a rational relation to a valid state objective. . . . If the Texas statute were to prohibit an abortion even where the mother's life is in jeopardy, I have little doubt that such a statute would lack a rational relation to a valid state objective . . . .

The Court eschews the history of the Fourteenth Amendment in its reliance on the "compelling state interest" test. . . .

. . . [T]he adoption of the compelling state interest standard will inevitably require this Court to examine the legislative policies and pass on the wisdom of these policies in the very process of deciding whether a particular state interest put forward may or may not be "compelling." The decision here to break pregnancy into three distinct terms and to outline the permissible restrictions the State may impose in each one, for example, partakes more of judicial legislation than it does of a determination of the intent of the drafters of the Fourteenth Amendment.

The fact that a majority of the States . . . have had restrictions on abortions for at least a century is a strong indication, it seems to me, that the asserted right to an abortion is not "so rooted in the traditions and conscience of our people as to be ranked as fundamental." Even today, when society's views on abortion are changing, the very existence of the debate is evidence that the "right" to an abortion is not so universally accepted as the appellant would have us believe.

. . . By the time of the adoption of the Fourteenth Amendment in 1868, there were at least 36 laws enacted by state or territorial legislatures limiting abortion. . . .

. . . The only conclusion possible from this history is that the drafters did not intend to have the Fourteenth Amendment withdraw from the States the power to legislate with respect to this matter.

QUESTIONS

1. Why does Justice Rehnquist believe that privacy rights are not involved in this case?

2. What other objections does Justice Rehnquist have to the Court's decision?

Planned Parenthood of Southeastern Pennsylvania v. Casey (1992)

Justice O'Connor, Justice Kennedy, and **Justice Souter** announced the judgment of the Court and delivered the opinion of the Court with respect to Parts I, II, III, V-A, V-C, and VI, an opinion with respect to Part V-E, in which **Justice Stevens** joins, and an opinion with respect to Parts IV, V-B, and V-D.

EXCERPT 1

Liberty finds no refuge in a jurisprudence of doubt. Yet 19 years after our holding that the Constitution protects a woman's right to terminate her pregnancy in its early stages, *Roe v. Wade*, that definition of liberty is still questioned. Joining the respondents as *amicus curiae*,[4] the United States, as it has done in five other cases in the last decade, again asks us to overrule *Roe*.

At issue in these cases are five provisions of the Pennsylvania Abortion Control Act of 1982 as amended in 1988 and 1989. . . . The Act requires that a woman seeking an abortion give her informed consent prior to the abortion procedure, and specifies that she be provided with certain information at least 24 hours before the abortion is performed. For a minor to obtain an abortion, the Act requires the informed consent of one of her parents, but provides for a judicial bypass option if the minor does not wish to or cannot obtain a parent's consent. Another provision of the Act requires that unless certain exceptions apply, a married woman seeking an abortion must sign a statement indicating that she has notified her husband of her intended abortion. The Act exempts compliance with these three requirements in the event of a "medical emergency," [as] defined in . . . the Act. In addition to the above provisions regulating the performance of abortions, the Act imposes certain reporting requirements on facilities that provide abortion services.

. . . The Court of Appeals found it necessary to follow an elaborate course of reasoning even to identify the first premise to use to determine whether the statute enacted by Pennsylvania meets constitutional standards. And at oral argument in this Court, the attorney for the parties challenging the statute took the position that none of the enactments can be upheld without overruling *Roe v. Wade*. We disagree with that analysis; but we acknowledge that our decisions after *Roe* cast doubt upon the meaning and reach of its holding. . . . State and federal courts as well as legislatures throughout the Union must have guidance as they seek to address this subject in conformance with the Constitution. Given these premises, we find it imperative to review once more the principles that define the rights of the woman and the legitimate authority of the State respecting the termination of pregnancies by abortion procedures.

After considering the fundamental constitutional questions resolved by *Roe*, principles of institutional integrity, and the rule of *stare decisis*,[5] we are led to conclude this: the essential holding of *Roe v. Wade* should be retained and once again reaffirmed.

It must be stated at the outset and with clarity that *Roe*'s essential holding, the holding we reaffirm, has three parts. First is a recognition of the right of the woman to choose to have an abortion before viability and to obtain it without undue interference from the State. Before viability, the State's interests are not strong enough to support a prohibition of abortion or the imposition of a substantial obstacle to the woman's effective right to elect the procedure. Second is a confirmation of the State's power to restrict abortions after fetal viability, if the law contains exceptions for pregnancies which endanger a woman's life or health. And third is the principle that the State has legitimate interests from the outset of the pregnancy in protecting the health of the woman and the life of the fetus that may become a child. These principles do not contradict one another; and we adhere to each.

... We give this summary:

(a) To protect the central right recognized by *Roe v. Wade* while at the same time accommodating the State's profound interest in potential life, we will employ the undue burden analysis as explained in this opinion. An undue burden exists, and therefore a provision of law is invalid, if its purpose or effect is to place a substantial obstacle in the path of a woman seeking an abortion before the fetus attains viability.

(b) We reject the rigid trimester framework of *Roe v. Wade*. To promote the State's profound interest in potential life, throughout pregnancy the State may take measures to ensure that the woman's choice is informed, and measures designed to advance this interest will not be invalidated as long as their purpose is to persuade the woman to choose childbirth over abortion. These measures must not be an undue burden on the right.

(c) As with any medical procedure, the State may enact regulations to further the health or safety of a woman seeking an abortion. Unnecessary health regulations that have the purpose or effect of presenting a substantial obstacle to a woman seeking an abortion impose an undue burden on the right.

(d) Our adoption of the undue burden analysis does not disturb the central holding of *Roe v. Wade*, and we reaffirm that holding. Regardless of whether exceptions are made for particular circumstances, a State may not prohibit any woman from making the ultimate decision to terminate her pregnancy before viability.

(e) We also reaffirm *Roe*'s holding that "subsequent to viability, the State in promoting its interest in the potentiality of human life may, if it chooses, regulate, and even proscribe, abortion except where it is necessary, in appropriate medical judgment, for the preservation of the life or health of the mother."

These principles control our assessment of the Pennsylvania statute. . . .

QUESTIONS

1. *What is the "essential holding" of the* Roe *decision that the writers of the opinion wish to uphold?*

2. *Where do they feel that* Roe *can be challenged?*

3. *What do they mean by using "undue burden" as a criterion for allowing abortion? What do you think of this idea?*

Justice Scalia, with whom the **Chief Justice, Justice White,** and **Justice Thomas** join, concurring in the judgment in part and dissenting in part.

EXCERPT 2

. . . The States may, if they wish, permit abortion-on-demand, but the Constitution does not require them to do so. The permissibility of abortion, and the limitations upon it, are to be resolved like most important questions in our democracy: by citizens trying to persuade one another and then voting. . . . A State's choice between two positions on which reasonable people can disagree is constitutional even when (as is often the case) it intrudes upon a "liberty" in the absolute sense. Laws against bigamy, for example—which entire societies of reasonable people disagree with—intrude upon men and women's liberty to marry and live with one another. But bigamy happens not to be a liberty specially "protected" by the Constitution.

That is, quite simply, the issue in this case: not whether the power of a woman to abort her unborn child is a "liberty" in the absolute sense; or even whether it is a liberty of great importance to many women. Of course it is both. The issue is whether it is a liberty protected by the Constitution of the United States. I am sure it is not. I reach that conclusion not because of anything so exalted as my views concerning the "concept of existence, of meaning, of the universe, and of the mystery of human life." Rather, I reach it for the same reason I reach the conclusion that bigamy is not constitutionally protected—because of two simple facts: (1) the Constitution says absolutely nothing about it, and (2) the longstanding traditions of American society have permitted it to be legally proscribed.

. . . I do not see how ["reasoned judgment"] could possibly

have produced the answer the Court arrived at in *Roe v. Wade* [as the joint opinion maintains]. . . . "[R]easoned judgment" does not begin by begging the question, as *Roe* and subsequent cases unquestionably did by assuming that what the State is protecting is the mere "potentiality of human life." The whole argument of abortion opponents is that what the Court calls the fetus and what others call the unborn child is a human life. Thus, whatever answer *Roe* came up with after conducting its "balancing" is bound to be wrong, unless it is correct that the human fetus is in some critical sense merely potentially human. There is of course no way to determine that as a legal matter: it is in fact a value judgment. . . .

The emptiness of the "reasoned judgment" that produced *Roe* is displayed in plain view by the fact that, after more than 19 years of effort by some of the brightest (and most determined) legal minds in the country, after more than 10 cases upholding abortion rights in this Court, and after dozens upon dozens of amicus briefs submitted in this and other cases, the best the Court can do to explain how it is that the word "liberty" must be thought to include the right to destroy human fetuses is to rattle off a collection of adjectives that simply decorate a value judgment and conceal a political choice. The right to abort, we are told, inheres in "liberty" because it is among "a person's most basic decisions"; it involves a "most intimate and personal choice"; it is "central to personal dignity and autonomy"; it "originates within the zone of conscience and belief"; it is "too intimate and personal" for state interference; it reflects "intimate views" of a "deep, personal character"; it involves "intimate relationships," and notions of "personal autonomy and bodily integrity"; and it concerns a particularly "important decision." But it is obvious to anyone applying "reasoned judgment" that the same adjectives can be applied to many forms of conduct that this Court . . . has held are not entitled to constitutional protection—because, like abortion, they are forms of conduct that have long been criminalized in American society. Those adjectives might be applied, for example, to homosexual sodomy, polygamy, adult incest, and suicide, all of which are equally "intimate" and "deeply personal" decisions involving "personal autonomy and bodily integrity," and all of which can constitutionally be proscribed because it is our unquestionable constitutional tradition that they are proscribable. It is not reasoned judgment that supports the Court's decision; only personal predilection. . . .

. . . [The undue burden] standard is inherently manipulable and will prove hopelessly unworkable in practice.

. . . Defining an "undue burden" as an "undue hindrance" (or a "substantial obstacle") hardly "clarifies" the test. Consciously or not, the joint opinion's verbal shell game will conceal raw judicial policy choices concerning what is "appropriate" abortion legislation. . . .

. . . [T]he approach of the joint opinion is, for the most part, simply to highlight certain facts in the record that apparently strike the three Justices as particularly significant in establishing (or refuting) the existence of an undue burden; after describing these facts, the opinion then simply announces that the provision either does or does not impose a "substantial obstacle" or an "undue burden." We do not know whether the same conclusions could have been reached on a different record, or in what respects the record would have had to differ before an opposite conclusion would have been appropriate. The inherently standardless nature of this inquiry invites the district judge to give effect to his personal preferences about abortion. By finding and relying upon the right facts, he can invalidate, it would seem, almost any abortion restriction that strikes him as "undue"—subject, of course, to the possibility of being reversed by a Circuit Court or Supreme Court that is as unconstrained in reviewing his decision as he was in making it. . . .

QUESTIONS

1. *Justice Scalia clearly indicates his fundamental reason for objecting to* Roe. *Why does he find* Roe *wanting? How does he think the legality of abortion should be decided?*

2. *What is Justice Scalia's objection to the idea that the right to abort inheres in the concept of liberty?*

3. *Why does Justice Scalia object to the "undue burden" idea of the joint opinion posited in* Casey?

The opinion of **Justice Blackmun**.

EXCERPT 3

At long last, The Chief Justice admits it. Gone are the contentions that the issue need not be (or has not been) considered. There, on the first page, for all to see, is what was expected: "We believe that *Roe* was wrongly decided, and that it can and should be overruled consistently with our traditional approach to *stare decisis* in constitutional cases." If there is much reason to applaud the advances made by the joint opinion today, there is far more to fear from The Chief Justice's opinion.

The Chief Justice's criticism of *Roe* follows from his stunted conception of individual liberty. While recognizing that the Due Process Clause protects more than simple physical liberty, he then goes on to construe this Court's personal-liberty cases as establishing only a laundry list of particular rights, rather than a principled account of how these particular rights are grounded in a more general right of privacy. This constricted view is reinforced by The Chief Justice's exclusive reliance on tradition as a source of fundamental rights. . . .

Under [The Chief Justice's] standard, States can ban abortion if that ban is rationally related to a legitimate state interest— a standard which the United States calls "deferential, but not toothless." Yet when pressed at oral argument to describe the teeth, the best protection that the Solicitor General could offer to women was that a prohibition, enforced by criminal penalties, with no exception for the life of the mother, "could raise very serious questions." Perhaps, the Solicitor General offered, the failure to include an exemption for the life of the mother would be "arbitrary and capricious." If, as The Chief Justice contends, the undue burden test is made out of whole cloth, the so-called "arbitrary and capricious" limit is the Solicitor General's "new clothes."

Even if it is somehow "irrational" for a State to require a woman to risk her life for her child, what protection is offered for women who become pregnant through rape or incest? Is there anything arbitrary or capricious about a State's prohibiting the sins of the father from being visited upon his offspring?

But, we are reassured, there is always the protection of the democratic process. While there is much to be praised about our democracy, our country since its founding has recognized that there are certain fundamental liberties that are not to be left to the whims of an election. A woman's right to reproductive choice is one of those fundamental liberties. Accordingly, that liberty need not seek refuge at the ballot box.

QUESTIONS

1. *Why does Justice Blackmun believe that the Chief Justice has a "stunted conception of individual liberty"?*

2. *What fundamental liberties does Justice Blackmun believe are protected by the* Roe *decision?*

Language and the Abortion Debate

It is easy to feel that most people take sides in the abortion issue depending on simple emotional reactions; they get attached to the "abortion is murder" label and come away feeling that it is wrong, or they get attached to a "woman's rights" label and feel that abortion should be legal. Even the chosen labels of the movement suggest the emotional appeal of each position. Who could resist being "pro-life"? And what American could resist being "pro-choice"? Because each label covers a huge variety of positions, the labels hardly give us any information by themselves. There is little doubt that they are extremely misleading as well, for few pro-choice advocates are in favor of limitless choice and even the phrase "pro-life" makes one wonder whose life they are considering.

It has been said that whether one approves of abortion or not depends on whether you call the procedure "murder of an unborn child" or "pregnancy termination." And lest one believe that euphemism is a late twentieth-century invention, one should know that the favorite phrase used for pregnancy by nineteenth-century purveyors of over-the-counter abortions was "menstrual blockage." Indeed, no present-day pro-choice phrase comes close to presenting abortion in that light.

George Orwell, in his famous essay "Politics and the English Language," notes that political orthodoxy seems to demand a certain style of writing and speaking. The style he says, is lifeless and mechanical, infested with clichés and virtually devoid of meaning. In 1984, Orwell calls this type of talking "duckspeaking," meaning to quack like a duck. He further notes that, in the ultra-orthodox totalitarian state imagined in his novel, to call someone a duckspeaker is a phrase of approbation when applied to an ally and a phrase of scorn when applied to an enemy.

It is fascinating to notice the extent to which duckspeaking is practiced by both sides in the abortion debate. In fact, any rational observer will note that for the most part the debate is not a debate at all. Both sides rally forces to the call of duty with duckspeak and clashes then take place. The "pro-life" people seem determined to prevent forcibly what they consider murder; the "pro-choice" people seem determined not to allow even the more self-controlled "pro-lifers" to make their opponents uncomfortable by marching in front of abortion clinics.

Language in these cases is used not for the content of what is said but for emotional arousal, and clichés and jargon are extremely useful in achieving this end. They are familiar and therefore comforting, and the use of cliché and jargon identify speaker and listener as members of the same group. This achieves the immediate "we are in this together" mood that is so necessary to arouse collective hatred and unthinking conformity.

Orwell, in noticing this, thought that perhaps one way to encourage more intelligent and rational debate would be to cultivate the careful and perceptive use of language. Conversely, in 1984, he imagined a society in which language was controlled in order to limit thought—a society in which there were no words available to create intelligent thought. It is difficult to know, however, whether bad language or sloppy thought comes first, and the issue has many of the characteristics of a chicken-and-egg question. Certainly, the accounts of the ancient Athenians suggest that humans have long been seduced by bad language that plays on emotions and that makes people feel that thinking is unnecessary. Although abortion is, by its very nature, an emotional hot spot, it is only through a serious reasoned consideration of the historical, legal, and medical realities of the situation that we can even make an informed judgment about where we stand on the issue.

QUESTIONS

1. *What do you think of Orwell's idea that, if you limit language, you can limit thought? How realistic is it to assume that we can limit language?*

ACTIVITIES

❶   Find some examples of clichés or meaningless phrases used by a politician in some speech given recently. Analyze the clichés in terms of the emotional tone used. Name the actual intent of the speech.

Endnotes for Chapter 8

1. *appellant*: legal term referring to the party that appeals a decision to a higher tribunal.

2. *amici*: in Latin, friend.

3. *appellee*: the defendant in an appeals proceeding.

4. *amicus curiae*: literally, a friend of the court, or, a person who is invited by the court to give advice upon some matter pending before it.

5. *stare decisis*: in law, a doctrine that states that principles of law on which the court rested a previous decision are authoritative in all future cases in which the facts are substantially the same.

CHAPTER 9

ETHICS AND EDUCATION:
Inculcating Values

We initially consider the question of whether it is, in fact, possible to inculcate values in children. After a general consideration of the problem, we include a passage from John Stuart Mill's Autobiography, *in which he deals with the relationship between his own education and the development of his value system. We next look at the ways values can be inculcated through even the most basic presentation of facts, as we examine the approaches to the War of 1812 offered in an American and a Canadian history textbook. We end with the selections from Plato's* Republic *that discuss education; here, Plato actively advocates the inculcation of values.*

The Aims of Education

Throughout history, education has served two purposes: to impart information and to inculcate values. As we shall see, these roles overlap to a greater degree than we would suspect, but it should really not disturb anyone that they do. A stated aim of the common-school movement in America, which advocated and established state-supported schools in the nineteenth century, was to assimilate and Americanize children; in other words, to help establish a common culture. It would be virtually impossible to measure such things, but there also can be little doubt that the national character of people has been strongly influenced by the different ways they have been educated. The humanistic and peculiarly rigid French educational system seems thoroughly at one with the French national character, whereas the different behaviors and beliefs of the various classes in England seem easily understandable in view of the vast differences in the way they are educated.

In recent years, there has been a significant debate on the issue of inculcating values in schools. Some have wondered about which values should be inculcated in a pluralistic society. Although all would argue that virtues, such as tolerance, concern for fellows, and a sense of civic duty should be expressed, there is a great deal of disagreement on how these ideas should be spread, and what they mean in practical terms. There was controversy over a recent book introduced in New York City schools which seemed to suggest tolerance for a homosexual lifestyle by telling the story of a child who lived with his father and his father's "roommate." Some have argued that such books actually promote a homosexual lifestyle.

There are also those who believe that the mandated separation of church and state in America has led to an antireligious prejudice in school curriculum. These people usually believe that schools should promote Christian values, by which they virtually mean the promotion of Christianity itself. They are indignant at mention of historical information that may put Christianity in a bad light.

What is interesting about these debates is the unstated assumption that children's attitudes will be strongly influenced by the values taught in schools. In fact, we have no firm evidence that values, stated in school, have that much influence on what children do, and the extent of influence that education has on children would be almost impossible to measure convincingly. The issue is exceedingly complex, because we also would have to wonder what values are inculcated unconsciously; for example, by the teacher's behavior, by the unconscious cultural assumptions embedded in the text, by the bias of the writers, and by the atmosphere of the school and its setting. These factors must influence the way children think and feel, but the relative weights of each factor is almost impossible to separate out.

It seems obvious that any exploration of the ethical responsibilities of a teacher, or of education in general, must begin with an exploration of the unconscious and the instinctive ways in which we impart our values. Therefore, this section will begin with a fascinating account by John Stuart Mill of his own unique education, taken from his *Autobiography*. He freely discusses the values inculcated in him by his father; it also becomes clear that as overwhelming an influence as his father was in his life, as an adult Mill embraced a somewhat different set of values.

After noting this personal account of the influence of a unique education on one individual, we shall see how an allegedly objective account of the same historical event can be deeply value-laden and can imply not only a different perspective on the same event, but a different way of thinking altogether. We shall also look at a prescription for the education of people by Plato, who clearly believed that the inculcation of values was an essential, lifelong task.

This chapter explores different ways in which values are inculcated through education. The Mill selection shows how values can be induced on a personal level; the selection from history texts on the War of 1812 show how values can be conveyed unconsciously; and the selection by Plato shows how value can be overtly and deliberately taught. In fact, all of us are exposed to all three approaches, for we learn through individual instruction, unconscious absorption of values, and systematic advocacy of points of view.

John Stuart Mill

The Moral Education of John Stuart Mill[1]

My father's moral convictions, wholly dissevered from religion, were very much of the character of those of the Greek philosophers; and were delivered with the force and decision which characterized all that came from him. Even at the very early age at which I read with him the *Memorabilia* of Xenophon, I imbibed from that work and from his comments a deep respect for the character of Socrates; who stood in my mind as a model of ideal excellence: and I well remember how my father at that time impressed upon me the lesson of the "Choice of Hercules." At a somewhat later period the lofty moral standard exhibited in the writings of Plato operated upon me with great force. My father's moral inculcations were at all times mainly those of the "Socratici viri": justice, temperance (to which he gave a very extended application), veracity, perseverance, readiness to encounter pain and especially labour; regard for the public good; estimation of persons according to their merits, and of things according to their intrinsic usefulness; a life of exertion in contradiction to one of self-indulgent ease and sloth. These and other moralities he conveyed in brief sentences, uttered as occasion arose, of grave exhortation, or stern reprobation and contempt.

But though direct moral teaching does much, indirect does more; and the effect my father produced on my character, did not depend solely on what he said or did with that direct object, but also, and still more, on what manner of man he was.

In his views of life he partook of the character of the Stoic, the Epicurean, and the Cynic, not in the modern but the ancient sense of the word. In his personal qualities the Stoic predominated. His standard of morals was Epicurean, inasmuch as it was utilitarian, taking as the exclusive test of right and wrong the tendency of actions to produce pleasure or pain. But he had (and this was the Cynic element) scarcely any belief in pleasure; at least in his later years, of which alone, on this point, I can speak confidently. He was not insensible to pleasures; but he deemed very few of them worth the price which, at least in the present state of society, must be paid for them. The greater number of miscarriages in life, he considered to be attributable to the over-valuing of pleasures. Accordingly, temperance, in the large sense intended by the Greek philosophers—stopping short at the point of moderation in all indulgences—was with him, as with them, almost the central point of educational precept. His inculcations of this virtue fill a large place in my childish remembrances. He thought human life a poor thing at best, after the freshness of youth and of unsatisfied curiosity had gone by. This was a topic on which he did not often speak, especially, it may be supposed, in the presence of young persons: but when he did, it was with an air of settled and profound conviction. He would sometimes say, that if life were made what it might be, by good government and good education, it would be worth having: but he never spoke with anything like enthusiasm even of that possibility. He never varied in rating intellectual enjoyments above all others, even in value as pleasures, independently of their ulterior benefits. The pleasures of the benevolent affections he placed high in the scale; and used to say, that he had never known a happy old man, except those who were able to live over again in the pleasures of the young. For passionate emotions of all sorts, and for everything which has been said or written in exaltation of them, he professed the greatest contempt. He regarded them as a form of madness. "The intense" was with him a bye-word of scornful disapprobation. He regarded as an aberration of the moral standard of modern times, compared with that of the ancients, the great stress laid upon feeling. Feelings, as such, he considered to be no proper subjects of praise or blame. Right and wrong, good and bad, he regarded as qualities solely of conduct—of acts and omissions; there being no feeling which may not lead, and does not frequently lead, either to good or to bad actions: conscience itself, the very desire to act right, often leading people to act wrong.

Consistently carrying out the doctrine, that the object of praise and blame should be the discouragement of wrong conduct and the encouragement of right, he refused to let his praise or blame be influenced by the motive of the agent. He blamed as severely what he thought a bad action, when the motive was a feeling of duty, as if the agents had been consciously evil doers. He would not have accepted as a plea in mitigation for inquisitors that they sincerely believed burning heretics to be an obligation of conscience. But though he did not allow honesty of purpose to soften his disapprobation of actions, it had its full effect on his estimation of characters. No one prized conscientiousness and rectitude of intention more highly, or was more incapable of valuing any person in whom he did not feel assurance of it. But he disliked people quite as much for any other deficiency, provided he thought it equally likely to make them act ill. He disliked, for instance, a fanatic in any bad cause, as much or more than one who adopted the same cause from self-interest, because he thought him even more likely to be practically mischievous. And thus, his aversion to make intellectual errors, or what he regarded as such, partook, in a certain sense, of the character of a moral feeling. All this is merely saying that he, in a degree once common, but now very unusual, threw his feelings into his opinions; which truly it is difficult to understand how anyone who possesses much of both, can fail to do. None but those who do not care about opinions, will confound this with intolerance. Those, who having opinions which they hold to be immensely important, and their contraries to be prodigiously hurtful, have any deep regard for the general good, will necessarily dislike as a class and in the abstract, those who think wrong what they think right, and right what they think wrong: though they need not therefore be, nor was my father, insensible to good qualities in an opponent, nor governed in their estimation of individuals by one general presumption, instead of by the whole of their character. I grant that an earnest person, being no more infallible than other men, is liable to dislike people on account of opinions which do not merit dislike; but if he neither himself does them any ill office, nor connives at its being done by others, he is not intolerant: and the forbearance which flows from a conscientious sense of the importance to mankind of the equal freedom of all opinions, is the only tolerance which is commendable, or, to the highest moral order of minds, possible.

It will be admitted that a man of the opinions, and the character above described was likely to leave a strong moral impression on any mind principally formed by him, and that his moral teaching was not likely to err on the side of laxity or indulgence. The element which was chiefly deficient in his moral relation to his children was that of tenderness. I do not believe that this deficiency lay in his own nature. I believe him to have had much more feeling than he habitually showed, and much greater capacities of feeling than were ever developed. He resembled most Englishmen in being ashamed of the signs of feeling, and by the absence of demonstration, starving the feelings themselves. If we consider further that he was in the trying position of sole teacher, and add to this that his temper was constitutionally irritable, it is impossible not to feel true pity for a father who did, and strove to do, so much for his children, who would have so valued their affection, yet who must have been constantly feeling that fear of him was drying it up at its source. This was no longer the case later in life and with his younger children. They loved him tenderly: and if I cannot say so much of myself, I was always loyally devoted to him. As regards my own education, I hesitate to pronounce whether I was more a loser or gainer by his severity. It was not such as to prevent me from having a happy childhood. And I do not believe that boys can be induced to apply themselves with vigour, and what is so much more difficult, perseverance, to dry and irksome studies, by the sole force of persuasion and soft words. Much must be done, and much must be learnt, by children, for which rigid discipline, and known liability to punishment, are indispensable as means. It is, no doubt, a very laudable effort, in modern teaching, to render as much as possible of what the young are required to learn, easy and interesting to them. But when this principle is pushed to the length of not requiring them to learn anything *but* what has been made easy and interesting, one of the chief objects of education is sacrificed. I rejoice in the decline of the old brutal and tyrannical system of teaching which, however, did succeed in enforcing habits of application; but the new, as it seems to me, is training up a race of men who will be incapable of doing anything which is disagreeable to them. I do not, then, believe that fear, as an element in education, can be dispensed with; but I am sure that it ought not to be the main element; and when it predominates so much as to preclude love and confidence on the part of the child to those who should be the unreservedly trusted advisers of after years, and perhaps to seal up the fountains of frank and spontaneous communicativeness in the child's nature, it is an evil for which a large abatement must be made from the benefits, moral and intellectual, which may flow from any other part of the education.

QUESTIONS

1. *What are the ancient meanings of the words* stoic, epicurean, *and* cynic? *What do you imagine John Stuart Mill's father was like, based on your understanding of these terms and on what the essay says?*

2. *What effect do you think John Mill's temperance, lack of passion, and love of rationality had on his son?*

3. *In John Stuart Mill's twentieth year he suffered a crisis of faith and felt the lack of emotional and aesthetic stimulation in his life. From what you read about his background, do you think Mill was deprived in these ways? Explain your answer.*

Two Perspectives on the War of 1812

Mill's discussion of his own education is as remarkable for what it implies as for what it tells us. There seems to be a subtle undertone of resentment towards his father, for although he says that his severity "was not such as to prevent me from having a happy childhood" one wonders what was happy about a childhood that so deliberately and thoroughly isolated one child from his peers. He admits that he did not love his father tenderly, but remained devoted to him. Mill seems to have had an attitude of respect rather than love towards his father.

His later philosophical works moved away from the thinking he was brought up with, but one can always sense the strong underpinning of the values inculcated in his childhood. It is to the underpinning of values as presented in historical accounts that we now turn. The following two selections are descriptions of the War of 1812. The first selection is from a standard American history text, the second from a Canadian history text. It is fascinating to look at the different emphasis and tone of the two writers. As you read the following passages, try to think of the values that are suggested but not stated by each author.

A U. S. Perspective[2]

The conflict ostensibly arose over the commercial issues of impressment and neutral rights. However, Federalist merchants and seamen vigorously opposed the declaration of war, as did a majority of voters in the Atlantic Coast states. Conversely, about twenty-eight Republican congressmen, "war hawks" from the frontier political districts of the South and West, strongly supported it. These congressmen acted from a variety of motives. Some thought the British blockade had cut agricultural prices. Others wanted territorial spoils in Florida and the final defeat of the Western Indian Confederacy. A few politicians dreamed of annexing British Canada. Beyond these motives, many Republicans thought war was the only way to preserve American honor. As President Madison proclaimed in his second inaugural address, "national honor is national property of the highest value."

The War of 1812

Republican hopes for a series of rapid military victories quickly collapsed. American privateers captured scores of merchant vessels during the first months of the war, but then the Royal Navy redeployed its fleet and British commerce moved in relative safety. By 1813, the British had seized the maritime initiative. A flotilla of British warships moved up and down the American coastline, harassing shipping and threatening seaport cities. In 1814, this fleet sailed up Chesapeake Bay. British forces stormed ashore and set fire to most of the government buildings in the District of Columbia, the new United States capital. The British then advanced on Baltimore but were repulsed by the courageous American resistance at Fort McHenry, inspiring Francis Scott Key, a Washington attorney, to compose "The Star-Spangled Banner." After two years of sporadic warfare, United States forces stood on the defensive in the East.

In the West, the United States failed to exploit its geographical advantage. Republican politicians had predicted an easy military advance into Canada, but they underestimated the difficulties of transportation and supply. General William Hull, the governor of the Michigan Territory, invaded western Canada in the summer of 1812. He quickly retreated because of a lack of reinforcements. By quickly building ships, the United States won naval superiority on the Great Lakes. Commodore Oliver Perry defeated a small British flotilla on Lake Erie, permitting General

William Henry Harrison to launch an attack on British and Indian forces near Detroit. Harrison killed his old rival Tecumseh, now an officer in the British army. Another American expedition captured and burned the Canadian capital of York (now Toronto).

These minor victories were poor substitutes for a major invasion of Canada. Political opposition in the northeastern states prevented such a military stroke. New England governors prohibited state militiamen from fighting outside the United States. Boston merchants and banks declined to lend money to the national government; they invested in British funds instead. Ordinary citizens likewise refused to buy American bonds. New England Federalists actively opposed the war effort in other ways as well. Led by Daniel Webster, a young, dynamic congressman from New Hampshire, they voted against the higher taxes and tariffs needed to finance the fighting. To force a negotiated peace, Webster and his Federalist colleagues discouraged army enlistments and prevented the conscription of state militiamen into the American army.

Section opposition to the war reached its height in 1814. The Massachusetts legislature called for a convention "to lay the foundation for a radical reform in the National Compact." In December, Federalists from all the New England states gathered in Hartford, Connecticut. Some delegates to the Hartford convention proposed secession from the Union, but the majority called for revision of the Constitution. Their goal was to reverse the declining role of their party—and of New England— in an expanding nation. To end the "Virginia Dynasty" of presidents, delegates proposed a constitutional amendment limiting the presidency to one four-year term and rotating the office among citizens from different states. Other Federalists suggested amendments restricting commercial embargoes to sixty days and requiring two-thirds majorities in Congress to declare war, prohibit commerce, and admit new states to the Union.

During the winter of 1814, the United States government faced the threat of internal secession and external invasion. In the north, the Hartford convention called for substantial revision of the Constitution. Far to the south, British transports landed thousands of seasoned veterans for an attack on New Orleans. A single ray of hope broke the darkness. Britain had finally defeated Napoleon in Europe. To end its war with the United States as well, the British entered negotiations with an American delegation at Ghent in Belgium. The American commissioners—John Quincy Adams, Albert Gallatin, and Henry Clay—initially demanded an end to British impressment and territorial gains in Canada and

Florida. The British insisted on a native American buffer state between the United States and Canada. In the end, neither side won significant concessions. The Treaty of Ghent, signed on Christmas Eve of 1814, required both nations to give up their territorial gains and to decide the Canadian-American boundary in subsequent negotiations.

The result of the war hardly justified three years of costly fighting and a sharply divided nation. It confirmed the judgment of contemporary critics and later historians that the War of 1812 was unnecessary, undertaken at the wrong time and for partisan reasons. But a final victory in combat lifted American morale and seemed to justify the fighting. Before news of the Treaty of Ghent reached the United States, newspaper headlines proclaimed an "ALMOST INCREDIBLE VICTORY!! GLORIOUS NEWS." Troops commanded by General Andrew Jackson had dealt a crushing defeat to the British force attacking New Orleans.

Whatever its other results, the war had created a new group of political leaders—Henry Clay, Daniel Webster, and John Calhoun—and, in Andrew Jackson, a national hero. Jackson, a rugged slaveowning planter from Tennessee, came to public attention as a controversial Indian-fighter and expansionist. In 1814, he led a troop of militia against the Creek Indians. After defeating them in the Battle of Horseshoe Bend, his men mercilessly slaughtered the women and children of the tribe. Jackson then ordered his troops into Spanish Florida, overwhelming a Creek settlement near Pensacola.

At New Orleans, Jackson commanded a mixed force of regular troops, city militiamen, and frontier fighters. They fought behind carefully constructed breastworks and were amply supplied with cannon. "Our artillery fired upon their whole columns . . . with grapeshot and cannister bombs," reported one American observer. "The slaughter must have been great." The British lost thousands of their finest troops, suffering about seven hundred killed and ten thousand wounded or captured. American casualties totaled only thirteen killed and fifty-eight wounded.

Jackson's triumph was the only significant victory of the entire war for either side. The Battle of New Orleans seemed to testify, as one headline put it, to the "RISING GLORY OF THE AMERICAN REPUBLIC!" It redeemed the nation's battered pride and, along with the coming of peace, undercut Federalist demands for a revision of the Constitution. The political institutions of the republic had survived a generation of strife.

ACTIVITIES

❶   List the main events and campaigns of the War of 1812 as given in the above (U. S.)selection.

A Canadian Perspective[3]

The War of 1812 was a complex, like other historical events. It was a complex of the historical relations of the two countries that fought it, of the judgments and ambitions of men, of the logic of international law, and of the historical situation in the West. Among all these factors, the greatest weight should perhaps be attached to the international situation at sea and its derivatives. No country of the pretensions of the United States could accept the dictation of another. The pressure from the West screwed the courage of principle to the sticking point, and so war followed. It was to give the United States its first lesson on the impossibility of isolation, a position with which insistence on "sailors' rights" and the freedom of the seas accords. That lesson the Americans did not learn, and it was to take two more wars before the republic would understand that no nation, no matter how far removed or strong it may be, can play a lone hand.

The war itself was satisfactory to all parties in that both sides won it: the American tradition is one of glorious victories and so is the Canadian. The British, who did most of the fighting and whose navy was the major instrument in ending the war, have no tradition at all, and there are few English people who have ever heard of it. The war was no fight to the death, and it produced no Marlboroughs or Nelsons. It was a succession of timorous advances and hasty retreats, of muddle-headed planning and incompetent generalship, interspersed with a few sharp actions and adroit manoeuvers which reflected credit on a few individuals and discredit on many. Except for the uninformed and for the professional patriots, time has almost turned its melodrama into farce.

There had certainly been enough examples of how a war between Canadians and Americans ought to be fought. Sea power must be used to contain the adversary within his own coasts and the army then employed to cut him in two along the vital St. Lawrence-Hudson highway. Strategy was just the same for both parties, excepting that one marched south and the other north. The side that had no navy must march all the more quickly. If it had no army, it must use its navy that much more vigorously. The British had a navy, but no army worth speaking of in Canada; and the Americans had little navy, but a relatively inexhaustible supply of manpower. Since the British navy was busy all over the world, it did not really get round to blockading the American coast until 1814. Part of the delay was to be ascribed to policy, for internal division within the United States gave the British a trump card and it would have been foolish to throw this away by rigorous naval action upon the coasts of New England, where sentiment was strongly against the war. The Americans, who should have been able to take Montreal in 1812 as Montgomery had done in 1775, did not undertake a serious offensive against that decisive spot in the entire struggle but, instead, devoted most of their efforts to outposts whose possession could settle nothing.

The key points of Canada, in order of importance, were Quebec, Montreal, Kingston, Niagara, the Detroit River. The order in which the Americans attacked was Detroit River, Niagara, Kingston, Montreal. Without a navy, they could not get at Quebec from the sea, but a mild degree of competence would have given them Montreal, for which they would have had a fair chance at Quebec. At it was, they aimed for the fingers and toes, not the heart. They did not really do much harm to fingers and toes. This may be explained on two counts. The first lay in sheer military incompetence and in the inability to grasp the strategical situation (which must have argued great ignorance of history). Strategical ignorance was associated with neglect of primary objects. The American Secretary for War, General Armstrong, seems to have contemplated the taking of Montreal but to have let himself be distracted by objectives in the interior. The second explanation lay in the state of that American community, Upper Canada: it was so American that it would surely welcome the invaders. This the British authorities as well as the American expected, and it explains Hull's easy-going operations around Detroit on the opening of the war. He believed that his proclamation would win the war, without any fighting.

What changed the whole situation was that classic of the Canadian school-room: Queenston Heights (October 14, 1812). The doggerel verse, sung by generations of young Canadians, in which that "dark October day-y-y" has been celebrated, has possibly detracted from the significance of the occasion. As a battle, it was just a big skirmish "and ere the setting sun Canadians held the Queenston Heights", thanks in large part to British regulars.[4] Yet by showing that the British were going to make a fight for it, that they could hit hard, and that things might not be a walkover for the Americans, Queenston Heights changed the whole picture, confirming the doubters in their allegiance, strengthening the wavering, and forcing the pro-Americans to change their tune. There is nothing like a good display of successful force for making people decide which side it is their patriotic duty to support. After Queenston Heights, there was little danger of fifth columnism swinging the province into the Republic. Isaac Brock, the only commanding officer on either side to show any marked ability throughout the war, who was killed in the gallant but injudicious charge up the face of the Heights, as every school child knows, deserves his monument there at Queenston. Without him, Upper Canada would have been taken.

In the campaigns of 1813 and 1814, the Americans displayed more military efficiency but not much advance in co-ordination and in generalship. The main effort was still directed at Upper Canada, its points of departure being Sacket Harbour and Oswego on Lake Ontario, Niagara, and the harbours of western Lake Erie. The military achievements of either side, apart from the occasional brilliant incident, such as Col. Fitzgibbon's at Beaver Dams or such engagements as Chrysler's Farm and Chateauguay, were inconsiderable and inconclusive. The only engagement of the war to be fought out in hard blows, with credit to both sides, was at Lundy's Lane, June 25, 1814. In this battle British losses were heavier, and it might be called a tactical victory for the Americans; but as they afterwards withdrew, and the battle prevented their campaign against the Niagara district from coming to anything, it amounted to a British win.

The decisive aspect of the struggle was not military but naval: the side which could secure and hold control of Lakes Champlain, Ontario, and Erie, in the order named, would be able to dominate the St. Lawrence valley; the side which could control the Atlantic coast would win the war. In 1814, the Americans had the stronger forces on Lake Champlain, but with the opportunity in his hands to alter the situation, General Prevost, the British commander, with characteristic ineptitude let it slip. On Lake Ontario the two fleets remained fairly evenly matched throughout the war, causing both commanders to take the view that discretion was the better part of valour; there was no decisive engagement on that lake. On Lake Erie was fought the only freshwater engagement of the war (and one of the few in history) that amounted to anything, when Commodore Perry, with half a dozen ships built on the spot, met the British in the battle of Put-in Bay, Sept. 10, 1813, and destroyed them.[5] This naval victory gave the Americans command of Lake Erie and was followed by Harrison's march into Upper Canada and his victory at Moraviantown, Oct. 5, 1813. The victories came at the wrong end of the line and decided nothing, except that the Americans sat in Amherstburg instead of the British sitting in Detroit. The American invaders did not even cut communication with the west, for a new route was improvised overland from York to Nottawasaga and thence by boat and schooner to Michilimackinac, which port had been taken by the British at the beginning of the war and was held throughout.

It was British sea power that decided the war. As Napoleon's giddy career drew to a close, British ships were able to give more attention to the American war. The arrival of some thousands of veteran reinforcements in the St. Lawrence (who were to be mishandled at Plattsburg, Sept 11, 1814, by Prevost) was followed by an intensified blockade of the American coast, culminating in the burning of Washington in August, 1814, an act which had no military significance and whose only excuse was the previous American burning of Newark and York. The British would have acted more sensibly and much more effectively if they had taken and held New York. Some territory they did seize: that part of Maine adjacent to New Brunswick, down as far as the Penobscot. There they required the inhabitants to take an oath of allegiance and it is related that "they showed no unwillingness to remain permanently British subjects".

The vast weight of her sea-power, as it stood in 1814, would have enabled Great Britain to do almost anything she wished in the United States, short of actual permanent conquest of the inhabited areas. Her statesmen were not unaware of this. If peace was to be achieved, it looked as if the Americans would have to eat humble pie, and for peace they were most anxious. Two years of unsuccessful war following upon the frictions of the previous period had gone far towards disintegrating national unity. New England was talking secession. Victory was impossible; defeat close. In negotiation lay wisdom. The American government had arrived at this conclusion as early as the winter of 1813, after one campaign, when it accepted the Czar's offer to mediate. Thanks to the European situation, the British at no time desired to go on with a war which had been forced upon them and from which they neither expected nor desired anything. They refused to accept mediation but showed no indisposition to direct negotiation. Madison accepted their offer of November, 1813, with alacrity, and peace preliminaries may be considered as commencing with the New Year, 1814.

QUESTIONS

1. *What were the main events of the War of 1812, according to the Canadian selection?*

2. *After comparing the lists of events in the two articles you have read, to what do you attribute the differences in these lists?*

A Comparison of Attitudes

The two preceding selections were respectively taken from an American and a Canadian standard history text. Even allowing for the inevitable difference of perspective, at times one may wonder if the two writers were discussing the same events. However, from our perspective, what is really fascinating is the way these selections were structured, and the tone of the presentation in each case. One familiar with the differing national characters of Canadians and Americans can feel that the emotional needs of their people were satisfied by the way each selection was written. Note the cynical carefulness of the opening of the Canadian selection, ending with a phrase that could never be uttered in an American history text, intended for the impressionable. "Except for the uninformed and for the professional patriots, time has almost turned its melodrama into farce." The author then goes on to underline the stupidity of the military strategy used, to poke fun at a battle of some patriotic significance to his fellow country-men, and to continue to list various silly failings and indecisive battles, but ends with a suggestion that the British could have made a total mess of the United States if they had wanted to, and simply decided that it was not worth the trouble. There is no sense of heroism or glory in this account, no explanations offered for failures, only a litany of stupid and occasionally incomprehen-sible actions with grudging praise for only one person, General Brock. One is left with a sense of the futility of the operation, the indifference of the Canadian and British people to the war effort, and the pretentiousness of the American attempt.

In contrast, the American account fairly bristles with ex-cuses for American failure, underplays the American interest in overtaking Canada (an effective way of making the American fail-ure to do so into less of a failure), and ends with an upbeat, positive account of a great American victory late in the fighting. The cru-cial detail that the war was over before the Battle of New Orleans and that the battle had no effect on the peace treaty is mentioned only in passing. The final paragraph shows the relationship of the war to the future of America.

The American account is as free of cynicism as the Canadian is permeated by it, as measured and fair as the Canadian is subtly emotionally toned, as carefully structured to a happy ending as the Canadian is left inconclusive, and as heroic as the Canadian is antiheroic. Surely, this is accomplished at subconscious level, and yet it so deeply reflects the national cultures and so deeply incul-cates these cultures in others that it cannot be ignored, if we are to get a grip on the fundamental question of how ethical values are formed and developed.

ACTIVITIES

❶   Find some examples of the ways in which values are uncon-sciously inculcated in movies or television shows. Describe the effect that you think this unconscious inculcation has on you personally.

Plato

The idea of educating for values is an old one; Plato expresses it clearly in *The Republic*, which was written about 388 B.C., a work in which he establishes the boundaries of what he would consider an ideal state. Plato's thought is difficult and complex, and is of sufficient importance to the history of philosophy for Alfred North Whitehead, the English philosopher/mathematician, to have said that all philosophy is a footnote to Plato. What Whitehead probably meant is that the great problems of philosophy are first expressed somewhere in Plato's work, and we have spent the last two thousand-odd years unpacking the implications of his thought.

The Republic, written when Plato was forty, stands both at the halfway point in his life and as the central work in his philosophical *oeuvre*. Plato's early dialogues were genuine philosophical discussions, with his beloved teacher Socrates playing the role of one who prods others to think, taking on positions, showing the weakness of other arguments, and often leaving the problems unsolved. *The Republic* is a transitional work, in which Socrates sometimes continues to act as a catalyst to the discussion, but more often states positions which are then uncritically agreed to by other participants in the discussion. The effect is less a discussion than a sycophantic admiration session, but Plato was sufficiently addicted to the form of dialogue that he did not think to write these passages out as didactic treatise, which, in fact, they are. The passages we are looking at from *The Republic* are of this type, and present a coherent picture of the practical aspects of Plato's view of education. Socrates is speaking to Adeimantus as the passage begins.

Education in *The Republic*[6]

EXCERPT 1

What is this education to be, then? Perhaps we shall hardly invent a system better than the one which long experience has worked out, with its two branches for the cultivation of the mind and of the body. And I suppose we shall begin with the mind, before we start physical training.

Naturally.

Under that head will come stories;[7] and of these there are two kinds: some are true, others fictitious. Both must come in, but we shall begin our education with the fictitious kind.

I don't understand, he said.

Don't you understand, I replied, that we begin by telling children stories, which, taken as a whole, are fiction, though they contain some truth? Such story-telling begins at an earlier age than physical training; that is why I said we should start with the mind.

You are right.

And at the beginning, as you know, is always the most important part, especially in dealing with anything young and tender. That is the time when the character is being molded and easily takes any impress one may wish to stamp on it.

Quite true.

Then shall we simply allow our children to listen to any stories that anyone happens to make up, and so receive into their minds ideas often the very opposite of those we shall think they ought to have when they are grown up?

No certainly not.

It seems, then, our first business will be to supervise the making of fables and legends, rejecting all which are unsatisfactory; and we shall induce nurses and mothers to tell their children only those which we have approved, and to think more of moulding their limbs to make them strong and shapely. Most of the stories now in use must be discarded.

What kind do you mean?

If we take the great ones, we shall see in them the pattern of all the rest, which are bound to be of the same stamp and to have the same effect.

No doubt; but which do you mean by the great ones?

The stories in Hesiod and Homer and the poets in general, who have at all times composed fictitious tales and told them to mankind.

Which kind are you thinking of, and what fault do you find in them?

The worst of all faults, especially if the story is ugly and immoral as well as false—misrepresenting the nature of gods and heroes, like an artist whose picture is utterly unlike the object he sets out to draw.

That is certainly a serious fault; but give me an example.

A signal instance of false invention about the highest matters is that foul story, which Hesiod repeats, of the deeds of Uranus and the vengence of Cronos;[8] and then there is the tale of Cronos's doings and of his son's treatment of him. Even if such tales were true, I should not have supposed they should be lightly told to thoughtless young people. If they cannot be altogether suppressed, they should only be revealed in a mystery, to which access should be as far as possible restricted by requiring the sacrifice, not of a pig, but of some victim such as very few could afford.[9]

It is true: those stories are objectionable.

Yes and not to be repeated in our commonwealth, Adeimantus. We shall not tell a child that, if he commits the foulest crimes or goes to any length in punishing his father's misdeeds, he will be doing nothing out of the way, but only what the first and greatest of the gods have done before him.

I agree; such stories are not fit to be repeated.

Nor yet any tales of warfare and intrigues and battles of gods against gods, which are equally untrue. If our future Guardians are to think it a disgrace to quarrel lightly with one another, we shall not let them embroider robes with the Battle of the Giants or tell them of all the other feuds of gods and heroes with their kith and kin.[10] If by any means we can make them believe that no one has ever had a quarrel with a fellow citizen and it is a sin to have one, that is the sort of thing our old men and women should tell children from the first; and as they grow older, we must make the poets write for them in the same strain. Stories like those of Hera being bound by her son, or of Hephaestus flung from heaven by his father for taking his mother's part when she was beaten, and all those battles of the gods in Homer, must not be admitted into our state, whether they be allegorical or not. A child cannot distinguish the allegorical sense from the literal, and the ideas he takes in at that age are likely to become indelibly fixed; hence the great importance of seeing that the first stories he hears shall be designed to produce the best possible effect on his character.

Yes, that is reasonable. But if we were asked which of these stories in particular are of the right quality, what should we answer?

I replied: You and I, Adeimantus, are not, for the moment, poets, but founders of a commonwealth. As such, it is not our business to invent stories ourselves, but only to be clear as to the main outlines to be followed by the poets in making their stories and the limits beyond which they must not be allowed to go.

True; but what are these outlines for any account they may give of the gods?

Of this sort, said I. A poet, whether he is writing epic, lyric, or drama, surely ought always to represent the divine nature as it really is. And the truth is that nature is good and must be described as such.

Unquestionably.

Well, nothing that is good can be harmful; and it cannot do harm, it can do no evil; and so it cannot be responsible for any evil.

I agree.

Again, goodness is beneficent, and hence the cause of well-being.

Yes.

Goodness, then, is not responsible for everything, but only for what is as it should be. It is not responsible for evil.[11]

Quite true.

It follows, then, that the divine, being good, is not, as most people say, responsible for everything that happens to mankind, but only for a small part; for the good things in human life are far fewer than the evil, and, whereas the good must be ascribed to heaven only, we must look elsewhere for the cause of evils.

I think that is perfectly true.

So we shall condemn as a foolish error Homer's description of Zeus as the 'dispenser of both good and ill.'[12] We shall disapprove when Pandarus' violation of oaths and treaties is said to be the work of Zeus and Athena, or when Themis and Zeus are said to have caused strife among the gods. Nor must we allow our young people to be told by Aeschylus that 'Heaven implants guilt in man, when his will is to destroy a house utterly.' If a poet writes of the sorrows of Niobe or the calamities of the house of Pelops or of the Trojan war, either he must not speak of them as the work of a god, or, if he does so, he must devise some such explanation as we are now requiring: he must say what the god did was just and good, and the sufferers were the better for being chastised. One who pays a just penalty must not be called miserable, and his misery then laid at heaven's door. The poet will only be allowed to say that the wicked were miserable because they needed chastisement, and the punishment of heavens did them good. If our commonwealth is to be well-ordered, we must fight to the last against any member of it being suffered to speak of the divine, which is good, being responsible for evil. Neither young nor old must listen to such tales, in prose or verse. Such doctrine would be impious, self-contradictory, and disastrous to our commonwealth.

I agree, he said, and I would vote for a law to that effect.

Well then, that shall be one of our laws about religion. The first principle to which all must conform in speech or writing is that heaven is not responsible for everything, but only for what is good.

I am quite satisfied.

God implants a fault in a man, when he wishes to destroy a house utterly.[13]

No: we must forbid anyone who writes a play about the sufferings of Niobe (the subject of the play from which these last lines are quoted), or the house of Pelops, or the Trojan war, or any similar topic, to say they are acts of god; or if he does he must produce the sort of interpretation we are now demanding, and say that god's acts were good and just, and that the sufferers were benefited by being punished. What the poet must not be allowed to say is that those who were punished were made wretched through god's action. He may refer to the wicked as wretched because they needed punishment, provided he makes it clear that in punishing them god did them good. But if a state is to be run on the right lines, every possible step must be taken to prevent anyone, young or old, either saying or being told whether in poetry or prose, that god, being good, can cause harm or evil to any man. To say so would be sinful, inexpedient, and inconsistent.

I should approve of a law for this purpose and you have my vote for it.

Then of our laws laying down the principles which those who write or speak about the gods must follow, one would be this: *God is the cause, not of all things, but only of good.*

I am quite content with that.

Then you agree that dialectic is the coping-stone that tops our educational system; it completes the course of studies and there is no other study that can rightly be placed above it.

I agree.

QUESTIONS

1. *What sort of stories should be told to children at the start of their education? Why must their education begin in this way?*

2. *What sort of stories about gods did Plato consider unsuitable for a well-ordered state? What sort of stories about gods did he consider suitable?*

3. *What do you think of the restrictions on stories that Plato proposes? Can you think of any contemporary examples of people who would like to restrict children's exposure to literature in a similar way?*

EXCERPT 2

It only remains, then, to draw up a scheme showing how, and to whom, these studies are allotted.

Clearly.

You remember what sort of people we chose earlier to be Rulers?[14]

Of course I do.

In most respects, then, natures of that quality are to be selected: we shall prefer the steadiest, the bravest, and, so far as possible, the handsomest persons. But, besides that, we must look not only for generous and virile characters, but for gifts fitting them for this sort of education. They must be eager students and learn with ease, because the mind is more apt to shrink from severe study than from hard physical exercise, in which part of the burden falls upon the body. Also we must demand a good memory and a dogged appetite for hard work of every kind. How else can you expect a man to undergo all the hardships of bodily training and, on the top of that, to carry through such a long course of study?

He will certainly need every natural advantage.

At any rate, this explains what is wrong now with the position of Philosophy and why she has fallen into disrepute: as I said before,[15] she ought never to have been wooed by the base-born, who are unworthy of her favours. To begin with, the genuine aspirant should not be one-sided in his love of work, liking one half of it and neglecting the other; as happens with one who throws himself into athletics, hunting, and all sorts of bodily exertion, but hates the trouble of learning anything from others or of thinking for himself. His industry goes halting on one foot; and so the other does too if it takes the opposite direction.

Quite true.

Also with regard to truth, we shall count as equally crippled a mind which, while it hates deliberate falsehood, cannot bear to tell lies, and is very angry when others do so, yet complacently tolerates involuntary error and is in no way vexed at being caught wallowing in swinish ignorance. We must be no less on the watch to distinguish the base metal from the true in respect of temperament, courage, highmindedness, and every kind of virtue. A state which chooses its rulers, or a man who chooses his friends, without a searching eye for these qualities will find themselves, in respect of one or another of them, cheated by a counterfeit or leaning on a broken reed. So all such precautions are very much our concern. If we can find, for this long course of training and study, men who are at all points sound of limb and sound in mind, then Justice herself will have no fault to find with us and we shall ensure the safety of our commonwealth and its institutions. We should only ruin it by choosing pupils of a different stamp; and moreover we should bring down upon philosophy an even greater storm of ridicule.

That would be a discreditable result.

It would. But at the moment I seem to be inviting ridicule myself.

In what way?

By speaking with so much warmth and forgetting that these speculations are only an amusement for our leisure. As I spoke, I seemed to see Philosophy suffering undeserved insults, and was so vexed with her persecutors that I lost my temper and became too vehement.

I did not think so as I listened.

No, but I felt it myself. However, here is something we must not forget. When we spoke earlier of selecting Rulers, we said we should choose old men;[16] but that will not do for the selection we are making now. We must not let Solon persuade us that a man can learn many things as he grows old;[17] he could sooner learn to run. Youth is the time for hard work of all sorts.

Undoubtedly.

Arithmetic, then, and geometry and all branches of the preliminary education which is to pave the way for Dialectic should be introduced in childhood; but not in the guise of compulsory instruction, because for the free man there should be no element of slavery in learning. Enforced exercise does no harm to the body, but enforced learning will not stay in the mind. So avoid compulsion, and let your children's lessons take the form of play. This will also help you to see what they are naturally fitted for.

That is a reasonable plan.

You remember, too, our children were to be taken to the wars on horseback to watch the fighting, and, when it was safe, brought close up like young hounds to be given a taste of blood.

I remember.

Then we must make a select list including everyone who shows forwardness in all these studies and exercises and dangers.

At what age?

As soon as they are released from the necessary physical training. This may take two or three years, during which nothing else can be done; for weariness and sleep are unfavourable to study. And at the same time, these exercises will provide not the least important test of character.

No doubt.

When that time is over, then, some of those who are now twenty years old will be selected for higher privileges. The detached studies in which they were educated as children will now be brought together in a comprehensive view of their connexions with one another and with reality.

Certainly that is the only kind of knowledge which takes firm root in the mind.

Yes, and the chief test of a natural gift for Dialectic, which is the same thing as the ability to see the connexions of things

I agree.

You will keep an eye, then, on these qualities and make a further selection of those who possess them in the highest degree and show most steadfastness in study as well as in warfare and in other duties. When they reach thirty they will be promoted to still higher privileges and tested by the power of Dialectic, to see which can dispense with sight and the other senses and follow truth into the region of pure reality. And here, my friend, you will need the greatest watchfulness.

Why in particular?

You must have seen how much harm is done now by philosophical discussion—how it infects people with a spirit of lawlessness.

Yes, I have.

Does that surprise you? Can you not make allowances for them? Imagine a child brought up in a rich family with powerful connexions and surrounded by a host of flatterers; and suppose that, when he comes to manhood, he learns that he is not the son of those who call themselves his parents and his true father and mother are not to be found. Can you guess how he would feel towards his supposed parents and towards his flatterers before he knew about his parentage and after learning the truth? Or shall I tell you what I should expect?

Please do.

I should say that, so long as he did not know the truth, he would have more respect for his reputed parents and family that for the flatterers, and be less inclined to neglect them in distress or to be insubordinate in word or deed; and in important matters the flatterers would have less influence with him. But when he learnt the facts, his respect would be transferred to them; their influence would increase, and he would openly associate with them and adopt their standards of behaviour, paying no heed to his reputed father and family, unless his disposition were remarkably good.

Yes, all that would be likely to happen. But how does your illustration apply to people who are beginning to take part in philosophical discussions?

In this way. There are certain beliefs about right and honourable conduct, which we have been brought up from childhood to regard with the same sort of reverent obedience that is shown to parents. In opposition to these, other courses attract us with flattering promises of pleasure; though a moderately good character will resist such blandishments and remain loyal to the beliefs of his fathers. But now suppose him confronted by the question, What does 'honourable' mean? He gives the answer he has been taught by the lawgiver, but he is argued out of his position. He is refuted again and again from many different positions of view and at last reduced to thinking that what he called honourable might just as well be called disgraceful. He comes to the same conclusion about justice, goodness, and all the things he most revered. What will become now of his oldest respect and obedience?

Obviously they cannot continue as before.

And when he has disowned these discredited principles and failed to find the true ones, naturally he can only turn to the life which flatters his desires; and we shall see him renounce all morality and become a lawless rebel. If this is the natural consequence of plunging the young into philosophical discussion, ought we not to make allowances, as I said before?

Yes, and be sorry for them too.

Then, if you do not want to be sorry for those pupils of yours who have reached the age of thirty, you must be very careful how you introduce them into such discussions. One great precaution is to forbid their taking part while they are still young.

You must have seen how youngsters, when they get their first taste of it, treat argument as a from of sport solely for the purposes of contradiction. When some one has proved them wrong, they copy his methods to confute others, delighting like puppies in tugging and tearing at anyone who comes near them. And so, after a long course of proving others wrong and being proved wrong themselves, they rush to the conclusions that all they once believed is false; and the result is that in the eyes of the world they discredit, not themselves only, but the whole business of philosophy. An older man will not share this craze for making a sport of contradiction. He will prefer to take for his model the conversation of one who is bent on seeking the truth, and his own reasonableness will bring credit on the pursuit. We meant to ensure this result by all that we said earlier against the present practice of admitting anybody, however unfit, to philosophic discussions, and about the need for disciplined and steadfast character.

Certainly.

If a man, then, is to devote himself to such discussion as continuously and exclusively as he gave himself up earlier to the corresponding training of his body, will twice as long a time be enough?

Do you mean six years or four?

No matter; let us say five. For after they must be sent down again into that Cave we spoke of and compelled to take military commands and other offices suitable to the young, so that they may not be behind their fellow citizens in experience. And at this stage they must once more be tested to see whether they will stand firm against all seductions.

How much time do you allow for this?

Fifteen years. Then when they are fifty, those who have come safely through and proved the best at all points in action and in study must be brought at last to the goal. They must lift up the eye of the soul to gaze on that which sheds light on all things; and when they have seen the Good itself, take it as a pattern for the right ordering of the state and of the individual, themselves included. For the rest of their lives, most of their time will be spent in study; but they will all take their turn at the troublesome duties of public life and act as Rulers for their country's sake, not regarding it as a distinction, but as an unavoidable task. And so, their place as Guardians of the commonwealth, they will depart to dwell in the Islands of the Blest. The state will set up monuments for them and sacrifices, honouring them as divinities, if the

Pythian Oracle approves, or at least as men blest with a godlike spirit.

That is a fine portrait of our Rulers, Socrates.

Yes, Glaucon, and you must not forget that some of them will be women. All I have been saying applies just as much to any women who are found to have the necessary gifts.

Quite right, if they are to share equally with the men in everything, as we said.

Well then, said I, do you agree that our scheme of a commonwealth and its constitution has not been a mere day-dream? Difficult it may be, but possible, though only on the one condition we laid down, that genuine philosophers—one or more of them—shall come into power in a state; men who will despise all existing honours as mean and worthless, caring only for the right and the honours to be gained from that, and above all for justice as the one indispensable thing in whose service and maintenance they will reorganize their own state.

How will they do that?

They must send out into the country all citizens who are above ten years old, take over the children, away from the present habits and manners of their parents, and bring them up in their own ways under the institutions we have described. Would not that be the quickest and easiest way in which our polity could be established, so as to prosper and be a blessing to any nation it might arise?

Yes, certainly; and I think, Socrates, you have satisfactorily explained how, if ever, it might come into being.

Have we now said enough, then about this commonwealth and also about the corresponding type of man; for it must be clear what sort of person we shall expect him to be?

It is clear; and, to answer your question, I believe our account is complete.

QUESTIONS

1. *What characteristics should a person possess to be trained for serious higher-level study? What characteristics should be avoided?*

2. *How should arithmetic and geometry be taught, according to Plato?*

3. *After the age of thirty, Plato recommends that selected students begin the study of dialectic, which for Plato meant the study of philosophical argument and reasoning. Why does he consider the study of dialectic especially dangerous for the young?*

4. *How will men and women of the highest character spend their lives after the age of fifty?*

5. *What do you think of Plato's educational scheme? Do you think it would ensure, as he clearly does, that the rulers of the state will be good rulers?*

Relevance to Contemporary Education

Although Plato's *Republic* was written 2,500 years ago, there is much in his thinking that reminds one of contemporary debates in education—the concern for appropriate education, and the belief in the importance of education in developing character. The emphasis he places on making sure that one is the proper age to study the chosen subject matter leads him to some surprising ideas, but the idea that a ruler of a state should study until the age of fifty was as strange then as it is today.

Plato was sensitive to the many subtle ways that people's thinking can be affected by the way they are taught, and he believed that values could be taught. That still leaves the question open for us though, and perhaps it will never be answered: Can values be taught, and how much of people's value system is indoctrinated through education?

Endnotes for Chapter 9

1. Reprinted from the *Autobiography*, by John Stuart Mill. Longmans, Green, Reader and Dyer, 1873.

2. Reprinted with the permission of James A. Henretta from *America's History*, 1st edition, by James A. Henretta, W. Elliot Brown Lee, David Brody, and Susan Ware. Copyright 1987, The Dorsey Press, pp. 236–240.

3. Reprinted by permission of the Longman Group, U. K. Ltd., from *Colony to Nation: A History of Canada: The Evolution of a Nation* by Arthur R. M. Lower, Longmans, Canada, 1964.

4. The Canadian militia, both French and English, once it got some training, fought well during the war, but in British North America in 1812, there were only a few thousand trained Canadians available and 4,000 British regulars. See William Wood, *The War with the United States* (Vol. 14 of *Chronicles of Canada*), 36ff., and C. P. Stacey, "The War of 1812 in Canadian History," *Ontario History*, (Summer, 1958), 153–159.

5. Perry's ships were manned by saltwater sailors, those of the British by the sailors of the backwoods; the result was not in doubt.

6. Reprinted with permission of Oxford University Press from *The Republic of Plato*, translated by F. M. Cornford. Copyright 1945, Oxford University Press.

7. In a wide sense, tales, legends, myths, narratives in poetry or prose.

8. Hesiod, *Theogony*, I54 ff. A primitive myth of the forcing apart of the sky (Uranus) and Earth (Gaia) by their son Cronos, who mutilated his father. Zeus, in turn, took vengeance on his father, Cronos, for trying to destroy his children. These stories were sometimes cited to justify ill-treatment of parents.

9. The usual sacrifice at the Eleusisian Mysteries was a pig, which was cheap. In a mystery, unedifying legends might be given an allegorical interpretation, a method which had been applied to Homer since the end of the sixth century B.C.

10. Such a robe was woven by maidens for the staute of Athena at the Great Panathenaea.

11. The words of Lachesis in the concluding myth (617 E, p.357) illustrate Plato's meaning.

12. Some further instances from Homer are here omitted.

13. Frag. 160.

14. 412 B ff.

15. 495 c.

16. At 412 c.

17. Solon, frag. 22 (Diehl) : "I go on learning many things as I grow old."

CHAPTER 10

ETHICS AND SCIENCE:
The Question of
Objectivity

This chapter asks the question: Can those who work in the hard sciences divorce themselves from ethical questions because of the "objectivity" of their work? In order to answer this question, we must first consider whether the hard sciences are capable of being as objective as they claim to be. We look at the writing of two people, Arthur Koestler and Paul Feyerabend, who argue that scientific discovery and scientific belief are complex, emotionally tinged enterprises that involve a great deal of intuition and a world-view that is not all-embracing. Feyerabend consider the dangers inherent in the belief in objectivity through an analysis of the "Statement Against Astrology" by one hundred eighty-six leading scientists.

T he objectivity of the hard sciences has long been an article of faith among many people. According to their beliefs, a scientist is a seeker after truth who creates hypotheses that purport to explain the universe, and then confirms these hypotheses in a rigorous, mathematically precise manner. Historians of science have long recognized that the discovery of what we call scientific truth is a much more complex, uncertain, and controversial process than this initial idea would suggest. Scientists are people, living at particular times in particular places, of differing ambitions and expectations, having various aesthetic tastes, religious beliefs, and experiences. It would be absurd to suggest that one can totally divorce oneself from these factors, for they will influence one's thoughts, and affect the style in which one looks for ways to confirm theories.

What does this have to do with science and ethics? Everything. It is easy to state, or to have people believe, that scientific discovery is amoral by nature. An astronomer or physicist seeks only to explain the world, not to justify it. It is trivial, but true, to note that discoveries of scientific laws can have practical implication. The role of Einsteinian physics in the creation of the atomic bomb is exceptionally well documented. But there is an even deeper sense in which a scientific theory is a product of the people who created it, and therefore cannot be separated from what the scientists believe is right, good, and beautiful. For what one considers worth discovering and the form the discovery takes are vitally influenced by the personality and interest of the discoverer.

We are not raising silly questions, such as whether or not one can be a good Christian and believe in the theory of evolution. There is no reason to assume that a person's Christianity would affect their ability to do exemplary scientific work; in fact, countless cases can be cited of Christians who put the Bible aside while in the laboratory. But their Christianity will affect their world view, and can interact with other factors—their career ambitions, their aesthetic sensibilities, who they talk to and work with, their personality and mood. These factors may well determine what they will look for, what evidence they will see, and what they will ignore. It is not only Galileo's persecutors who refuse to look through the telescope.

Johannes Kepler

What is perhaps even more interesting is that the process of scientific discovery is littered with false starts, strange guesses, and technical errors; it is far from a smooth process. It is fascinating to read Arthur Koestler's classic account of the process that Johannes Kepler undertook to discover his famous laws of planetary motion. Here, we have the first examples of truly modern science—mathematically precise descriptions of the universe that explain what we see and that can be used to predict the future. The path to discovery, however, was not only unclear, but was strewn with an amazing combination of guesses, intuitions, and errors. Koestler's vivid prose brings the process to light in a fascinating way.

The Sleepwalkers[1]

EXCERPT 1

The First Assault

The task before him [Kepler] was to define the orbit of Mars by determining the radius of the circle, the direction (relative to the fixed stars) of the axis connecting the two positions where Mars is nearest and farthest from the sun (perihelion and aphelion), and the positions of the sun (S), orbital centre (C), and *punctum equans* (E), which all lie on that axis. Ptolemy had assumed that the distance between E and C was the same as between C and S, but Kepler made no such assumption, which complicated his task even more.

He chose out of Tycho's[2] treasure four observed positions of Mars at the convenient dates when the planet was in opposition to the sun. The geometrical problem which he had to solve was, as we saw, to determine, out of these four positions, the radius of the orbit, the direction of the axis, and the position of the three central points on it. It was a problem which could not be solved by rigorous mathematics, only by approximation, that is, by a kind of trial-and-error procedure which has to be continued until all the pieces in the jig-saw puzzle fit together tolerably well. The incredible labour that this involved may be gathered from the fact that Kepler's draft calculations (preserved in manuscript) cover nine hundred folio pages in small handwriting.

At times he was despairing; he felt, like Rheticus, that a demon was knocking his head against the ceiling, with the shout: "These are the motions of Mars." At other times, he appealed for help to Maestlin (who turned a deaf ear), to the Italian astronomer, Magini (who did the same), and thought of sending an S.O.S. to Francois Vieta, the father of modern algebra: "Come, oh Gallic Appollonius, bring your cylinders and spheres and what other geometer's houseware you have. . . ." But in the end he had to slog it out alone, and to invent his mathematical tools as he went along.

Half-way through that dramatic sixteenth chapter, he bursts out:

> "If thou [dear reader] art bored with these wearisome methods of calculation, take pity on me who had to go through with at least seventy repetitions of it, at a very great loss of time; nor wilst thou be surprised that by now the fifth year is nearly past since I took on Mars . . . . "

Now, at the very beginning of the hair-raising computations in chapter sixteen, Kepler absentmindedly put three erroneous figures for three vital longitudes of Mars, and happily went on from there, never noticing his error. The French historian of astronomy, Delambre, later repeated the whole computation, but, surprisingly, his correct results differ very little from Kepler's faulty ones. The reason is, that toward the end of the chapter Kepler committed several mistakes in simple arithmetic—errors in division which would bring bad marks to any schoolboy—and these errors happen very nearly to cancel out his earlier mistakes. We shall see, in a moment, that, at the most crucial point of the process of discovering his Second Law, Kepler again committed mathematical sins which mutually canceled out, and "as if by miracle" (in his own words), led to the correct result.

At the end of that breathtaking chapter, Kepler seems to have triumphantly achieved his aim. As a result of his seventy-odd trials, he arrived at values for the radius of the orbit and for the three central points which gave, with a permissible error of less than 2', the correct positions of Mars for all the ten oppositions recorded by Tycho. The unconquerable Mars seemed at last to have been conquered. he proclaimed his victory with the sober words:

> "Thou seest now, diligent reader, that the hypothesis based on this method not only satisfies the four positions on which it was based, but also correctly represents, within two minutes, all the other observations. . . ."

There follow three pages of tables to prove the correctness of his claim; and then, without further transition, the next chapter starts with the following words:

> "Who would have thought it possible? This hypothesis, which so closely agrees with the observed oppositions, is nevertheless false. . . ."

QUESTIONS

1. *What was Kepler trying to do? How did he go about getting information?*

2. *What was astonishing about his discovery of the radius of the orbit for the three central points of Mars?*

EXCERPT 2

The Eight Minutes Arc

In the two following chapters Kepler explains, with great thoroughness and an almost masochistic delight, how he discovered that the hypothesis is false, and why it must be rejected. In order to prove it by a further test, he had selected two specially rare pieces from Tycho's treasury of observations, and lo! they did not fit; and when he tried to adjust his model to them, this made things even worse, for now the observed positions of Mars differed from those which his theory demanded by magnitudes up to eight minutes arc.

This was a catastrophe. Ptolemy, and even Copernicus could afford to neglect a difference of eight minutes, because their observations were only accurate within a margin of ten minutes, anyway. "But," the nineteenth chapter concluded, "but for us, who, by divine kindness were given an accurate observer such as Tycho Brahe, for us it is fitting that we should acknowledge this divine gift and put it to use. . . . Henceforth I shall lead the way toward that goal according to my own ideas. For, if I had believed that we could ignore these eight minutes, I would have patched up my hypothesis accordingly. But since it was not permissible to ignore them, those eight minutes point the road to a complete reformation of astronomy: they have become the building material for a large part of this work. . . ."

It was the final capitulation of an adventurous mind before the "irreducible, obstinate facts." Earlier on, if a minor detail did not fit into a major hypothesis, it was cheated away or shrugged away. Now this time-hallowed indulgence had ceased to be permissible. A new era had begun in the history of thought: an era of austerity and rigour. As Whitehead has put it:

> "All the world over and at all times there have been practical men, absorbed in 'irreducible and stubborn facts': all the world over and at all times there have been men of philosophic temperament who have been absorbed in the weaving of general principles. It is this union of passionate interest in the detailed facts with equal devotion to abstract generalization which forms the novelty in our present society."

This new departure determined the climate of European thought in the last three centuries, it set modern Europe apart from all other civilizations in the past and present, and enabled it to transform its natural and social environment as completely as if a new species had arisen on this planet.

The turning point is dramatically expressed in Kepler's work. In the *Mysterium Cosmographicum* the facts are coerced to fit the theory. In the *Astronomia Nova*, a theory, built on years of labour and torment, was instantly thrown away because of a discord of eight miserable minutes arc. Instead of cursing those eight minutes as a stumbling block, he transformed them into the cornerstone of a new science.

What caused this change of heart in him? I have already mentioned some of the general causes which contributed to the emergence of the new attitude: the need of navigators, and engineers, for greater precision in tools and theories; the stimulating effects on science of expanding commerce and industry. But what turned Kepler into the first law-maker of nature was something different and more specific. It was *his introduction of physical causality into the formal geometry of the skies* which made it impossible for him to ignore the eight minutes arc. So long as cosmology was guided by purely geometrical rules of the game, regardless of physical causes, discrepancies between theory and fact could be overcome by inserting another wheel into the system. In a universe moved by real, physical forces, this was no longer possible. The revolution which freed thought from the stranglehold of ancient dogma, immediately created its own, rigorous discipline.

The Second Book of the *New Astronomy* closes with the words:

> "And thus the edifice which we erected on the foundation of Tycho's observations, we have now again destroyed. . . . This was our punishment for having followed some plausible, but in reality false, axioms of the great men of the past."

QUESTION

1. *What made Kepler's attempt to understand the motion of Mars an exercise in "modern" science?*

EXCERPT 3

The Wrong Law

The next act of the drama opens with Book Three. As the curtain rises, we see Kepler preparing himself to throw out more ballast. The axiom of *uniform* motion has already gone overboard, Kepler feels, and hints that the even more sacred one of *circular* motion must follow. The impossibility of constructing a circular orbit which would satisfy all existing observations, suggests to him that the circle must be replaced by some other geometrical curve.

But before he can do that, he must make an immense detour. For if the orbit of Mars is not a circle, its true shape can only be discovered by defining a sufficient number of points on the unknown curve. A circle is defined by three points on its circumference; every other curve needs more. The task before Kepler was to construct Mars's orbit without any preconceived ideas regarding its shape; to start from scratch, as it were.

To do that, it was first of all necessary to re-examine the motion of the earth itself. For, after all, the earth is our observatory; and if there is some misconception regarding its motion, all conclusions about the motions of other bodies will be distorted. Copernicus had assumed that the earth moves at uniform speed—not, as the other planets, only "quasi-uniformly" relative to some equant or epicycle, but *really* so. And since observation contradicted the dogma, the inequality of the earth's motion was explained away by the suggestion that the orbit periodically expanded and contracted, like a kind of pulsating jellyfish. It was typical of those improvisations which astronomers could afford so long as they felt free to manipulate the universe as they pleased on their drawing boards. It was equally typical that Kepler rejected it as "fantastic", again on the grounds that no physical cause existed for such a pulsation.

Hence his next task was to determine, more precisely than Copernicus had done, the earth's motion round the sun. For that purpose he designed a highly original method of his own. It was relatively simple, but it so happened that nobody had thought of it before. It consisted, essentially, of the trick of transferring the observer's position from earth to Mars, and to compute the motions of the earth exactly as an astronomer on Mars would do it.

The result was just as he had expected: the earth, like the other planets, did not revolve with uniform speed, but faster or slower according to its distance from the sun. Moreover, at the two extreme points of the orbit, the aphelion and perihelion, the earth's velocity proved to be, simply and beautifully, inversely proportional to distance.

At this decisive point, Kepler flies off the tangent and becomes air-borne, as it were. Up to here he was preparing, with painstaking patience, his second assault on the orbit of Mars. Now he turns to a quite different subject. "Ye physicists, prick your ears," he warns, "for now we are going to invade your territory." The next six chapters are a report on that invasion into celestial physics, which had been out of bounds for astronomy since Plato.

A phrase seems to have been humming in his ear like a tune one cannot get rid of; it crops up in his writings over and again: there is a force in the sun which moves the planet, there is a force in the sun, there is a force in the sun. And since there is a force in the sun, there must exist some beautifully simple relation between the planet's distance from the sun and its speed. A light shines the brighter the nearer we are to its source, and the same must apply to the force of the sun: the closer the planet to it, the quicker it will move. This is his instinctive conviction, already expressed in the *Mysterium Cosmographicum*; but now, at last, he has succeeded in proving it.

In fact he has not. He has proved the inverse ratio of speed to distance only for the *two extreme points* of the orbit; and his extension of this "Law" to the entire *orbit* was a patently incorrect generalization. Moreover, Kepler knew this, and admitted it at the end of the thirty-second chapter, before he became airborne; but immediately afterwards, he conveniently forgot it. This is the first of the critical mistakes which "as if by a miracle" canceled out, and led Kepler to the discovery of his Second Law. It looks as if his conscious, critical faculties were anaesthetized by the creative impulse, by his impatience to get to grips with the physical forces in the solar system.

Since he had no notion of the *momentum* which makes the planet persist in its motion, and only a vague intuition of *gravity* which bends that motion into a closed orbit, he had to find, or invent, a force which, like a broom, sweeps the planet around its path. And since the sun causes all motion, he let the sun handle the broom. This required that the sun rotate round its own axis— a guess which was only confirmed much later; the force which it emitted rotated with it, like the spokes of a wheel, and swept the planets along. But if that were the only force acting on them, the planets would all have the same angular velocity, they would all complete their revolutions in the same period—which they do not. The reason, Kepler thought, was the laziness or "inertia" of the planets, who desire to remain in the same place, and resist the sweeping force. The "spokes" of that force are not rigid; they allow the planet to lag behind; it works rather like a vortex or whirlpool. The power of the whirlpool diminishes with distance, so that the farther away the planet, the less power the sun has to overcome its laziness, and the slower its motion will be.

It still remained to be explained, however, why the planets moved in eccentric orbits instead of always keeping the same distance from the centre of the vortex. Kepler first assumed that apart from being lazy, they performed an epicyclic motion in the opposite direction under their own steam, as it were, apparently out of sheer cussedness. But he was dissatisfied with this, and at a later stage assumed that the planets were "huge round magnets" whose magnetic axis pointed always in the same direction, like the axis of a top; hence the planet will periodically be drawn closer to, and be repelled by the sun, according to which of its magnetic poles faces the sun.

Thus, in Kepler's physics of the universe, the roles played by gravity and inertia are reversed. Moreover, he assumed that the sun's power diminishes in direct ratio to distance. He sensed that there was something wrong here, since he knew that the intensity of light diminishes with the *square* of distance; but he had to stick to it, to satisfy his theorem of the ratio of speed to distance, which was equally false.

The Second Law

Refreshed by this excursion into the *Himmelsphysik*, our hero returned to the more immediate task in hand. Since the earth no longer moved at uniform speed, how could one predict its position at a given time? (The method based on the *punctum equans* had proved, after all, a disappointment.) Since he believed to have proved that its speed depended directly on its distance from the sun, the time it needed to cover a small fraction of the orbit was always proportionate to that distance. Hence he divided the orbit (which, forgetting his previous resolve, he still regarded as a circle) into 360 parts, and computed the distance of each bit of arc from the sun. The sum of all distances between, say 0° and 85°, was a measure of the time the planet needed to get there.

But this procedure was, as he remarked with unusual modesty, "mechanical and tiresome." So he searched for something simpler:

> "Since I was aware that there exists an infinite number of points on the orbit and accordingly an infinite number of distances [from the sun] the idea occurred to me that the sum of these distances is contained in the area of the orbit. For I remembered that in the same manner Archimedes too divided the area of a circle into an infinite number of triangles."

Accordingly, he concluded, the area swept over by the line connecting planet and sun AS–BS is a measure of the time required by the planet to get from A to B; *hence the line will sweep out equal areas in equal times.* This is Kepler's immortal Second Law (which he discovered before the First)—a law of amazing simplicity at the end of a dreadfully confusing labyrinth.

Yet the last step which had got him out of the labyrinth had once again been a faulty step. For it is not permissible to equate an area with the sum of an infinite number of neighbouring lines, as Kepler did. Moreover, he knew this well, and explained at length why it was not permissible. He added that he had also committed a second error, by assuming the orbit to be circular. And he concluded: "But these two errors—it is like a miracle—cancel out in the most precise manner, as I shall prove further down."

The correct result is even more miraculous than Kepler realized, for this explanation of the reasons *why* his errors cancel out was once again mistaken, and he got, in fact, so hopelessly confused that the argument is practically impossible to follow—as he himself admitted. And yet, by three incorrect steps and their even more incorrect defence, Kepler stumbled on the correct law.

QUESTIONS

1. *What was the first of the critical mistakes that Kepler made, which miraculously did not matter, that helped him to discover the laws of planetary motion?*

2. *What other notions in Kepler's physical theory were incorrect?*

3. *What other mistakes did Kepler make in the process of discovering his second law of planetary motion?*

Paul Feyerabend

The incident referred to in the next selection has achieved a certain notoriety in the literature. The fact that the scientific community regarded astrology as a threat is very interesting, as is the tone of the manifesto. Feyerabend, incidentally, has claimed that he finds astrology stupid and boring. He is interested merely in preserving its right to be heard; he is concerned about a tyranny of scientists imposing on everyone else what they think is "truth."

In this context, it is interesting to note that one of the prime reasons that many scientists consider their work superior to the work of astrologers is that the calculations of scientists have predictability. Astrologers claim predictability, but these claims are pretty feeble according to most studies. However, most of the scientists, who signed the antiastrology manifesto, did not know these studies; in fact virtually all of them were abysmally ignorant of astrology. It is the arrogance of this ignorance that excited Feyerabend to write his article.

The Strange Case of Astrology[3]

To drive the point home I shall briefly discuss the 'Statement of 186 Leading Scientists Against Astrology,' which appeared in the September/October 1975 issue of *Humanist*. This statement consists of four parts. First, there is the statement proper which takes about one page. Next come 186 signatures by astronomers, physicists, mathematicians, philosophers, and individuals with unspecified professions, eighteen Nobel Prize Winners among them. Then we have two articles explaining the case against astrology in some detail.

Now what surprises the reader whose image of science has

been formed by the customary eulogies which emphasize rationality, objectivity, impartiality and so on is the religious tone of the document, the illiteracy of the 'arguments' and the authoritarian manner in which the arguments are being presented. The learned gentlemen have strong convictions, they use their authority to spread these convictions (why 186 signatures if one has arguments?), they know a few phrases which sound like arguments, but they certainly do not know what they are talking about.

Take the first sentence of the 'Statement'. It reads: 'Scientists in a variety of fields have become concerned about the increased acceptance of astrology in many parts of the world.'

In 1484 the Roman Catholic Church published the *Malleus Maleficarum*, the outstanding textbook on witchcraft. The *Malleus* is a very interesting book. It has four parts: phenomena, aetiology, legal aspects, theological aspects of witchcraft. The description of phenomena is sufficiently detailed to enable us to identify the mental disturbances that accompanied some cases. The aetiology is pluralistic, there is not just the official explanation, there are other explanations as well, purely materialistic explanations included. Of course, in the end only one of the offered explanations is accepted, but the alternatives are discussed and so one can judge the arguments that lead to their elimination. This feature makes the *Malleus* superior to almost every physics, biology, chemistry textbook of today. Even the theology is pluralistic, heretical views are not passed over in silence, nor are they ridiculed; they are described, examined, and removed by argument. The authors know the subject, they know their opponents, they give a correct account of the positions of their opponents, they argue against these positions and they use the best knowledge available at the time in their arguments.

The book has an introduction, a bull by Pope Innocent VIII, issued in 1484. The bull reads: 'It has indeed come to our ears, not without afflicting us with bitter sorrow, that in . . . '—and now comes a long list of countries and counties—'many persons of both sexes, unmindful of their own salvation have strayed from the Catholic Faith and have abandoned themselves to devils . . .' and so on. The words are almost the same as the words in the beginning of the 'Statement', and so are the sentiments expressed. Both the Pope and the '186 leading scientists' deplore the increasing popularity of what they think are disreputable views. But what a difference in literacy and scholarship!

Comparing the *Malleus* with accounts of contemporary knowledge the reader can easily verify that the Pope and his learned authors knew what they were talking about. This cannot be said of our scientists. They neither know the subject they attack, astrology, nor those parts of their own science that undermine their attack.

Thus Professor Bok, in the first article that is attached to the statement writes as follows: "All I can do is state clearly and unequivocally that modern concepts of astronomy and space physics give no support—better said, negative support—to the tenets of astrology' i.e. to the assumption that celestial events such as the positions of the planets, of the moon, of the sun influence human affairs. Now, 'modern concepts of astronomy and space physics' include large planetary plasmas and a solar atmosphere that extends far beyond the earth into space. The plasmas interact with the sun and with each other. The interaction leads to a dependence of solar activity on the relative positions of the planets. Watching the planets one can predict certain features of solar activity with great precision. Solar activity influences the quality of short wave radio signals hence fluctuations in this quality can be predicted from the position of the planets as well.

Solar activity has a profound influence on life. This was known for a long time. What was not known was how delicate this influence really is. Variations in the electric potential of trees depend not only on the *gross* activity of the sun but on *individual flares* and therefore again on the positions of the planets. Piccardi, in a series of investigations that covered more than thirty years found variations in the rate of standardized chemical reactions that could not be explained by laboratory or meteorological conditions. He and other workers in the field are inclined to believe 'that the phenomena observed are primarily related to changes of the structure of water used in the experiments'. The chemical bond in water is about one tenth of the strength of average chemical bonds so that water is 'sensitive to extremely delicate influences and is capable of adapting itself to the most varying circumstances to a degree attained by no other liquid.' It is quite possible that solar flares have to be included among these 'varying circumstances' which would again lead to a dependence on planetary positions. Considering the role which water and organic colloids play in life we may conjecture that 'it is by means of water and the aqueous system that the external forces are able to react on living organisms.'

Just how sensitive organisms are has been shown in a series of papers by F. R. Brown. Oysters open and close their shells in accordance with the tides. They continue their activity when brought inland, in a dark container. Eventually they adapt their rhythm to the new location which means that they sense the very weak tides in an inland laboratory tank. Brown also studied the metabolism of tubers and [found a lunar period though the potatoes were kept at constant temperature, pressure, humidity, illumination]: man's ability to keep conditions constant is smaller than the ability of a potato to pick up lunar rhythms and Professor Bok's assertion that 'the walls of the delivery room shield us effectively from many known radiations' turns out to be just another case of a firm conviction based on ignorance.

The 'Statement' makes much of the fact the 'astrology was part and parcel of (the) magical world view' and the second article that is attached to it offers a 'final disproof' by showing that 'astrology arose from magic.' Where did the learned gentlemen get *this* information? As far as one can see there is not a single anthropologist among them and I am rather doubtful whether anyone is familiar with the more recent results of this discipline. What they do know are some older views from what one might call the 'Ptolemaic' period of anthropology when post-17th century Western man was supposed to be the sole possessor of sound knowledge, when field studies, archaeology and a more detailed examination of myth had not yet led to the discovery of the surprising knowledge possessed by ancient man as well as by modern 'Primitives' and when it was assumed that history consisted in a simple progression from more primitive to less primitive views. We see: the judgment of the '186 leading scientists' rests on an antediluvian anthropology, on ignorance of more recent results in their own fields (astronomy, biology, and the connection between the two) as well as on a failure to perceive the implications of results they do know. It shows the extent to which scientists are prepared to assert their authority even in areas in which they have no knowledge whatsoever.

There are many minor mistakes. 'Astrology,' it is said 'was dealt a serious death blow' when Copernicus replaced the Ptolemaic system. Note the wonderful language: does the learned writer believe in the existence of 'death blows' that are not 'serious'? And as regards the content we can only say that the very opposite was true. Kepler, one of the foremost Copernicans, used the new discoveries to improve astrology, he found new evidence for it, and he defended it against opponents. There is a criticism of the dictum that the stars incline, but do not compel. The criticism overlooks that modern hereditary theory (for example) works with inclinations throughout. Some specific assertions that are part of astrology are criticized by quoting evidence that contradicts them; but every moderately interesting theory is always in conflict with numerous experimental results. Here astrology is similar to highly respected scientific research programmes. There is a longish quotation from a statement by psychologists. It says: 'Psychologists find no evidence that astrology is of any value whatsoever as an indicator of past, present, or future trends of one's personal life. . . .' Considering that astronomers and biologists have not found evidence *that is already published, and by researchers in their own fields*, this can hardly count as an argument. 'By offering the public the horoscope as a substitute for honest and sustained thinking, astrologers have been guilty of playing upon the human tendency to take easy rather than difficult paths' —but what about psychoanalysis, what about the reliance upon psychological tests which long ago have become a substitute for 'honest and sustained thinking' in the evaluation of people of all ages? And as regards the magical origin of astrology one need only remark that science once was very closely connected with magic and must be rejected if astrology must be rejected on these grounds.

The remarks should not be interpreted as an attempt to defend astrology as it is *practiced now* by the great majority of astrologists. Modern astrology is in many respects similar to early mediaeval astronomy: it inherited interesting and profound ideas, but it distorted them, and replaced them by caricatures more adapted to the limited understanding of its practitioners. The caricatures are not used for research; there is no attempt to proceed into new domains and to enlarge our knowledge of extra-terrestrial influences; they simply serve as a reservoir of naive rules and phrases suited to impress the ignorant. Yet this is not the objection that is raised by our scientists. They do not criticize the air of stagnation that has been permitted to obscure the basic assumptions of astrology, they criticize these basic assumptions themselves and in the process turn their own subjects into caricatures. It is interesting to see how closely both parties approach each other in ignorance, conceit and the wish for easy power over minds.

QUESTIONS

1. *Why does Feyerabend consider the* Malleus Maleficarum *to be a fairer treatment of opposing views than the statement against astrology?*

2. *Why does Feyerabend consider Professor Bok's opening statement ill-considered?*

3. *Why does Feyerabend believe that scientists do not help their case by arguing that a serious objection to astrology can be induced from the statement that astrology was part of a magical world-view?*

Ethical Standards
in Science

The danger of scientific arrogance, from an ethical standpoint, is that other points of view, some that may have worth, are suppressed. In a sense, then, science is capable of behaving much like a religion that claims a monopoly on the truth. All other points of view are false and must be suppressed. Even within the scientific community, unorthodox positions have a difficult time being heard, and often for political, rather than scientific, reasons.

Scientists must remember that, though they have powerful "magical" tools for discovering things about the universe, these tools do not always give us certainty. There is always an Einstein who comes along to supersede Newton, and there is always someone who can put doubt into the perfection of Einstein's vision. In fact, there are experiments going back over fifty years, conducted by D. C. Miller and others, that, if taken seriously, could significantly compromise our acceptance of the theory of relativity. Science as a vision of the world has great elegance and insight. But, when dealing with human beings, it is always best to make sure that the power of any group over others is restricted.

Of course, it can be argued that what we are objecting to here is not science but scientists, and that is certainly true. But it must be remembered that science is practiced by people, and professional ethics is related to how people behave in their professional capacity. In the case of the "Statement of Leading Scientists," what was particularly fascinating is the dissonance between the ideals of scientific practice and the behavior of the scientists. We may not accept the veracity of astrology. In fact,

Feyerabend himself does not. But the objections expressed to astrology in the "Statement of Leading Scientists" did not come from a serious study of the weaknesses of astrology. We should note that many prominent scientists refused to sign the manifesto because of its authoritarian tone and unscientific hysteria. It also seems strange that scientists feel sufficiently threatened by astrology that they need to write manifestos condemning it.

I do not want to imply that Feyerabend's position is the last word on the subject, or that we should think of scientists as a bunch of authoritarian zealots. Feyerabend's prose is designed to provoke and there is an element of rhetoric in his writing. The idea is, however, that he does get you to think. If nothing else, one should be aware of science as a process that helps us understand our world, and as an understanding it continually evolves and changes. Further, we can understand scientific insight as human insight, interesting and imperfect, perennially fascinating and forever evolving.

Endnotes for Chapter 10

1. Reprinted with the permission of Peters, Fraser, and Dunlop from *The Sleepwalkers*, by Arthur Koestler. Copyright 1959, Arthur Koestler.

2. Tycho Brahe was an astronomer who developed many tools for observing the heavens and who undertook a great series of calculations of planetary and stellar positions. Kepler worked at his observatory for a time.

3. Reprinted with the permission of Verso Publishers, from *Science in a Free Society*, by Paul Feyerabend. Copyright 1978, Verso Publishers.

❖ INDEX

309

S

Sacks, Howard R., 23–24
Sanitation, 79–81
Sartre, Jean-Paul, 117, 128–31
Scalia, Antonin, 254–56
Schools, inculcating values, 262–63
Schweitzer, Dr. Albert, 98
Science
  ethics and, 291–308
  Feyerabend, Paul, on, 302–7
  Kepler, Johannes, and, 293–302
  process of discovery in, 308
    errors canceling out, 301
    laws of planetary motion, 293–302
  theory in, 292, 297
Scientists, 292, 307, 308
  and antiastrology manifesto, 302–8
Scipio, 235
Sea power, War of 1812, 272, 275
Self-interest
  and business ethics, 46, 48
  Kant, Immanuel, on, 59, 67
  and religious ethics, 133, 134
Self-regard, 31, 34
Self-sacrifice, 102, 126
Semmelweis, Ignaz, 79–80
Servetus, Michael, 79
Sexual attitudes, 152, 153, 244
Sexual promiscuity, 96, 97
Sharp, Philip R., 207, 208, 209
Shaw, Robert, 225
Shephardizing, 22
Siddhartha Gautama, 135
Silent Spring (Carson), 203
Slavery justification, 107
Sleepwalkers, The (Koestler), 293–302
Smith, Adam, 46
Smog, 202
Smokestacks, 204, 205
Socialism, lawyers under, 4, 42, 43
Society
  agricultural, and mental illness, 152
  and alienation, 197–98
  class, problems, and, 151
  and individual
    ethics and the law, 1–44
    medical-ethics issues, 99–100
    psychosurgery issue, 95–97
  pluralistic, and education, 262–64
  and thought control, 217–23
Socrates, 264, 278, 288
Solar system, 298–301
Solon, 284

Soto school, 137
Souter, David H., 251
Sterilization, 80
Stevens, John Paul, 251
Stewart, Potter, 250
Stoicism, 265
Storytelling, 279–80
Studies in Hysteria (Breuer, Freud), 149
Suffering, 104–5
  Machiavelli on, 231, 233
  in obedience experiments, 157–97
  Plato on, 281, 282
  Zen Buddhism on, 137
Suicide, 94–95, 151
Sumerians, 85
Supreme Court, abortion, 246–58
Surgery. *See also* Psychosurgery
  and Hippocratic Oath, 71, 73
  needless, 88, 89
Sutra, 137, 141
Suzuki, D. T., 139, 140
Sydenham, Thomas, 84
Szasz, Dr. Thomas, 100–112
  on freedom and responsibility, 101–3
  on medical theory and religion, 101,
    107–8
  on medicine and the First Amendment,
    106–8
  on priest and physician, 109–10
  on suffering and salvation, 104–5

T

Taoism, 75
Tao Te Ching. See Dao de Jing
Teaching
  and ethical responsibility, 263
  and inculcating values, 261–89
  indirect, 264
  methods of, 267, 284
Technological advances, 76, 108, 205
Tecumseh, 270
Temperance, 265
Terminal illness, 92
Terrorism, Central America, 221, 222
Theravada Buddhism, 135, 136
Thomas, Clarence, 254
Thought
  astrology and, 306
  control of, 217–23
  existentialism and, 115, 118
  functionalism and, 155–56
  language and, 259
  mechanical, 154–55

and scientific process, 293–302
Time, 217
Tischbein, Johann Heinrich, 124
Tolerance, 42, 43, 154, 155, 263, 266
Tortious, 22
Torture, 157, 221, 222
Totalitarian society
  distrust of information in, 217
  lawyers in, 4, 42, 43
  party line in, 218
  propaganda in, 223
Tragic hero, 125, 126
Trauma, 149
Treaty of Ghent, 271
Trial and error in scientific process, 294–95
Truth
  and constitutional rights, 5–6
  and journalism ethics, 215–30, 239
  Kant, Immanuel, on, 64
  and media, 217, 239
  Mill, John Stuart, on, 37
  nature of, 114, 115–16, 119
  and patient/physician relationship, 92
  Plato on, 281, 284, 286, 287
  and science, 292, 302, 307
  and Zen Buddhism, 137
  in Zen story, 143

U

Unconscious, 149
USA Today, 225
Utilitarianism, 26
Utopia, 75, 76

V

Vergil, 234
Victimless crimes, 41
Vietnam Syndrome, 220
Vietnam War, 194–95, 218–20
Voluntarism, 184–85

W

Wade-Giles transliteration, 211
War
  authority and conformity in, 194–95
  behavior causing, 155

ethics and, 132, 198–99
  media manipulation in, 239
  Plato on, 285
  propaganda, 218–20
War of 1812, 264
  Canadian perspective on, 268, 272–77
  U. S. perspective on, 268–71, 276–77
Warren, Earl, 6
Washington Post, 221
Wealth, 133, 211
Webster, Daniel, 270
White, Byron Raymond, 5, 254
Whitehead, Alfred North, 278, 296
Will, 62, 63, 65, 101
Wines, Michael, 229–30
Witchcraft, 303
Women
  and abortion controversy, 242–60
  in obedience experiments, 177–78
    table, 180, 181, 182
  Plato on, 288
World-view
  in Chinese philosophy, 210, 211–13, 214
  religion and, 134
  science and, 307
  in Zen Buddhism, 135
Wrong actions
  and abortion controversy, 242
  Hippocratic Oath on, 73
  Kant, Immanuel, on, 67
  Mill, John Stuart, on, 39, 265, 266
  and obedience, 196
  and religious ethics, 132
  in Vietnam War, 219, 220

Y

Yale University, obedience experiments, 160, 173

Z

Zen, 136
Zen Buddhism, 135–45
  characteristics of, 139–42
  development of, 135–39
  existentialism compared with, 138–39, 145
  stories, 137, 140, 142–44